Transforming
Narcissism

Psychoanalytic Inquiry Book Series

Volume 28

Psychoanalytic Inquiry
Book Series

Transforming *Narcissism*

Reflections on Empathy, Humor, and Expectations

Frank M. Lachmann

The Analytic Press
Taylor & Francis Group

New York   London

The Analytic Press
Taylor & Francis Group
270 Madison Avenue
New York, NY 10016

The Analytic Press
Taylor & Francis Group
27 Church Road
Hove, East Sussex BN3 2FA

Printed in the United States of America on acid-free paper
10 9 8 7 6 5 4 3 2

International Standard Book Number-13: 978-0-88163-479-2 (Softcover) 978-0-88163-468-6 (0)

Library of Congress Cataloging-in-Publication Data

Lachmann, Frank M.
   Transforming narcissism : reflections on empathy, humor, and expectations / Frank
Lachmann.
      p. ; cm. -- (Psychoanalytic inquiry book series ; v. 28)
   Includes bibliographical references and index.
   ISBN 978-0-88163-479-2 (alk. paper) -- ISBN 978-0-88163-468-6 (alk. paper)
   1. Kohut, Heinz. 2. Self psychology. 3. Psychoanalysis. 4. Narcissism. 5. Empathy.
6. Ego. 7. Mother and infant. I. Title. II. Series.
   [DNLM: 1. Kohut, Heinz. 2. Narcissism. 3. Empathy. 4. Humor. 5. Mother-Child
Relations. 6. Psychotherapeutic Processes. W1 PS427F v.28 2008 / WM 460.5.E3
L138t 2008]

RC489.S43L33 2008
616.89'17--dc22

sp; 2007041592

Visit the Taylor & Francis Web site at
http://www.taylorandfrancis.com

and The Analytic Press Web site at
http://www.analyticpress.com

To

Annette

Peter, Suzanne, Gene,

Brendan, Dylan, Matthew,

and Collin

Contents

Preface

Oh, no! Not another book about narcissism! I know no one has directly said this to me, but I'll bet some people are thinking it. So here is my response to them.

Why do we need another book on narcissism and why did I want to write it? In spite of Kohut's heroic efforts and those of many other analysts who have tried, discussions of narcissism in patients have tended to retain pejorative moralistic connotations of obnoxious arrogance, insufferable self-centeredness, and intolerable conceit. Yet, a wealth of literature has been produced that speaks of the subtleties of the self-pathology that underlies the overt "haughty behavior" that has given narcissism such a bad name. Yet, this literature has had little effect. How often in both common and professional usage is someone described as "a total narcissist"? Although there is a clear difference in having such a person as a parent, an employer, a friend, or a patient, that difference is not always apparent when I hear colleagues and students describe treatments of "narcissistic disorders" or, using Kohut's later terminology, which I prefer, "self-pathology." Will this book make a difference? All I can do is to try.

Using Kohut's seminal paper, "Forms and Transformations of Narcissism," as a springboard, in the chapters to follow I update his proposals for contemporary clinicians with a particular recognition of the extent to which actions and attitudes usually called "narcissistic" serve self- and interactive regulatory functions. This book elaborates, expands on, and modifies Kohut's thesis that archaic narcissism is *transformed* in the course of development or through treatment into empathy, humor, creativity, an acceptance of transience, and wisdom.

Right away we bump head-on into a problem. Kohut did not provide a clear discussion of the process whereby these transformations take place. What is required to bring about such transformations as he proposed? I was intrigued by this question and came up with a proposal derived from Kohut's essay: A treatment that would have the kind of end-products that Kohut envisioned ought to have the very same elements in it as it goes along. That is, the process of treatment itself ought to embody or contain or otherwise reflect empathy, humor, creativity, an acceptance of transience, and wisdom. If the process of treatment—the analyst–patient interaction—did contain these qualities, then it would not be surprising if these qualities, the now transformed narcissism, became the permanent acquisition of the patient.

But can we really expect treatment to contain these qualities? It's a tall order. As I reflect on my day's work, do I wonder how much wisdom there was in my office today? I don't think so. How much acceptance of transience there was? I don't think so. On the other hand, I do reflect on the place of empathy in the treatment of one or another patient. And some of us may note with self-approval that there was indeed a modicum of humor and some creativity that went into this or that hour.

So, I have made my proposal into a springboard for these reflections. However, I can't simply map Kohut's list of five transformations onto treatment in any lock-step way. Rather, this book is a series of reflections on themes by Heinz Kohut.

The reflections in this book on therapeutic process have another basis as well. I will be updating Kohut's proposals by looking at therapeutic process through the lens of dyadic processes, especially studies of mother–infant interactions. I will be relying not only on clinical work— my own and that of others—but also on what we have learned about dyadic interactions in the past three decades of developmental research. Very briefly, a description of the organization of the book follows. It is divided roughly into three parts.

Part I, "Transformation," covers the clinical domain derived from Kohut's proposition about the transformation of archaic narcissism. This section follows most closely the line of inquiry I have just mapped out.

Chapter 1 considers the questions: How do transformations occur? What is it that gets transformed? Utilizing a number of sources from the empirical infant literature, I illustrate transformation as a bidirectional process.

In chapter 2, I shift toward examining the implicit, nonverbal, and procedural dimensions of therapeutic exchange. This emphasis is retained throughout the book, although not to the exclusion of dynamic contents. In this chapter I cover both verbal and nonverbal implicit communications as they further therapeutic action, specifically considering how the implicit dimension of the therapist's verbal communications transforms the analytic relationship.

In chapters 3 and 4 I tackle empathy. Chapter 3 considers the precursors of empathy: implicit nonconscious communications that are necessary but not sufficient for empathic understanding. In chapter 4, I turn to empathic understanding proper and consider some challenges associated with it before taking up its place in the therapeutic process.

In chapter 5, I place the role of humor side by side with empathy in furthering therapeutic action. The inclusion of the patient's and the therapist's senses of humor can provide a unique view into how an affective violation of expectation can further the transformative aspects of the therapeutic encounter. One of the two cases included is that of a patient with a great sense of humor, who wrote about his experience with me as his therapist. To balance the usual tilt in clinical presentations, there is also a section on humor and spontaneity gone awry. This chapter ushers in a second theme of this book: the role of expectations and their violation in furthering therapeutic action.

In part 2, "Expectations," I change my strategy of presentation in that the chapters of this section are organized around concepts derived from the developmental literature, which is then utilized to clarify a variety of clinical issues related to the transformation of self-pathology. Chapter 6 details the place of expectancies in development and the consequences of violations of expectations, as are found in the studies of depressed mothers and their infants. A range of violations of expectations is proposed. Telling lies is one kind of typical violation of another's expectations and is illustrated through a case example.

Chapters 7 and 8 address the transformative power of violations of expectations in certain perversions and in certain creative works, respectively. Chapter 7 considers perversions of sexuality and what I call perversions of aggression from the vantage point of the place that violations of expectations have contributed to organizing the perverse behavior. A portion of the chapter is devoted to the development and history of a 15-year-old mass killer whose diary and home movies document a vicious cycle of parent and child violating each other's expectations, leading to an escalating spiral of despair and resulting in the killings.

In chapter 8, using autobiographies and other sources, I propose that, for certain creative artists, near-death experiences at or shortly after birth violated their families' expectations that they would not survive. Being told of the circumstances of their survival led the artists-to-be to absorb into their lives and work a family myth: "I lived when everyone expected me to die; I defied expectations and survived." The theme of violating expectations with delight then subsequently emerged in their work and in their lives. My goal in this chapter is to illustrate the transformative power of violations of expectations and thereby shed some light on creativity and some creative artists.

In part 3, I change my strategy of presentation yet again to a more discursive style—hence the section title, "Reflections." In chapter 9 I return via clinical material to the acceptance of transience as a goal of transformation. However, acceptance of transience per se is unlikely to be a feature of psychoanalytic treatment. Rather, treatment is more likely to address disorders of time. I translate the acceptance of transience into a person's relationship to time such as a fear of imminent death. Death anxiety is examined in the treatment of a man whose presenting symptom, "impatience," was "transformed" into an interest in gardening, in particular in growing perennials.

Chapter 10, "In Search of Wisdom," required a similar revision of Kohut's original thesis. Rather than investigating wisdom as a transformation of archaic narcissism, I address the search for wisdom, a more modest endeavor, and propose that the search can be affectively transformative.

Chapter 11 synthesizes the theoretical and clinical proposals offered. I revisit the concepts and cases described and advance a psychoanalytic theory that focuses predominantly on the implicit, procedural, and nonverbal dimensions of therapeutic action that are engaged in the transformative process.

However, following Kohut's "list" of the five transformations, even as loosely as I do, creates further problems since I consider them to be interacting dimensions of the therapeutic relationship. It is difficult to illustrate one—for example, empathy—in isolation or apart from, for example, humor. With that in mind, if it were possible, reading all the chapters simultaneously would provide optimal entrée for grasping how the therapeutic relationship absorbs and transforms the affective interaction of analyst and patient. Placing the chapters into a sequence is somewhat arbitrary but, alas, necessary.

So far I have responded to the question, "Why is this book necessary?" I turn now to another question, "Why make all this fuss about Kohut?" It's a personal bias. I like the feeling of continuity with figures from the past. In this book that figure is Kohut because his paper stretched from psychoanalytic treatment to the arts, and all along the continuum of life from early development to mortality. That's elegant.

Unlike music, art, and literature, where an appreciation of the giants of the past continues into the present, psychoanalysis is quick to grant each generation of psychoanalysts supremacy over bygone eras. Even Freud hasn't been doing so well these days. How many institutes include courses in their curricula that address the evolution of psychoanalytic thought? The collection of papers gathered by Martin Bergmann and Frank Hartman (1976), as well as the *Essential Papers* series (for example, Hanly, 1995), stand out as notable exceptions in offering an excellent collection of psychoanalytic contributions organized from historical and topical perspectives. Reading the papers of Strachey, Alexander, Ferenczi, Reich, Jacobson, and others fosters an appreciation for how they struggled with problems very similar to the ones with which present-day analysts struggle. And their patients from 60 and 70 years ago are remarkably similar to the patients about whom Kohut wrote 40 years ago.

In the years since Kohut published the proposals that provide the springboard for this book, our understanding of both narcissism and the origins of pathology in early development has undergone revision. In updating, modifying, expanding, and, yes, challenging Kohut's ideas I hope that they will thereby remain relevant and alive in current psychoanalytic conversations. It is my hope that the contributions of Kohut can be acknowledged while the specific developments in the evolution of self psychology and psychoanalysis in general can amplify and expand his ideas to make them clinically applicable for a new audience of analysts.

The style of the book is conversational. I talk to the reader. I want my ideas to be accessible and clinically useful. I provide many illustrations from my clinical work. In presenting the work of others, whether research studies or cases, I include why I think a particular contribution is fascinating or challenging.

The identities of the patients whose treatments I discuss have been disguised. Aspects of their lives not relevant to the point I make have been altered. But, that being said, I believe all case presentations, mine as well as those of my colleagues, are works of fiction. Even if I try to consciously present them in a fair and unbiased way, I have still picked these patients to discuss. In doing so, I have not picked others. To bring in some balance, I did try to present case material where I missed the boat or "blew it." Under the circumstances, it's probably the best we can do short of shooting ourselves in the foot in public.

In these chapters I use *analyst* and *therapist* interchangeably, as well as *analysis, therapy,* and *treatment.* At the level at which I am writing, my ideas are equally applicable to once a week and four times a week treatment. For this reason I have not always indicated how often a patient was seen.

Much of the material presented in these chapters has not appeared in print before, with the following exceptions: Sections of chapters 1 and 2 appeared in the *International Journal for Psychoanalytic Self Psychology* (2008), Vol. 3. Early versions of chapter 2 appeared in *Selbstpsychologie* (2005), Vol. 6, pp. 327–356 and of chapter 5 in the *Canadian Journal of Psychoanalysis* (2003), Vol. 11, pp. 287–312. Selections from chapters 6, 7, and 8 appeared in *Psychoanalytic Inquiry* (2006), Vol. 26, pp. 362–386.

Acknowledgments

J oe Lichtenberg provided immeasurable support in shepherding
  my various talks and papers toward this book. I thank him for his
encouragement, advice, and criticism with respect both to style and content. Earlier versions of many of the chapters were presented at confer-
ences, seminars, and ad hoc meetings arranged by my colleagues. I thank
them and appreciate the many opportunities they gave me to hear how
my work sounds and to raise questions for me to think about. I thank
the following colleagues for their many and generous invitations: Erwin
Bartosch and Andrea Harms (Vienna), Michael Klöpper (Hamburg),
Lotte Koehler and Ron Bodansky (Munich), Jane Jordan (San Francisco),
Alan Kindler (Toronto), Gianni and Suzi Nebbiosi (Rome). Versions of
these chapters were read and critiqued by colleagues and members of
some of my study groups. I thank them all for their thoughtful and generous commentary. In particular, I thank Beatrice Beebe, Ruth Gruenthal,
Pauline Pinto, Doris Silverman, and David Wyner, as well as Phyllis
Ackman, Tom Menaker, and Girard Franklin for their careful read-
ing of numerous chapters and their criticism and suggestions. I thank
the members of my study groups, on whom I inflicted several chapters
in the past few years. Thank you, Susan Brown, Carolyn Clement,
Michael Clifford, Barbara Feld, Bonnie Goodman, Arthur Gray, Diane
Greene, Ellen Gussaroff, Dianne Kaminsky, Andrew Karpf, Linda
Klempner, Larrie Majors, Ann Morris, Harriet Pappenheim, Merrill

Schneiderman, Gertrude Schwartzman, Manny Shapiro, Dorienne Sorter, Ann Sullivan, Ellen Synan, Shake Topalian, Marie Weinstein, Harriet Werner, Jane Wilkins, and Denise Zalman.

I am most indebted to John Kerr, who, with pen and scalpel, tweezers, and chisel, conscientiously read and, with empathy, good humor, extraordinary creativity, and a touch of wisdom, edited my manuscript and helped me to write the book that I wanted to write.

PART 1

Transformation

1 The Process of Transforming

The year was 1953. I was a psychology intern at Bellevue Hospital in New York. As an intern I was able to attend a seminar led by a training analyst from New York Psychoanalytic Institute. The other members of the seminar were psychiatric residents and psychiatrists, a number of whom were already in psychoanalytic training. The analyst opened one meeting of the seminar by relating the following incident: "Tell me what you think about this," he said to the group. "Last weekend I went to a restaurant with my wife and several other couples, colleagues from the institute. At a nearby table sat a patient of mine. We exchanged greetings through eye contact. When he left, the patient came over to say good-bye and that it was good to see me. When my friends and I were ready to leave and asked for our bill, the waiter told us it had already been paid, for all of us, by the gentleman who had just left." The analyst then turned to us and asked, "What do you all think of this?"

Very privately, I thought to myself that this patient must have liked his analyst very much. Fortunately, I kept quiet. The next thing I remember is that terms were flying past me from all directions. This patient was narcissistic, grandiose, competitive, controlling, demeaning, hostile, and destructive. He was defending against castration anxiety by submitting passively to his father's phallus, as well as expressing castrative hostility toward his father. The analyst looked very pleased with the psychoanalytic formulations of his students. They understood that narcissism and object relationships, self-centeredness, and an ability to relate to others were on a seesaw and that this patient's unbridled grandiosity and manipulativeness—his "narcissism"—had drained his ability to be concerned about others. Therefore, they contended his aggression was given free rein and he acted it out by paying for the dinners, thereby elevating himself and demeaning his analyst.

I was glad I had said nothing because I would obviously have been all wrong. I said to myself, "So this is what psychoanalysis is all about." One looks underneath or behind a person's actions to find the "real" motivation. Behaviors that appear kind, generous, or perhaps even an expression of gratitude and appreciation actually conceal baser, unconscious motivations that are aggressive and narcissistic.

This was in 1953, and if it weren't for the contributions of Heinz Kohut, we might still be understanding and treating patients from this perspective today. But in 1953 Kohut had not yet become a self psychologist, although his extraordinary ideas were already beginning to coalesce. In 1959 he would publish "Introspection, Empathy and Psychoanalysis," breaking new ground in redefining the analytic task as one of understanding and explaining patients' experiences from within their perspective rather than from the vantage point of an outside, "objective" observer. But in his essay on Thomas Mann's *Death in Venice*, which was published in 1957, Kohut had already begun to rethink narcissistic pathology and to conceptualize destructive impulses as secondary to the disintegration of a narcissistic self-organization. This formulation would eventually move therapists to a position vastly different from the one held by the analyst at Bellevue and the participants in his seminar. Rather than viewing narcissism as a character structure to be confronted, analysts could address the person's vulnerable sense of self and the protection, defense, and compensation that the person sought.

Not only did Kohut's perspective offer a radically new slant on narcissism, but it also changed our understanding of aggression. In the self psychology tradition, following Kohut (1972), aggression was thought of and treated as a reaction to narcissistic injuries. I elaborated this view of aggression in *Transforming Aggression* (Lachmann, 2000), where I distinguished between reactive and eruptive aggression. Both types of aggression are responses to narcissistic injuries in the broadest sense. Their manifestations differ and they reflect injuries to the sense of self over different time frames. Reactive aggression is comparatively a more short-range phenomenon (though obviously it has its own history), while eruptive aggression is a long-term phenomenon. Reactive aggression comes about in response to narcissistic injuries, experiences of deprivation, rejection, and frustration. However, aggression becomes "eruptive" like a volcano lying in wait quietly, ready to erupt at some slight atmospheric change, and functions *as though* it is innate, as a consequence of early persistent emotional and physical abuse and neglect. Aggression then appears for "no apparent reason" (A. Freud, 1972). Expressions of anger, rage, or hostility and other variations of aggression then become a prominent and dominant mode of affect expression. Under these circumstances aggression can become a way of expressing anxiety, shame, despair, sexual excitement, and any number of other affects and combinations of affects. Furthermore, eruptive aggression can become self-perpetuating and acquire a life of its own. A habitual link between narcissistic vulnerability and aggressive reactions is thereby established and maintained.

In his theoretical contributions, Kohut ultimately linked aggression and narcissism by considering aggression a "breakdown product" of the self, a form of self-pathology. In his clinical contributions, Kohut (Lachmann, 2000; Miller, 1985) spelled out these theoretical contributions by formulating "leading edge" and "trailing edge" interpretations. Kohut never wrote directly about these edge interpretations, but his then-supervisee, Jule Miller, did. In the case material in the chapters that follow, leading edge interpretations are implicitly and explicitly presented. However, sequences of trailing edge interpretations, when relevant, are neither avoided nor omitted. However, since they are the more familiar psychoanalytic interventions, in these chapters I pay more attention to the therapeutic action of leading edge interpretations. A more detailed description of these interventions now follows.

When Jule Miller (1985) was supervised by Heinz Kohut, Miller discussed the interventions suggested by Kohut that were in contrast to the ones he had been offering to his patient. Coming from a traditional psychoanalytic perspective, Miller had been addressing his patient's competitive and regressive behaviors based on the patient's childhood experiences. In the course of these supervisory sessions Kohut distinguished between leading and training edge interpretations. The leading edge interpretations address the "evolving and developing aspects of the transference relationship, as well as other factors of the patient's progress—how he handles conflict, what new or different tactics he uses to manage it" (p. 19). In the spirit of leading edge interpretations Kohut also advised that "one should always take analytic material first in a 'straight' manner, as if it means what it seems to mean" (p. 15).

Kohut referred to Miller's interventions as "trailing edge" interpretations. These included the genetic basis for a particular associative or behavioral sequence as well as what the patient might be afraid or ashamed to reveal—for example, his competitiveness, hostility, or envy—as well as what was subject to repression, negation, rationalization, denial, or other forms of defensiveness and resistance. These interventions were not to be excluded, but rather offered along with the leading edge interpretations, when appropriate.

In an example Miller described a sequence in which the patient had come an hour early to his analytic session and, upon seeing an unfamiliar person in the waiting room, felt dislocated and anxious. Miller focused on the patient having "set up" this situation by coming an hour early. In contrast Kohut proposed a leading edge formulation—namely, that the patient, like a young child eager to see his father (of particular importance in this instance), came early to the session. Kohut suggested that "the patient's motivation should be regarded first as one of an intense childlike wish rather than as an attempt to 'set up' a situation of disappointment" (Miller, pp. 15–16).

Leading edge interpretations take into account patients' heightened sensitivity to shame and criticism, attempts at mastering painful situations on their own, and attempts at restoring self-cohesion. Furthermore, they attempt to recognize the naturalness of the patient's response from within the patient's subjective framework.

Previously (Lachmann, 2000), I have suggested that leading edge interpretations are framed to recognize the extent to which a patient's thoughts, fantasies, and behaviors are necessary for and strive toward self-protection, self-restoration, self-righting, or self-regulation. These interpretations are particularly powerful in recognizing and validating aspects of a patient's communications that may be contained within self-defeating behaviors but yet are in the service of attempting to achieve self-cohesion.

To formulate a leading edge interpretation for the man who paid for the dinners of his analyst and colleagues, the treating analyst would investigate the man's experience as he observed him with his colleagues at the other table. Not having access to the man's experience, we might speculate here that he may have felt hurt and humiliated in that his tie to his analyst—his idealizing "selfobject" transference in Kohut's later (1971, 1977) terminology—was ruptured. A leading edge formulation would recognize the necessity for the patient to restore this connection, to feel anew his inclusion in his analyst's world, by paying the bill for his analyst and his fellow diners. Yet, Kohut also recognized the traditional psychoanalytic trailing edge meanings of narcissism—what the patient tried to ward off and avoid through repetition of self-defeating patterns and defense. In this instance, we might speculate that he may have been warding off feelings of humiliation at being excluded by "competitors."

Kohut's work shifted psychoanalysis by reconfiguring surface behaviors and their underlying motivations. He uprooted narcissism from its moorings in pathology and moralistic judgments based on "the altruistic value system of Western civilization" (Kohut, 1966, p. 427) and gave narcissism respectability as a metapsychological construct.

Until its rehabilitation in the works of Kohut, the term "narcissism" had a sad history in psychoanalysis. It had been, and to some extent still is, applied pejoratively to patients who behaved in a conceited, self-centered, insufferably entitled manner, unaware of or unconcerned about their effect on relationships with others and yet demanding recognition or some form of tribute from them. This was the view that the seminar participants seemed to have held about the man who paid for all the dinners. The prevailing wisdom was all too clear: Narcissism and object relations stood in an inverse relation to one another. In contrast Kohut proposed that the antithesis of narcissism is not object relations but object love. Making this distinction allowed him to clarify that we use objects for the contribution they make to our sense of self, a legitimate psychological need that had its own history and was open to analytic investigation. Recognizing the vicissitudes of these needs, how they were met and thwarted, and when and by whom led to a new definition of transference to include this "narcissistic" tie to objects that functioned to regulate self-esteem. Kohut's revolution consisted of the recognition that it was no longer tenable to suppose that narcissistic patients failed to form transferences; rather, the issue was to understand and investigate the kinds of transferences they did form.

I emphasize this way of thinking about Kohut's contribution because it shifts our thinking about the analytic dyad and the processes whereby it evolves. That's the subject matter of this book. To recapitulate, in contrast to the prevailing wisdom that the antithesis of narcissism was object relatedness, Kohut proposed that the antithesis of narcissism was object love, not the object relations with which, traditionally, it had been linked in a seesaw relationship. Object relations, according to Kohut at that time, referred across the board to the whole range of a person's interpersonal relationships—not to how other people were subjectively experienced. Pursuing this idea further, Kohut (1971) went on to develop the concept of the "selfobject," to highlight the self-affirming way in which the analyst or another person was subjectively experienced. Various selfobject transferences referred to needed relational experiences that fulfilled vital self-sustaining, self-vitalizing, and self-organizing needs. In his later writings, however, Kohut focused less on object love than on articulating the lifelong need for selfobjects. He subsumed what he had earlier proposed about object love and narcissism in the selfobject concept.

It's not Kohut's overall theory that I consider here, but rather a specific aspect of it: his view of what might be achievable with respect to transforming archaic narcissism. In 1966 Kohut published "Forms and Transformations of Narcissism" and it is this paper that provides the overarching theme for this book. It's my favorite paper by Kohut. The chapters of this book are elaborations and variations on the "transformations of narcissism" he proposed. What I like so much about this paper is Kohut's application of insights derived from psychoanalysis and psychoanalytic treatment to communication with oneself and with others. In a sense it is a philosophical paper. It speaks of and to the human condition on a grand scale. Through maturation we can come to view ourselves and our world with empathy, humor, creativity, wisdom, and an acceptance of transience.

Clinically, the paper envisioned a novel fate for archaic narcissism. Kohut defined archaic narcissism as referring to the child's narcissism when it had not been met with favorable parental responses and had therefore been retained, in its archaic form, into adulthood. It had remained in a childlike grandiose and peremptory form, unavailable for tension regulation and self-esteem maintenance. Life experiences had not muted or transformed it into mature forms of narcissism, so now it was up to psychoanalysis to do so. Kohut proposed that archaic narcissism could be transformed into mature forms of narcissism: the traits that Kohut expected a patient to develop through analytic treatment. More generally, these can be thought of as the hallmarks of successful maturation and development over the course of life.

The transformations are discussed in greater detail in the chapters devoted to them. For now, in the order in which I will be discussing them in this book, the transformations of narcissism are

> *Empathy*: "The mode by which one gathers psychological data about other people and, when they say what they think or feel, imagines their inner experience even though it is not open to direct observation" (Kohut, 1966, p. 261). Kohut considered the groundwork for accessing another person's mind to be laid in the early inclusion of the mother's feelings, actions, and behaviors in oneself. He considered these assertions about empathy to be "speculative in essence and, for their verification, a psychoanalytically oriented experimental approach" (p. 260, footnote 13) to be needed.
>
> A *sense of humor*: Especially when combined with "cosmic narcissism, [humor] aids man in achieving ultimate mastery over the demands of the narcissistic self, i.e., to tolerate the recognition of his finiteness in principle and even of his impending end" (p. 267). Like Dickens, who considered a sense of humor to be a sense of proportion, Kohut also considered humor and especially irony to provide an invaluable perspective about the vicissitudes of life.
>
> *Creativity*: Kohut distinguished between two sides of the narcissism of the creative person, whether artist or scientist. On the one side is the hunger for acclaim of some artists. On the other side is the narcissism that is transformed into the creative act. Kohut links this latter side of narcissism with the blurring of a barrier between oneself and one's surroundings, leading to a heightened awareness of those aspects of the artist's surroundings that are relevant to creativity.
>
> *Transience*: Transience is a capacity to contemplate one's own impermanence, one's mortality as one ages. Transience entails a capacity to acknowledge one's mortality or, as Kohut put it, the

finiteness of existence, and to act in accordance with this painful discovery. He held this to constitute a great "psychological achievement despite the fact that it can often be demonstrated that a manifest acceptance of transience may go hand in hand with covert denials" (p. 264). Woody Allen (2006) expressed this tension between acceptance and denial of one's transience when he quipped: "I was born to the Hebrews but as I got older I converted to narcissism."

Wisdom: Achieved during the later phases of life, wisdom is preceded by the acquisition of information and knowledge during the earlier phases. Wisdom rests on an "acceptance of the limitations of [one's] physical, intellectual, and emotional powers" (p. 268). Kohut defined wisdom as a stable attitude toward life and the world, formed through the integration of humor and acceptance of transience and firmly held values and ideals. He held that wise people are able to contrast the "utter seriousness and unrelieved solemnity of approaching the end of life by transforming the humor of their years of maturity into a sense of proportion, a touch of irony toward the achievements of individual existence, including even their own wisdom" (p. 269).

Intuitively, we can feel the aptness and the relevance of Kohut's contrast of the limitations imposed by archaic narcissism with the expanded and enriched world of relationships with oneself and others depicted in these transformations. Empathy, humor, creativity, an acceptance of transience, and achieving wisdom, Kohut argued, all required overcoming the demands of the narcissistic self. He thereby placed the transformation of archaic narcissism at the center of becoming a mature human being.

Yet, Kohut did not spell out *how* these transformations were to be brought about in development generally. Nor did he say how they would be brought about through psychoanalysis in particular. He posits that transformations result in these traits or qualities but he does not spell out how this process happens. That is what I address in this book.

Much has happened in psychoanalysis since Kohut published this paper. For me, the contributions of empirical infant research (with special attention paid to the bidirectionality of interactive processes) are especially pertinent. They allow us to consider interactive processes, including therapeutic processes, with new precision. We can fill in some of the details in the picture that, in 1966, Kohut could only have painted in broad strokes.

Kohut's conceptualization of archaic narcissism and its transformations came from an era of theorizing in which one-way influence models predominated. That is, in development as well as in treatment, effects were predominantly studied in one direction: from parent to child and analyst to patient. Concepts like "co-creation" or "co-construction" were circling in the air but had not yet landed in the field of psychoanalysis. Co-creation means that each partner has made some contribution to what emerges through the partners' interaction, but their contributions are not necessarily similar, equal, or symmetrical.

Using Kohut's paper as a template, here is what I propose. First, extrapolating from recent empirical infant research, transformation is presented as a process that is bidirectional and co-created by therapist and patient. The transformed or mature forms of narcissism are thus not end-points or goals of analysis, but rather are embedded within the ongoing therapeutic process and are more or less present as part of the process throughout the treatment. Using empathy as an illustration, the analyst is more often the one who contributes empathic understanding, while the patient contributes a readiness to be empathically understood. This co-creation of empathy directly shapes the affective ambience of the treatment and can gradually transform the analytic experience for both partners.

Note again that "co-create" does not mean that each partner contributes similarly, equally, or symmetrically. In later chapters in this book, clinical vignettes will depict one partner as hardly making an explicit contribution. Yet, closer examination will reveal that the process is co-created—even when the contributions of one partner appear to be much more dramatic than those of the other. Another caveat: Co-created does not imply that the creation is planned, preconceived, or consciously intended. It is precisely because input of both participants is necessary that co-created interactions remain unexpected, unpredictable, and spontaneous, with an improvisation-like quality. "Co-creation emphasizes dynamic unpredictable changes of relationships that underlie their uniqueness" (Tronick, 2003, p. 476). That is, co-creation emphasizes the unique, increasingly differentiating aspect of an interaction that makes it unlike any other.

Second, I also propose that it is not archaic narcissism or, for that matter, a person's self-state or self-experience that is directly transformed; rather, it is *affect* that is transformed. However, affect may be impacted directly or, as is customary in psychotherapy, in the context of the therapist–patient dialogue. The process whereby affect is transformed will impact other dimensions of one's sense of self, as has been recognized in developmental studies and self psychological treatment. As Karlen Lyons-Ruth (1999) stated, "Psychoanalysis has always been concerned with understanding the organization of meaning, with affects viewed as central guides and directors of meaning" (p. 577). The pivotal role of affective transformation in self-development is a theme that both developmentalists and psychoanalysts have come to embrace. Specifically, with respect to development, Demos and Kaplan (1986) reported that as the infant's recurrent affect states are responded to by caregivers, the infant's sense of self develops. In a similar vein with respect to adult treatment, Stolorow, Brandchaft, and Atwood (1987) stated that as the analyst's affective responsivity furthers the patient's affect integration, the patient's sense of self develops.

In my focus on affect, I use this term in a most inclusive way to cover the whole range of affect states, including feelings as well as emotions. Some theorists have offered distinctions between different affect states. For example, Fonagy, Gergely, Jurist, and Target (2002) consider emotions to be hard-wired, biological, and universal, whereas feelings are subjective and influenced by culture and individual idiosyncrasies. For my purposes in this book, however, such distinctions, useful as they may be in other contexts, do not help very much in day-to-day clinical work. Thus, pleasure, pain, sadness, anger, fear, and disgust will be considered as *both* hard-wired *and* customized through lived experience. One further point: Affect—one's emotional state—can be transformed directly without requiring symbolic thought. I will spell this out later.

The "How" and "What" of Transformation

Psychoanalysts, physicists, and mathematicians use the term transformation and often seem to assume its meaning to be self-evident. In these disciplines transformation is typically depicted as a one-directional process, with one person or one force acting upon another or on an inanimate entity, causing some change. Even the dictionary definition (Webster, 1976), "to change the form or outward appearance, condition, or function of," adds little to explain how transformation works. This was the definition of transformation that Kohut apparently utilized and thereby embodied a one-way influence model that was then customary in psychoanalytic writing. Transformation in any situation is liable to be a highly complex process, far more complicated than can be captured in a one-way influence model. Let's consider an analyst who considers his task to be to offer his patient a blank screen. We might compare this patient to a handball player. Imagine practicing handball, alone, against a wall. The player, like the patient in a one-way influence model, sets up, hits the ball, moves, hits it again, and so forth. Gradually, he gets better at it and to that extent the player is "transformed." The therapist, like the wall, stands still, unmoved, letting the ball bounce off.

In contrast, here is an illustration of bidirectional influence. Imagine a tennis game. Each time one player hits the ball, the stance of both players is altered, even if only momentarily. The players continually readjust their stance to be prepared for the next ball. Each player's stance is affected by anticipation, a prediction of how the opponent will respond. As in the analytic dyad, both players are affected: the one who adjusts to the anticipated ball—the "transformed" one—as well as the "transformer." But, as we will see later, the process of transforming and being transformed can also be circular and occur in the same person. The handball analogy is not all that inaccurate if we substitute a piano for the wall.

Psychologists Arnold Sameroff and Michael Chandler (Sameroff, 1983; Sameroff & Chandler, 1976) speak to the "how" in the process of transformation in bidirectional terms. These researchers showed that development is in a constant state of active reorganization. In the interactions between child and environment and, by extension, between patient and therapist, as Beatrice Beebe and I (2002) have discussed, each partner affects the other so that, from one point of time to the next, neither the child nor the environment, neither the patient nor the therapist, remains the same. Since each has influenced the other, each shifts the other, and each is shifted or transformed. That is, transformations are co-created by therapist and patient. As in the process of co-creation, in the process of transforming, each participant does not affect the other similarly, equally, or symmetrically.

Having proposed that in the process of transformation both participants are affectively engaged and impact each other and themselves, I now turn to the specifics of this process. To do so I draw on the three principles of salience that Beatrice Beebe and I culled from a wealth of empirical studies and that delineate how experience is organized from infancy onward.

These three principles of organization can also address the question, "How do transformations come about?" These principles are (1) ongoing regulations, (2) disruption and repair of ongoing regulations, and (3) heightened affective moments. They serve as key conceptual dimensions for understanding and revising the process of transformation as it occurs in psychotherapeutic treatment. I discuss them in increasing order of specificity, from a broad temporal sequence to a specific sequence to a moment in time.

Ongoing regulations address the most general patterns of interactions and include both how therapist and patient affect each other (interactive regulation) as well as how each regulates his or her own state (self-regulation). Self-regulation addresses regulation of affect and arousal, including physiological requirements, and also refers to bodily states such as sex and hunger by heightening attention or by diminishing vigilance. Self-regulation can establish and maintain a feeling of safety and stability or diminish tension and feelings of frustration.

Self-regulation also establishes and maintains expectancies. Expectancies refer to how interactions with the environment will transpire; for example, an infant comes to expect affective responsivity when playfully engaged with his or her mother. Through symbolic elaboration, self-regulation includes fantasy as well as access to, articulation of, and regard for one's self state. However, since self- and interactive regulation are simultaneous—two sides of the same coin—they constantly reorganize, update, negate, or reinforce the sense of self and the sense of self-with-other (Stern, 1983). Since both forms of regulation ultimately alter one's inner organization—one's sense of self—both contribute to the transformation of self-experience and behavior, while also impacting one's partner.

Both self-regulation and interactive regulation include the ways in which therapist and patient negotiate degrees of emotional closeness and distance, intimacy, and detachment. Through words, body language, tone, vocal rhythm, and, for example, expressions of empathic understanding, each partner can regulate his or her own and the other's level of arousal or distress.

In the treatment, ongoing regulations can alter or gradually transform the analytic ambience—for example, from mutually felt tension to greater comfort, or in the reverse direction. Ongoing regulations also entail transient shifts in the affective states of both partners. A co-created rhythm in the therapist–patient interactions can emerge that is the property of neither partner alone.

The second principle, disruption and repair, refers to ruptures or breaks in the sequence of ongoing interactions, applicable in therapy to the vicissitudes of a selfobject transference and lapses in empathy. But disruption and repair occur repeatedly in mother–infant interaction and studies of this pattern can shed light on similar patterns of interaction that occur in therapy and in life, generally. A classic illustration of the disruption and repair of affective communication is the "still face" study (Tronick, Als, Adamson, Wise, & Brazelton, 1978).

In the still face paradigm an event is studied that occurs innumerable times in the life of infants: namely, the violation of the infant's expectation of affective responsivity of the mother. In the experiment mothers were instructed to play with their 3-month-old infants for 2 minutes as they would at home. Typically, through facial expression, tone, vocal rhythm, and body movements, the mother and her infant establish an ongoing affective connection. The mother is then instructed to maintain an immobile, "still face"—that is, to show no reaction for 2 minutes— and then afterward to resume normal play.

During the 2-minute "still face" interval, the connection between mother and child is disrupted with a profound impact. The child's affect is precipitously transformed from joyful engagement to uncomprehending rejection and visible frustration, anger, and withdrawal. Nor is the child the only one affected. Studies of physiological indices of mothers under these conditions—for example, heart rate (Field et al., 1988)— show that her affect is also transformed. She too becomes anxious and distraught as she maintains a still face. In these studies, typically, both partners repair the disruption. The mother reengages with her child and the child reengages with his or her mother. Similarly, in psychotherapy, lapses in empathy can disrupt the ongoing process. Repair assumes, of course, that a lapse has been recognized. Such recognition can then lead to the restoration of the affective therapist–patient tie.

In the still face study the disruption is aversive to both partners. The transformations are from mutual engagement with expectations of affective responsivity, to a violation of expectations, to disengagement, to distress and anxiety, to reengagement. In the next chapter, in a clinical example I illustrate a comparable process of transformation in a patient and me in the reverse direction. We move from distress, anxiety, and disengagement, via a violation of expectations, to affective responsivity; the overall movement is from a detached to a more intimate state and the effect of the violation is positive, not negative. Violations of expectations both positive and negative play a major role in the process of transformation.

Tronick and colleagues' still face study is also an example of a stressful violation of expectations and thus stands in contrast to violations that are pleasurable, humorous, intimate, or joyful. Kohut's (1984) well-known comment to the psychiatric resident who drove so recklessly to his analytic appointment was that he "was going to give him the deepest interpretation he had so far received in his analysis: 'You are a complete idiot'" (p. 74). Kohut's interpretation was a violation of his analysand's expectations, using irony. Kohut added that after his interpretation, "a successful analysis of the events that triggered [the patient's] outbursts of narcissistic rage" (p. 75) followed. Unlike ongoing regulations in which changes are gradual, heightened moments—whether shock or humor, terror or joy, dissociation or intimacy—can produce dramatic and rapid transformation.

The third principle, heightened affect, concerns those moments that evoke strong emotions and become organizing beyond the brief time that they take. Kohut's comment to his patient became a heightened affective moment with an enduring impact on the treatment. Similarly, my experience in the Bellevue seminar was a heightened affective moment. It remained a powerful, organizing experience for me. Why? Not because it provided a model for how to do analysis. Rather, the experience challenged me directly by placing my admiration for psychoanalysis and the psychoanalyst who presided over the seminar into a conflict with my values and concern for the feelings of the patient, who I felt was not adequately understood or respected in the seminar's discussion. It retrospect, it was also a violation of my expectations.

These three principles were also utilized by Diana Fosha (2000) in proposing that affective experience has the power to transform by contributing to the emergence and development of a patient's sense of self. I mention Fosha's work here because it provides a lead-in to thinking about the "what" of transformation along with the "how." In her treatments, Fosha focuses quite directly on the patient's affect, which she tries to tap through such strategies as "mirroring validation," which she derived from an attachment paradigm. Her view of empathy is that it is a provision by the therapist to facilitate the patient making contact with and giving expression to inner affective experience. She views this direct, validating affective experience as transforming in itself.

My focus differs from Fosha's. She focuses on the transforming power of affect, whereas I propose that affect *is* transformed through the dyadic, therapeutic process. Qualities of both partners in addition to empathy are engaged as, for example, therapist's empathic understanding and the patient's capacity to receive it, integrate it, or fend it off. The therapist–patient dialogue also includes humorous, ironic, and creative interventions as vehicles for connecting with and transforming affect. In turn, the patient's rigidly restricted, vulnerable, or fragmentation-prone sense of self can be impacted. Certainly, affective experience is important and can trigger processes of self-transformation, but my focus is on how affect itself is transformed and the dimensions of the dyadic process that bring this about.

In exploring how affect is transformed in the dyad and also how affective states can trigger self-transformation, join me in a visit to the world of music. Musicians and musicologists use the term *transformation* in two ways. One definition, the familiar one-directional description, states that transformation is a process whereby a composer modifies "a theme so that in a new context it is different but yet manifestly made of the same elements" (Sadie & Tyrell, 2001, p. 694). In this usage, the composer "transforms" a musical theme.

According to a second usage of transformation, however, music directly transforms affect; that is, it impacts the emotional state or feelings of those who perform the music as well as those who listen to it. Steven Mithen (2006), writing from an evolutionary standpoint, has proposed that music and language probably share a common prehistoric origin. Utilizing dimensions of music such as pitch, rhythm, intensity, and time, he argues, provided some Neanderthals with an evolutionary advantage in communicating and bonding rituals. These dimensions of music impact affect. Hence, the title of Mithen's book is *The Sing-*

ing Neanderthals. In his view, music once provided underlying glue for human communication. Thus, music as an affective communication can both shape and be shaped by the evolving responses of the "players." Mithen reported that cross-cultural studies have demonstrated that music directly expresses emotions and similar musical conventions arouse similar emotions in listeners across the globe. In addition, attributes of music such as the interval between two notes can induce similar emotional states in listeners in diverse cultures. Here is an illustration of affect being *transformed* directly without language. In fact, Mithen, like composer–musicologist Leonard Bernstein (1976), considers music to be the language of emotion. According to Bernstein, music has no meaning per se; it's all evocation of emotion.

I am not proposing that the process of transformation is propelled *only* by affect. Even Beethoven saw the necessity for the use of language by drawing on Schiller's *Ode to Joy* to fully express his feelings about the brotherhood of mankind in the fourth movement of his Ninth Symphony. The same necessity applies to therapy. Both affect and language will be involved in therapist–patient interactions, no matter whether these are centered on empathy or humor, or incorporate a sense of transience, or are otherwise transformative.

Now to the question of whether interpretation can be transformative, a topic that traditionally was at the heart of a unidirectional model of treatment. Traditionally in psychoanalysis, complete and exact interpretations (Glover, 1959) at a point of affective urgency (Fenichel, 1941) have been credited with promoting insight, thereby bringing about transformations in the patient. However, in the course of this book I argue that what is transformed is the affect of both analyst and patient, both of whom are engaged in this process. Among the numerous categories of analytic interventions, interpretations are transformative precisely and only when they engage the affect of both participants. Both analyst and patient? Although it is conceivable that in an analytic dyad one partner is affectively moved while the other is not, it's just not likely that either the analyst or the patient is affectively moved—transformed—through the interaction, while the other sits there like a wall in handball, unmoved.

The transformation of affect generates the process of transformation in the analytic dialogue. This is the music of analytic communications. In fact, the direct connection between music and affect, outside linguistic-symbolic thought, informs my use of musical illustrations in examining the transformative process.

In spelling out the process of transformation, one further elaboration is necessary. Transformations are not only bidirectional and co-created by therapist and patient so that, in the process of transforming, both partners transform each other. Each partner also "self-transforms," a topic to which I now turn.

In line with the model of ongoing regulations, I have so far proposed that in the transformational process, as therapist and patient interact, each transforms the other's affect. Now, parallel to self-regulation, I add that each participant also inevitably self-transforms. Igor Stravinsky illustrated this self-transforming process as he composed *The Rite of Spring.*

In *The Rite of Spring*, Stravinsky drew heavily on folksong. What is particularly revolutionary in the *Rite of Spring* is not Stravinsky's borrowing of folk songs, but rather his transformation of the songs. He treated his sources as "raw material, excising and utilizing gestures, melodic fragments, and patterns as he saw fit.... [H]e *transformed* the original into something entirely new for the ballet" (Seitz, 2005, p. 21; italics added). In this music Stravinsky makes an unprecedented use of dissonance, even though he later maintained that the use of eight-note chords in that composition had not been particularly new. "The accents and displaced rhythms that he superimposed on the chords, however, made for something genuinely unique" (p. 21). He transformed the Russian folksongs into bombastic rhythms that aroused such powerful emotions that the audience was moved to riot when *The Rite of Spring* was first heard in Paris in 1913 (Bernstein, 1982).

So far my description of Stravinsky's endeavor has only illustrated the familiar, one-directional view of transformation; that is, he transformed the folksongs into something new. However, something more did happen. He himself was transformed in the process. His friend, the impresario Serge Diaghilev, described Stravinsky's facial expressions of increasing joy, ecstasy, and surprise as he watched him in the process of composing *The Rite of Spring* at his piano. Diaghilev came upon Stravinsky as he played those eight-note chords over and over for hours as he transformed the folksongs into those barbaric rhythms of *The Rite of Spring.* Apparently, Stravinsky banged away enthralled by the rhythmic cacophonies he was producing (Walsch, 2002). Hearing and feeling the music that he played affectively changed him and thereby propelled a process that was not really bidirectional, since he played to himself, but, rather, circular. His piano, inert until touched by Stravinsky, and the music that he and his piano produced were the co-creators. Creating this music visibly "transformed" Stravinsky and, thus "transformed," he composed music unlike he or anyone else had ever heard before.

Stravinsky interacted with and was affectively transformed by his own creativity and his creation. The folksongs were transformed but so was the composer in the act of transforming. Like a musician transforming a melody, when an analyst and patient transform a patient's behavioral pattern, a uniquely changed dyad emerges. Both participants have the opportunity to be engaged in and by the change.

Forms and Transformations of Narcissism Revisited

Recall that Kohut posited that archaic narcissism is transformed into empathy, humor, creativity, a sense of transience, and wisdom. Accordingly, the expectation is that in the course of self psychologically informed treatment, the therapist's attending to the maintenance, interpretation, and repair of disruptions of the selfobject transference can increase a person's self-regard; his or her access to the private experience of another person; his or her coming to view himself or herself with irony; and, in a larger perspective, his or her accepting the passage of time and perhaps even finding a place in the temporal flow of humanity. These explicit expectations, directly and indirectly, are contained in Kohut's descriptions of the transformations of archaic narcissism.

But Kohut did not posit any more specific details as to how these transformations might be brought about—that is, outside his general statements about managing and interpreting the selfobject transference as patient and analyst were engaged in the analysis. Rather, for these transformations to occur, the various qualities Kohut listed must themselves be embodied in the treatment process. Transformation can only occur via a therapeutic process that itself embraces empathy, humor, creativity, and recognition of transience.

In the course of this chapter I have begun to look at the process of transformation through the lens of self- and interactive regulation, disruption and repair, and heightened affective moments to address both the "what" and "how" of the transformation of self-pathology. "What" refers to the patient's and the analyst's affect. Such transformations are promoted with and without symbolic-linguistic accompaniment. Transforming affect then impacts other dimensions of the sense of self and self-pathology. "How" refers to the inclusion of empathy, humor, creativity, and acceptance of one's transience as part and parcel of the therapeutic processes. The transformations discussed by Kohut operate throughout the therapeutic relationship by continually engaging the patient's and the therapist's affect states. Transformations of the patient's and the therapist's self-experience are thus also circular. The chapters that follow reconceptualize the treatment of archaic narcissism as the treatment of self-pathology and as a process of self- and interactive transformation, and they discuss, illustrate, and augment these proposals.

One final note: Throughout this chapter I have avoided taking up wisdom as a topic. My avoidance is deliberate. Although it was listed by Kohut as a transformation, I have come to believe that wisdom is on a different conceptual level than the other four. However, wisdom may be embedded in empathy, humor, and creativity, and an acceptance of transience can be embedded in wisdom. Wisdom—not as a trait but as the search for wisdom—will be taken up in a later chapter.

2 Implicit and Explicit Communication

In this chapter I examine the process of transformation through implicit and explicit communication with special attention to the therapist's contribution to therapeutic action. Therapists and patients implicitly convey their vision of life, the world, human nature, "reality," their *Weltanschauung*, and associated affect in their dialogue. This level of implicit communication is part and parcel of the dyad's ongoing regulations. It often provides the background against which, for better or worse, expectations are met, surpassed, or violated.

The importance of exploring a patient's unconscious, implicitly conveyed *Weltanschauung* has long been recognized in psychoanalysis, although analysts today are more likely to think of *Weltanschauung* in terms of grim unconscious beliefs (Weiss & Sampson, 1986), unconscious organizing principles (Stolorow, Brandchaft, & Atwood, 1987), or unconscious fantasies (Arlow, 1969). However, the analyst's implicit verbal communication reflecting the analyst's vision of the world has its own role in co-creating the patient's emerging thoughts, feelings, and actions. The analyst's implicit worldview thus impacts the process of transformation and is the central concern of this chapter.

Embedded in the therapist's verbal communication is the therapist's vision of life, the world, and "reality." Whether the therapist articulates this view consciously or shares it with the patient, the therapist's view shapes his or her implicit communications. To explicate that the therapist's vision shapes implicit communications and thus impacts the patient, a detour is necessary. An experiment in social psychology demonstrates the subtle behavioral impact of "priming" in implicit, nonconscious, verbal communication.

Priming (Lashley, 1951) refers to a preparatory function of thought, a stirring up of thoughts that leads directly to a behavior. But "priming" can be activated by the impact of another person as well, through implicit communication.

What might be distributed among such topics as the therapist's transference, countertransference, bias, suggestion, or the therapist's influence on the patient is thus potentially subsumed by social psychologist John Bargh and his colleagues (Bargh, Chen, & Burrows, 1996; see also Gladwell, 2005) under the heading of "priming." Following William James (1890), these researchers assume that we all harbor certain stereotypes—unconscious attitudes, thoughts, or images that can be triggered by simple everyday events and then manifested in measurable, observable behavior. The researchers proposed that imagining or thinking about an action increases, to some degree, the likelihood of its activation, the likelihood of the thought appearing as behavior. Their study also illustrates transitory transformations manifested in behavior that are probably ubiquitous occurrences in life. When such priming communications are not reinforced by repetition, they tend to extinguish quite rapidly, without our becoming aware of the behavior that has been stirred up. Through priming, the researchers reasoned, a brief and immediate alteration in one's behavior can be activated. Bargh's study thus can provide a microcosm of transformation: a controlled study using linguistic-symbolic thought that, as we shall see, alters a person's behavior.

Thirty volunteer psychology students at New York University were asked to participate in a study of language proficiency. The task consisted of 30 sets of five-word combinations. The participants were instructed to write down a grammatically correct sentence using only four of the five words given in each set. Here are some examples of the five-word groups presented:

from are Florida oranges temperature
shoes give replace old the
be will sweat lonely they
us bingo sing play let

In these sets, the words "Florida," "old," and "lonely" were the priming words. Other words embedded in a five-word set were: "worried," "gray," "helpless," "dependent," "sentimental," "wise," "stubborn," "forgetful," "conservative," "alone," and so forth. The participants given these sets of words were referred to as the "elderly priming condition" group. A matched control group received word sets in which the elderly priming words were replaced with neutral words such as thirsty, clean, private, and so forth. Each participant worked alone with no time requirements. Upon completion of the task, the experimenter explained to each participant that the study investigated how individuals use words in various ways. When a participant had gathered his or her belongings together, he or she was directed toward the elevator down the hall and thanked for participating. Using a hidden stopwatch, a confederate of the experimenter, who sat in a chair in front of a nearby office and seemed to be waiting for a professor, recorded the amount of time in seconds that each participant spent walking to the elevator, a length of corridor of about 9.75 meters.

The participants were later asked whether they thought the sentence construction task might have affected them in any way. They all stated that it had not. Furthermore, they were asked if they had known the task contained words relevant to a stereotype of an elderly person. No participant expressed any knowledge of the relevance of the words to an elderly stereotype. The experimenter then gave the participant a complete debriefing and explained the experimental hypothesis.

Here is the amazing finding: The participants who were primed with the elderly stereotype words walked significantly more slowly down the corridor than the control group.

From the vantage point of social psychology, the study investigated the nonconscious activation of a presumably already existing stereotype in a person's mind through priming. An elderly stereotype is a relatively stable, coherent nonconscious image of a nonspecific elderly person. From the vantage point of psychoanalysis, however, there are several additional implications:

1. The study demonstrated cross-modal transfer: translating a word or image from a visual modality into a bodily experience.

Cross-modal transfer, a crucial precursor of empathy, will be taken up in the next chapter.

2. Although the volunteers were not aware of any change in their feelings in connection with the study, a point I will discuss further later, the role of affect can be inferred by examining the difference between the elderly stereotype words and the neutral words. The elderly stereotype words—for example, "lonely," "hopeless," "dependent," and "stubborn"—seem closely associated with strong affect. The neutral words were not devoid of associated affect, but "thirsty" and "clean" are not as compellingly affective as the words in the other group. Thus, the study also illustrates the power of affect, triggered by words, mediated by cross-modal transfer, in promoting behavioral change.

3. The link between primed ideation and behavior is nonconscious and automatic; what is affected are nonconscious procedures, such as walking, and procedural memory. Nonconscious refers to procedures that are out of awareness, yet accessible to consciousness; they are not repressed. They are thus not dynamically unconscious. Nevertheless, dynamically unconscious processes, representations, or fantasies can also be activated in a manner similar to the priming of stereotypes. Although nonconscious and unconscious are not identical, there can be overlap in this respect.

4. Implicit communications that are embedded in verbal content can exert a powerful effect, manifest in a visible and organized behavioral response. Bargh and his coworkers concluded that priming the participants with words linked to a particular stereotype influenced their behavior by activating the stereotype. Since there was no direct allusion to speed or movement, no words like "slow" or "halting" in the sets presented to the participants, some image of "elderly" had presumably resided in the memory of the participant and had been activated through priming. Those who had been primed then behaved in a way that was consistent with the activated stereotypic image. A parallel can be drawn between priming and suggestion through interventions dominated by theory implicitly embedded in a therapist's communications. The patient takes the therapist's cues but responds to them within the limits of his own repertoire.

In a follow-up study, presenting the implicit message explicitly had no effect on behavior. These findings replicate those found in studies of subliminal perception (Silverman, Lachmann, & Milich, 1982), when a subliminal message was presented supraliminally. Presenting messages containing personally sensitive or conflicted content at the level of normal perception, we argued, permits the subjects to fend off or defend against any threatening implications. Therefore, the person can nullify the content more readily and will not be affected by it.

What was the role of affect in the priming experiment? After completing the experiment, the researchers investigated whether the affect and arousal of the two groups differed with respect to the priming stimulus. Using a standardized questionnaire, they found that the participants who were exposed to the "elderly" words were *not* more likely to feel sad or less aroused when compared to the control group. They did not feel "slowed down" even though their walk was "slowed down." The lack of awareness of the participants with respect to their affect suggests that their feelings were not aroused, or that, if aroused, they did not reach the level of awareness, or that these feelings dissipated quickly when the volunteers resumed their usual gait. Their more sluggish walk, however, does suggest that their momentary mood had been affected. As I indicated earlier, the priming words such as "hopeless" or "stubborn" had strong affective connotations. However, the researchers did not press on to explore this or other possible implications.

In psychoanalysis the distinction between priming and suggestion can be murky. There is considerable overlap. Priming relies on an already existing stereotype in the patient whereas suggestion relies equally or more on the quality of the transference, the patient's compliance. Take the following illustration. A supervisee of mine described his treatment of an anxious and depressed man who had been an actor but who had changed careers to become a schoolteacher shortly after he began his treatment. The supervisee told me that he was sorry that this man had switched careers because he would have preferred having an actor as a patient rather than yet another schoolteacher.

After about a year of four sessions of analysis per week, this man started going to auditions again. For reasons unclear to my supervisee, the patient, or me, he again sought work on the stage. Although he had experienced some minor disappointments at his school, there seemed to be no external reason propelling his return to the stage. As my supervisee and I reviewed his process notes for the previous weeks of the treatment, which we had no longer been doing, we noted that whenever the patient spoke about some difficulty in his work in the school, his therapist had translated it into "show biz" language. For example, when the patient spoke of feeling anxious prior to the first day of classes as a new term began, the therapist said, "Ah, opening night jitters!" Is this priming or suggestion? Most likely, it is both.

Further investigation revealed that the patient had retained his desire to act and his pleasure in performing. Having felt more emboldened through his analysis, it did not take much prompting, priming, or suggesting by his therapist for him to translate these thoughts into behaviors. It is possible, too, that there had been a growing affective engagement between therapist and patient during this time. Through his show-biz interventions, my supervisee had raised his own level of engagement and also had begun to respond to the patient's faintly emerging desire to resume his acting career.

An unexpected mood or behavioral change is a good indication that a therapist has touched a patient in an unintended way. We often work backwards, first noting a change and then inquiring whether or not the patient is aware of it. Then we bring our observations to the patient's attention and investigate the possible sources of that change. Working in this way, we sometimes detect, after the fact, subtle changes in our own attitude and behavior that have emerged in interaction with the patient. In the foregoing illustration, explicitly and implicitly, an "unintended message" slipped through the therapist's conscious self-monitoring and coincided with the patient's dawning readiness to act again. In other instances the therapist's message and the patient's "stereotype" may obstruct treatment.

In Bargh's study the implicit communication to the participants was conscious on the part of the examiner. The findings are equally relevant if a therapist, like my supervisee, nonconsciously or unconsciously activates a particular stereotype, image, preconception, state of mind, fantasy, or representation from a patient's repertoire—or a therapist may implicitly activate a patient's feeling of shame, undesirability, or fear of intimacy. The therapist may also connect with a preferred self-image of the patient—for better or worse.

When a Therapist "Primes"

Judy consulted me about her analysis. She told me that her analyst said she was resistant in that whenever she moved closer to him in the course of the analysis, she then quickly withdrew. Furthermore, when she announced she was seeking this consultation with me, she was told that it was a hostile act and that she was fleeing from treatment when things got tough. She objected to this characterization, where-upon her analyst asked her whether she was on the debating team in high school. She reported that he then told her she has a problem with intimacy as manifested in their relationship. Judy explained to me that as soon as she confided in her analyst about a disappointing date she had had or a problem she had encountered in a college course, he offered her painful confrontations of her hostility and her withdrawal from him and others.

I had told Judy when she telephoned me that I would be able to offer her a consultation but did not have the time to work with her. We met for six sessions in the course of which I told her that it seemed to me that her withdrawal from her analyst was self-protective. I tried to balance his trailing edge interpretations with some leading edge formulations.

Judy told me that she had been spoiled by her parents and sought challenge in her life. She exercised vigorously and was an excellent runner. She said she tried to steel herself to compensate for what she felt was an excessively privileged life. However, she suffered from anxiety and debilitating depression, which were the reason for her entering analysis and for which her analyst was prescribing medications.

Since Judy's anxiety and depression increased in the course of her treatment, her mother, a therapist in another city, encouraged her to have a consultation. Judy's analyst, however, considered the increase in symptomotology to be a consequence of her resistance and tendency to withdraw from him. She told me that she argued a good deal with her analyst but that he offered the kind of "tough" approach that she felt she needed. The analyst's implicit and explicit conviction of what makes for change coincided with Judy's conviction about proving that she could be "tough."

Judy told me that she was well aware of her discomfort in intimate relationships. In fact, it had been another reason for seeking treatment. She also told me that her analyst's tone of voice was reminiscent of her frightening father. That, too, made her feel anxious but she was ashamed to tell her analyst. Thus, it was both the content of his interventions, his implicitly and explicitly harsh view of how analysis cures, as well as his affective-vocal communications that added to her distress. But implicitly and explicitly he ultimately fulfilled her wish to become tough and thereby to overcome her belief that her parents had spoiled her.

It appeared to me that Judy and her analyst shared a similar view of how therapy works or, rather, what therapy should accomplish: By enduring pain and suffering we become stronger, tougher, and healthier. I doubt whether Judy's analyst said this to her directly, but it seemed to be implicit in their interactions.

In a manner reminiscent of Bargh's priming experiment, Judy's analyst implicitly functioned as a "primer." Since I never spoke with him, what follows are my inferences based on Judy's account of her treatment. In his interpretations, he implicitly conveyed a view of the therapeutic process and of human nature that might be characterized as:

> People are basically competitive and hostile, but you, you would-be-high-school debater, are more so than other people because you deny, flee from, and defend against these truths. To become healthy ("tough") we must remove those defenses. You are anxious because of your own hostility and competitiveness. You must undergo the pain and frustration of facing yourself. Avoiding, resisting and running away are typical of your pathology and will only perpetuate your problems.

In implicitly shaming Judy for trying to flee from the tough treatment, her analyst concurred with her "stereotype" of a healthy, tough person who does not want to be "spoiled." Through something like "priming," he activated that stereotype in her.

Much of what I describe here I discussed with Judy during our consultation. I gave her the name of another analyst, but she never called. I presume she remained with her analyst, thereby demonstrating that in addition to whatever conscious alliance existed, a powerful, unrecognized, nonconscious, and unconscious bond had been forged between them. In part, I surmise, this connection was based on the similarity of their stereotypes: The world is a tough place and you have to be tough to make it. If it's painful, it's good medicine. Take it and you will become tough.

It seemed to me that Judy's analyst, as reported by her, was as specific in his implicit communications as Bargh and the researchers were in theirs. Judy's analyst's implicit (and explicit) communications connected with her stereotype of the tough person she wanted to be. And, I presume that my implicit (and explicit) leading edge formulations directed toward different ways of being in the world failed to connect with her on that level.

Bargh's research exposed the student volunteers to only one priming session after which they were "debriefed." Whatever transformations were set in motion were short lived. In contrast, the priming that accompanies analytic interventions can be continuous and without debriefing. Furthermore, the researchers were aware of the stereotype they were priming. This may or may not be true for therapists. Thus, an understanding and recognition of the potential effect of priming adds to the heavy burden therapists already carry with respect to self-reflection and self-monitoring.

What if the researchers had studied a different stereotype using other priming words, such as Florida, spring break, bikini, thong, t-shirts, and so forth? I would predict that a completely different stereotype might have been activated in the college student volunteers. They might have skipped down the hall, rather than dragging their feet. What if Judy had encountered an analyst who was not rigidly bound to a need-to-become-tough-through-facing-pain vision of human nature? What if Judy had encountered a consultant who could shift from leading edge formulations and offer trailing edge formulations more in tune with her "stereotype" of toughness and yet use these interventions paradoxically to perturb or challenge the stereotype as well? In either instance, a more flexible repertoire of assumptions might have offered opportunities to examine the "glue" that binds the implicit communication of the analyst and the preexisting stereotype or self-image of the patient. The dilemma of nonconscious, unarticulated compliance or disjunction between patient and therapist might then be better explored.

Judy and her analyst illustrate a particular conjunction—a view of life as a painful struggle—whereas the disjunction with me was presumably fostered by my less harsh and more optimistic view of the therapeutic process. This vignette ushers in a consideration of the various psychoanalytic visions of life, human nature, and "reality," and their contribution to the process of transformation of a person's self-experience and relationships with others.

The Analyst's Vision of Reality in Psychoanalytic Theory

The findings from Bargh's study and the consultation with Judy point to how a patient's affect and self-experience can be transformed through nonconscious processing of the analyst's implicitly communicated vision of human nature. Schafer (1976) has delineated four visions of life, the world, human nature, or "reality" derived from literary criticism and philosophy, from mythic and artistic products. Schafer's notion of "vision" is well captured by the term *Weltanschauung*. He showed how these visions are contained, more or less, in various psychoanalytic theories. These visions are also embedded and implicit in psychoanalytic practice. That is, these visions or subjective views of the world are not only contained in theories, but, as in the case of Judy's analyst (and of me as Judy's consultant), are also communicated in analytic formulations and interventions. These visions are the tragic, the romantic, the ironic, and the comic.

Analytic communications are colored, lightly or heavy handedly, with one or more of these perspectives. No theories and probably no analysts adhere exclusively to any one vision. Furthermore, these visions are not mutually exclusive. But since an analyst may rely more heavily on one of these visions, a therapeutic process similar to repetitive "priming" may come to characterize a treatment. While one priming experience may well have only a brief effect, repetitive priming, as may have been the case for Judy, may exert a longer lasting impact.

I particularly like these visions as a way of depicting implicit communication in nonpathological terms. Each vision is a legitimate perspective on "reality." Each is embedded, implicitly and, to some extent, explicitly, in an analyst's (as well as a patient's) verbal communications. The analyst's communications will reflect his or her worldview, including a view of treatment, and this can complement or conflict with a patient's implicit or explicit worldview. The therapeutic process is furthered or obstructed as these visions of patient and analyst reinforce or conflict with each other. These visions inform the communications of both therapist and patient and thus constitute a continual bidirectional priming, for better or worse. There are obviously different ways of cataloging such worldviews. In what follows I utilize the fourfold classification proposed by Schafer (1976), who distinguished a comic vision, tragic vision, romantic vision, and ironic vision.

The comic vision emphasizes optimism, progress, and amelioration of difficulties. My consultation with Judy may have conveyed aspects of this vision, in sharp contrast with her "curative fantasy" (Ornstein, 1995) of needing to become tough. Optimism, an emphasis on hope, finding security and pleasure through new beginnings, and progress through redoing the past via new relationships are essential to this vision. Fun, humor, laughter, and spontaneity are not essential but neither are they ruled out. A goal of treatment is to feel alive, to feel that one is worthy of being the recipient of caring attention, and to feel free to pursue and enjoy success. Think of Shakespeare's comedies. Enormous obstacles are overcome, at the end the proper lovers are united, and all's well that ends well.

In the romantic vision, life is an adventure and odyssey, and analysis is a journey of discovery in the face of anxiety, guilt, grief, yearning, and despair. This ordeal is to be lived through or "worked through" and the victory to be won (or the defeat to be endured) concerns not so much a hostile rigid environment but contact with one's inner world with its unique version of one's earlier relationships and experiences. Think of Eugene O'Neill's *Long Day's Journey into Night* (see F. Lachmann & A. Lachmann, 1992), in which the ordeal is located within Mary Tyrone's "inner world." Awareness of one's inner world and sharing are equally prized and each can often lead to the other. In the romantic vision, analyst and patient form an alliance in their descent into the abyss of the patient's life. Authenticity, individuality, and self-expression are all highly prized.

The tragic vision also entails intense emotional involvement but sharing gives way to confrontation and self-confrontation and is less important than facing the world as it is. Conflict, terror, and uncertainty are to be expected. Growth takes place through adversity, deprivation, and frustration. There is no gain without pain. The tragic vision is implicitly conveyed when the analyst confronts and frustrates the patient's resistance and implies that only by remaining in what may feel like a painful process is one on a path toward genuine growth. In an extreme form of this vision, psychoanalysis is not an adventure but an endurance contest or, better yet, a painful birth process from which one can only emerge bloodied.

The analytic process potentially evokes all four visions at different times in any treatment. We all have our own preferred vision, but I think that the tragic vision at times seems to hog the center stage. Think of Shakespeare's tragedies. Hardly ever do any of the protagonists remain alive at the end. But, Shakespeare knew that "comic relief" was essential in his tragedies. He regularly included characters like Falstaff or the grave diggers, or comic scenes such as Lear's blind leap over a "cliff" that is not there, to provide relief from the cascading tragic events. Through contrast, these comic interludes actually heighten the tragedy; they also enable the audience to bear it. As analysts we could all benefit from Shakespeare's wisdom.

The ironic vision, like the tragic vision, seeks out inevitable internal contradictions, but it does so through paradoxes, and ambiguities. It addresses the same subject matter as the tragic vision, but with a somewhat bemused detachment that works to keep things in perspective. Kohut's comment about acceptance and denial of transience illustrates this vision. Often, issues are framed as dialectics. Nothing is taken for granted. Firmly held beliefs, expectations, established traditions, and cherished illusions are all challenged. Irony is directed not only outward as a depiction of the unpredictability of the world, but also inward. Applied to oneself, irony is self-deprecatory, but it is not so strident or harsh as self-abasement or self-ridicule. Irony can even be self-enhancing. A good illustration is of not taking any single aspect of oneself too seriously for one's own good.

Every theory—Freudian, self psychological, Lacanian, Kleinian, relational—incorporates aspects of all four of these visions, though in different proportions. Controversies among psychoanalysts are often fueled by those who rigidly hold on to one or another of these visions. These four visions are implicit and, at times, explicit in what is verbalized in varying shades in the patient–therapist dialogue.

Implicit Relational Knowing

In addition to the implicit contributions of the visions of patient and analyst, which can at times be verbalized, there are multiple communicative pathways whereby nonverbal, procedural knowledge is brought into the therapeutic interaction. The most comprehensive discussion of the implicit, nonverbal, procedural contributions to therapeutic action has been put forward by the Boston Change Process Study Group (1998, 2002; Lyons-Ruth et al., 1998; Stern et al., 1998; Tronick et al., 1998) and by Karlen Lyons-Ruth (1999). Both the Boston Group and Lyons-Ruth have tried to integrate their understanding of therapeutic change with the same developmental findings that buttress the clinical work described in these chapters. In contrast to Bucci (1997), who argues that nonverbal representations must be connected to one another for full integration to occur, both the Boston Group and Lyons-Ruth have left the door open for significant change to occur without necessarily being accompanied by verbalized awareness.

Lyons-Ruth posits as a starting point that "meaning systems are organized to include implicit or procedural forms of knowing." It is possible that these meaning systems become available only through action, that they reside in an implicit or enactive domain, since "the organization of memory and meaning in the implicit or enactive domain only becomes manifest in the doing" (1999, pp. 577–578). Lyons-Ruth's emphasis on enactive procedures potentially links these nonconscious, prerepresentational patterns with the enactments that occur in psychoanalytic treatment. However, the same implicit procedures are active even when an enactment is not dominating the therapeutic relationship. As implicit procedures available only in the enactive domain are woven into the therapeutic relationship, change can occur without the enactment being articulated. "Enactive procedures become more articulated and integrated through participation in more coherent and collaborative forms of intersubjective interaction" (p. 579). In fact, Lyons-Ruth emphasizes that the organization of meaning is implicit in the organization of enacted relational dialogue and does not require reflective thought or verbalization to be known; it does not rely on translation of procedures into reflective symbolized knowledge. This collaborative intersubjective process is also referred to as "implicit relational knowing" (Lyons-Ruth et al., 1998) in that both partners—caretaker–infant and therapist–patient—get to know each other and themselves better implicitly through their interactive process. In psychotherapy, this is a silent process that accompanies the dialogue and remains so unless it is made explicit or makes its way into enactments.

Both Schafer in his discussion of the analyst's vision and Lyons-Ruth and her colleagues in their discussion of implicit relational knowing explore the interfaces between verbal and nonverbal and implicit and explicit domains. They both emphasize that what is implicit in our verbal interactions, even though it may remain unstated, exercises a powerful effect in shaping expectations, moods, attitudes, and behaviors in both patient and analyst. Additionally, we know from research (Bargh et al., 1996; Silverman et al., 1982) that implicit communications can be far more impactful than the communication made explicitly. In addition to the experimental literature making the case that implicit, nonverbal communication need not be made explicit, common sense tells us that there are situations in which it's better to let sleeping implicit, nonverbal procedures lie. As Dan Stern rhetorically asked at a conference, if after a kiss, you discuss where you held your nose, what you did with your tongue, and the like, would it improve the experience of the kiss?

Transformation of Affect and More

In these first chapters I present an array of proposals and constructs pertaining to the process of transformation through self- and interactive regulation of affect and arousal, through the disruption and repair of these interactions, and through heightened affective moments. In this chapter I presented an array of proposals and constructs pertaining to implicit communication through priming inherent in the worldview or vision of the analyst and through implicit relational knowing. The various proposals are now illustrated through a discussion of a portion of the treatment of Sally.

Sally was 42 years old when her husband precipitously left her because, as Sally and I came to see it, he could not devote himself to drinking while being married to her. She had been in therapy, on and off, for about 20 years. After her husband left she again sought therapy and after a brief failed therapy experience, she then entered treatment with me. She was skeptical about receiving any benefit and was reluctant to engage once again in what she anticipated would be another disappointing experience.

Her relationship with her husband had been idyllic, or at least so she felt. They often traveled separately during the week as part of their work, so he was able to drink while on the road. Being with his wife, however, prevented him from drinking as much as he liked and as much as he could drink while on the road. But she loved her life with him on the weekends, living in an upscale California community, playing tennis, and enjoying the warmth and adoration her husband expressed when with her. There was one regret: He did not want to have a child, so she gave up her desire to have children. Then, in a flash, after about 16 years of marriage, it was all gone.

Shortly prior to the breakup of the marriage, Sally and her husband had come to New York City for their work. Now, without a husband or child, she felt "stranded and trapped in dirty, cold, unfriendly New York." In the course of obtaining her divorce Sally met a very stable but rather rigid man. He was in his early 50s and had never been married, although he had had numerous relationships. Mostly, he preferred to spend his time going to the theater and to the opera. He had no interest in tennis. She had made her career in popular music, 180 degrees from the opera. She had little interest in seeing every play or going to the opera. Other than the major differences in their avocation and styles, the relationship worked. She knew she could trust him, though, alas, he was unlike her warm, demonstrative, and affectionate husband. And, even more importantly for her, as we later elaborated in her treatment, he was unlike her charismatic father.

When she was about 6 years old, Sally's parents separated and her father "abandoned" her with her mother. By the time Sally was 10 or 11, her mother had become dangerously psychotic; in one terrifying episode she had cracked Sally's skull and broken several of her ribs. Sally recalled that during her early teen years, she slept with one eye open because in the middle of the night, her mother would burst into her bedroom, in a delusional state, brandishing a knife. Sally would then run out of the house into the street wearing just her nightgown. Her older sister, who was "immune" to the mother's attacks, probably because it was Sally who had been the father's favorite, would then let her know when it was safe to return.

After leaving her mother, Sally's father married several times and had numerous children. He also made and lost fortunes in business. Sally recalled her father's sudden exciting appearances and just as sudden disappearances. Yet, most important, she felt adored by him. Alas, he died when she was in her mid-teens.

Sally feared that her mother would literally kill her. She made plans as best she could and fled from her home. With the help of a neighboring family she finally succeeded in getting the court to place her with that family as a foster home. They literally rescued her and she felt safe and loved. She loved that family, felt enormous gratitude, and has remained in contact with them over the years. In talking about her preteen years, a dramatic split appeared, reflecting the change in her outlook between the time of her mother's adequate functioning and her mother's psychosis. During her teen years, Sally felt her childhood had come to an abrupt end. She went to school and continued ballet and flute classes for a while, but could never feel relaxed enough to feel secure and to "play." With her marriage she had recaptured some of her lost feeling of optimism, security, and playfulness that was associated with her pre-psychotic mother, her father, and his world.

The vision of the world contained in Sally's narrative was essentially "comic," as odd as that may sound given how harrowing life with her mother had been during her teen years. Prior to the breakup of her marriage, Sally had regained her optimism about life and saw her life as progressing just as she desired. The "enemy" had been clearly external to her (her mother) as had been her "rescuer" (her father). Her hope and her expectation of an ultimately happy ending to her tortured childhood had been reinforced by the loving foster family she had found and this had carried her through difficult times. Her marriage, maintained through some compromises and trade-offs on her part, also sustained her comic vision. The breakup of the marriage shattered this vision and specifically her expectation of being adored by a charismatic man. The breakup repeated the abrupt shift from attachment to abandonment, and from safety to danger, that characterized her childhood.

To convey how her husband's abandonment felt to her, Sally spoke of her mother's homicidal rages in contrast to her father's exciting visits. Her husband's leaving replicated her father's painful departures when he would return to his new family. She was then left at the mercy of her dangerously unpredictable mother. The depression and despair she felt, the loss of hope, and the dread that she would be doomed to live life alone and in terror brought to mind the time when she felt so helpless about protecting herself from her mother. To address this experience in one session, I said to her that she was now in a better position to articulate the rage and fear that she felt about both her husband's abandonment and similar experiences stirred up in relation to her father. In retrospect, I seem to have been holding out a renewed possibility of a better ending. Judging by her response, my timing was off and she was not yet ready to consider her resources. In response she told me that in her past therapies she had spent endless time discussing her parents and she asked why she had to go through it again.

Implicit in my intervention was my expectation that she now had a perspective that could enable her to investigate more aspects of her experience of loss and rage in relation to both her father and her husband. In her response she told me that this did not happen in the past—so why should it work now? I therefore turned our attention to her affectionate attachment to her father and her husband and her attempt to hold on to them. Specifically, I thought that her experience with her husband evoked many positive feelings associated with her father. I added that just as she did not want to alienate her father by rebuking him for leaving her, she did not reveal her annoyance and silent rebukes about her husband's drinking. She told me that he sensed her judgmental side in that he told her, when he left, that he was not good enough for her.

During this period Sally had a dream about her apartment and her being overrun with cockroaches. She felt stuck in that infested apartment and, metaphorically speaking, was not yet ready to move. The cockroaches also depicted the terrors of her childhood. She felt that when her husband left, he took with him a protective shield that, as in the past in relation to her father, had made her feel safe from the violent intrusions of her mother, the cockroaches of her dream. She felt as defenseless and vulnerable now as she did then.

I thought that Sally was waiting for an "exterminator" to rescue her, as she felt her father had done on occasion. I also thought of the transference implications of this dream image—that is, her expecting to be rescued by me. I did not say any of this. Articulating my thought might have intruded me into her private world to a greater extent than she might be able to assimilate. Interpreting her implicit wish for an "exterminator" as a message to me might also perpetuate a rigidly held comic vision, albeit a fractured one, in that danger and rescue were both depicted as "outside of her." But I could sense that a comic vision of life was not working for Sally and indeed this was a large part of the problem. I doubt whether I could have articulated this verbally. I was not as clear at the time as I was in retrospect. At the time I sensed our tenuous relatedness that indicated a vulnerability on her part that would not tolerate much intrusion from me or from my optimism. Yet I felt that we had to contact the more optimistic side of Sally, her yearning for intimacy and recognition that had been so sustaining for her in the past.

My interventions shifted from a focus on the "cockroaches" to coping strategies against feeling so exposed. Rather than emphasizing the external world (her psychotic mother, the cockroaches) as her "enemy," I explored two areas: her compromises and her "trade-offs" in keeping her complaints about her father and her husband to herself so as not to alienate them, and her resourcefulness and skill in finding her foster family. In her life, her attraction to her father and her search for someone like him as a hoped-for source of comfort and happiness led her to forgo stability and seek a marriage partner who had her father's charisma but also his instability. The "trade-off" worked for 16 years. The emphasis on the trade-off shifted our attention from an "enemy" and rescuer who were external to her to an exploration of her subjective world. In retrospect, there was a shift in our shared visions—from comic (the promise of a happy ending) to romantic (the need to refind her charismatic father in spite of his instability) and tragic (the dread that, unless she finds her father, she is destined to live in the world of her psychotic mother). We explored her past relationships and the experiences that contributed to sustaining her trade-off, especially the joy she felt in her father's presence, no matter what the sacrifice.

Applying the perspective derived from the four visions of "reality" to Sally's treatment alerted me to the role that these visions are co-created as well as indigenous to each of us. They describe different expectations of the world, ranging from expectations of support and gentle teasing to detachment and "hard knocks." And so I reflected more carefully on the kinds of expectations each of us entertained at any given moment. I also noted when our visions coincided and when they were at odds: Both of these circumstances can further or obstruct the process of transformation.

The next phase of the treatment was dominated by Sally's ambivalent relationship with her boyfriend. He was stable, very kind and concerned, and their sexual relationship was very satisfying to her. "But," she said, "every play that opened on Broadway, the ballet—well, OK, the ballet, but the opera?" That last comment was very hard for me to tolerate, but nevertheless I was able to maintain my unwavering empathic connection with Sally.

These interests of her boyfriend and the intellectual world he valued not only were really foreign to Sally but also held no interest for her. The main tensions and fights in their relationship centered on her not knowing some "obvious" bit of cultural trivia, history, or current events. Her lack of knowledge evoked searing contempt for and humiliation of her on his part. He gradually came to see that his heavy-handed attempts to force opera on her had a reverse effect. During this period when I would tilt toward supporting her criticism and complaints, she would defend him. When I tilted toward defending him, she reported that all her girlfriends advised her to "dump him." Our exploration of this pattern led us to see how she valued his stability and thus the stability she derived from him. As such, whether to maintain the relationship or dump him was too close to call. I also addressed her fear that if she left him, she would never find anyone else. Who would want her? In these explorations there seemed to be an implicit expectation of a happy ending by both of us.

One day in the fourth year of her treatment Sally entered my office and commented, as she had on numerous previous occasions, about how cold and ugly New York was. New York was still a metaphor for many misfortunes: the wrong choices she had made throughout her life, the bad luck that followed her with respect to her work, the general miscalculations that characterized her relationships, and, especially, that her boyfriend lacked the charisma of her ex-husband. Fortunately, he also lacked his alcoholism. New York symbolized the world into which her adoring, now here, now gone again, father had abandoned her, a world populated by cockroaches and her mother's psychosis. So in the context of beginning a session with her usual complaints about dismal New York, it was an unusual and a heightened affective moment, at least for me, when I believe for the first time in her treatment Sally turned to me to ask a question: "Did you grow up in New York?" I began my response with, "Assuming I have grown up ..." and as I listened to myself, I stopped. We both roared with laughter. I went no further in my response. My comment had surprised both of us and I was reacting to my own surprising comment. This interaction constituted a moment in which our relationship was momentarily transformed from the cautious distance exercised by both of us to shared laughter. It was an unexpected "now" moment (Stern et al., 1998) for both of us.

Sally dropped her question and went on to talk of other things, such as obstacles in finding a new career. A freelance venture she had undertaken had collapsed and so had she. Feeling hopeless and despondent, she had been unable to get out of bed in the morning. She was still angry that colleagues she trusted had ignored her accurate assessments of people and business arrangements. Later on in the session, however, she returned to my comment, and said, "You know when we both laughed, that was intimate."

It really was an intimate moment. In my response to Sally's question I had nonconsciously and implicitly regulated my own affective state. I must have wanted to disrupt her repetitive recital of the disappointments in her life as symbolized by New York. I was also demonstrating an attitude of, "Let's not take ourselves so seriously." My comment, my verbal communication, had been chock full of implicit meanings.

By stopping my comment as I did, I implicitly conveyed a familiarity with Sally. I implied that I knew her in a way that she liked, as a potentially far more playful Californian rather than as an embattled, frightened, angry, and despondent New Yorker. I gave Sally an opportunity to have fun with me and (although I was not aware of this at the time) to revive a sense of intimacy associated with her ex-husband and her father. Implicitly, I said to her that being in New York (being with me) can be fun, too. Most important, I believe my comment challenged her rigidly held tragic vision, a rebound from her comic vision first prompted by her childhood abandonment and now powerfully reinforced by her husband leaving her. My comment jostled the somewhat stiff, depressed affect that frequently characterized the opening of the sessions by pitting an expression of an ironic view against her expectations of disaster.

When I later thought about this interaction I realized I was implicitly joining the ranks of her father and ex-husband. However, Sally's comment about experiencing our intimacy suggested that she heard my remark, in its context, as affectionate. That is, I would not be speaking with her in this manner if I did not feel warmly toward her. Furthermore, in spite of the potentially problematic aspect of my implicit communication, it may have subsequently contributed toward enabling her to work out a difficult situation with her boyfriend. I will pick this point up later.

Now another question: Why on earth did I make that comment? What possessed me? I can only speculate about that. Except to complain occasionally that she had not gotten any better, until that time Sally rarely if ever addressed direct statements to me, or asked questions about me, or expressed any personal interest in me. The transference, a tentative though frequently ruptured idealizing selfobject transference, had enabled her, gradually, to regain a somewhat more positive sense of herself and even to experience brief moments of the well-being that she had previously enjoyed during her marriage and that had been linked historically to the periodic appearances of her father. But an atmosphere of distance and fragility hung in the room.

Prior to our "assuming I have grown up" session Sally and I must have been paving a path toward greater intimacy. Implicit relational knowing had been in the background of the session and now emerged in the foreground as an enactment. In my comment I mirrored her continuing self-depreciation with ironic humor on the elusiveness of maturity. She evidently experienced our shared laughter as I did, as affection and a moment of intimacy. Through some slight self-mockery, through not taking myself so seriously, I illustrated a sense of bemused and reluctant recognition of the transience of life. I depicted myself as not having grown up and as mocking my desire to stay young, just as she had recently bemoaned her upcoming birthday. Inadvertently, I had included several of the dimensions of the process that furthers transformation, empathy, humor, and transience, just as Sally reorganized her experience with me to embrace greater intimacy.

Was I aware of any of this when I made my comment? Of course not. However, I was aware that there was something new and different in her question to me, a potentially new affective coloration in our relationship. This was her contribution to the transformative moment. In my response I pushed the envelope. I used the situation to further a connection, an expansion of her and my implicit awareness of ourselves and of each other. Later, volunteering the comment in which she explicitly acknowledged our "intimate" moment reflected her expanded self-awareness, and heralded what turned out to be a vastly different feeling about herself in relation to me as well as newly formed sense of herself. In this interaction we both altered our immediate affective experience of each other. That is, Sally's self-experience was transformed, as was mine. I felt a new connection, or perhaps better, we co-created a new way of connecting with each other. The new connection arose affectively, nonverbally, and implicitly; its crystallization was fostered by surprise, a violation of expectations for both of us, and by our shared laughter.

There were various subtle changes in Sally's life, in my feelings about her, and in our relationship after the "intimate" session. Several weeks later, Sally mentioned in the course of a session that she had just had the birthday we had spoken about, an event about which she had expressed notable ambivalence. At the end of that hour she said that she wanted to share some of her birthday chocolates with me and gave me the chocolates on her way out of the office.

In writing up the treatment of Sally I was now subsequently struck by the similarity between her bringing me the birthday chocolates and the actions of the patient, discussed at the Bellevue seminar, who paid for the dinners of his analyst and his colleagues. As Sally and I explored the meaning and implications of her giving me the chocolates, its "leading edge" became apparent. We understood this gift as reflecting her readiness now to let me in on aspects of her life other than disappointment, despair, and rage. In this instance trailing edge motives such as competitiveness with my having given more of myself or trying to stir up my anxiety about aging by inducing me to eat that chocolate-covered cholesterol would have taken the analysis in a different direction. I believe it would have derailed her burgeoning ability to regain a feeling of trust and tolerance for intimacy with others and me. In her associations to the birthday chocolates, she revealed an aspect of her current life that she had not spoken about, the surprisingly good time she had had enjoying the occasion with friends and her fiancée. We understood that she was ready to reveal another side of her life to me. During this period of time, her feelings of despair and lack of energy decreased. She could now get up in the morning, which she had been unable to do ever since the collapse of a freelance venture. Furthermore, she was able go to her health club and resume a long-standing exercise program.

Sally and her boyfriend had become engaged some months before our "intimate" session occurred. However, the disrespectful way in which, at times, he spoke to her resurfaced. She had complained to him and pointed out his unacceptable tone and manner on numerous occasions with only a brief effect. After our "intimate" session an incident occurred in which his "disrespect" again filled the air, but she handled herself differently. Now Sally, fearless and transformed, was able to tell him, whether or not they married, if he spoke to her like that again, she "is out of here." Apparently she was clear, and with some frequency he now asks her whether she notices how sweet he is. And, a year later, Sally told me that he is still as sweet as he was on the day they got married.

In assessing the therapeutic consequences of my comment, "assuming I have grown up," there are three possibilities. I list them because there is no way of confirming or disproving any of them. First, my intervention had no effect or at best a minimal affect. What occurred afterward, the soft signs of therapeutic change, came as a result of all our prior and subsequent painstaking work. Second, my comment occurred in an already subtly changing context. It furthered an intimacy that had slowly been building. A trend continued that had been evolving. My comment not only enhanced an ongoing process but also was quite consonant with it. It came at a time when Sally's sense of herself had shifted from needing to be rescued to being ready to recognize and own her resources. She shifted from feeling that she had to accept trade-offs to taking risks. Although I believe in the merits of this explanation, I also believe that a third possibility may better capture these circumstances. My intervention engaged both of us affectively and transformed our interaction in a dramatic way. The shift that occurred could not or would not have occurred had the treatment proceeded without that moment.

In this chapter, I have explored transformation within the therapeutic process with an emphasis on the therapist's implicit verbal communications. Both therapist and patient affectively impact each other as they communicate their implicit visions of life, the world, human nature, and "reality." By adopting literary terms to describe the four visions' reality, I am emphasizing that they are ubiquitous. One vision is not more desirable, therapeutic, or pathological than another. Their value lies in the checks and balances they provide in the treatment. But, if you have read carefully, you will have noticed that, implicitly, I do favor some visions over others, as I think we all do. But we had best know which they are.

3 The Road to Empathy

Transforming affect as emerging in a bidirectional process is now applied to empathy. As one of the constituents of the transformative therapist–patient interaction, empathy, too, requires clarification and unpacking.

Imagine asking a magician to describe how he transforms his assistant into an elephant. "I ask my assistant to step into a large black box. I pull a curtain over it; when I pull the curtain back, my assistant is gone and an elephant is there." This description of the transformation of the magician's assistant omits important details. These details occur offstage and hidden from view, and are analogous to the omissions in discussions of empathy in the transformation of self-pathology. In a moment, I will draw the curtain aside to examine some of the "details" that therapist and patient contribute to an empathic exchange and then to the eventual transformation of self-experience. These details are important in teasing apart what happens in an empathic exchange, but it is difficult to isolate them conceptually. To aid in illuminating these "details" I follow a somewhat circuitous route by examining first what might be called the "precursors" of "empathic understanding." In this chapter, these precursors are mapped out as situated along the road to empathy, while the following chapter addresses the empathic understanding proper.

To get started, some definitions: "Empathy" was American psychologist Edward Tichener's translation of the German word *einfühlung*, which indicates a mental process of feeling oneself into the experience of another person. The process of *einfühlen* depicts the activity of a single psychological subject. It implies a one-way model as one feels one's way into the subjectivity of another person, or a text, or a work of art. This one-way view passed imperceptibly into English and into its translated form, empathy. For better or worse, Kohut's name has now become inextricably associated with the role of empathy in psychoanalytic treatment. Although he explicitly acknowledged that analysts from various theoretical perspectives have relied on empathy as a means of accessing the experience of their patients, he nonetheless placed it at the center of his own definition of psychoanalysis. That is, for Kohut, psychoanalysis concerns itself only with what is accessible through introspection and empathy (Kohut, 1959). Clearly, empathy was around before Kohut, but to him empathy was the royal road to the inner life of another person. In keeping with established usage, however, Kohut assumed a one-directional model of empathy, a one-way street flowing from analyst to patient—and this led to confusion and misunderstanding in many quarters.

Just as supporters and colleagues of former President Clinton are referred to in some quarters as "friends of Bill," there is a group of analysts whom I like to think of as "friends of empathy." Michael Basch (1983), Anna and Paul Ornstein (1985), Virginia Demos (1984), Joe Lichtenberg, Jim Fosshage, and I (Lichtenberg, Lachmann, and Fosshage, 1992), and Judith Teicholz (2006) have attempted to clarify and rectify matters. They have provided detailed developmental, clinical, and conceptual emendations to our understanding of empathy. Although these friends, implicitly and explicitly, consider empathy to be bidirectional, much of the clinical literature still focuses on the one direction—from the analyst to the patient—or, alternatively, in empathic failures, on the analyst's failure to grasp empathically the patient's experience, which is also seen in terms of a one-way model.

The contributions of the friends of empathy have had remarkably little impact on the various misuses of empathy, especially in clinical practice, both within and outside the self psychology community. Perhaps empathy is one of those terms that is just so experience-near that therapists believe they have an intuitive grasp of it, as though empathy resides just in the realm of feelings—as though it is not thought about.

The friends of empathy have tried to set the record straight. Lichtenberg (1984) pointedly distinguished three interrelated uses of empathy:

1. A traditional use as a process or mode of perception—that is, a way of gathering information about the analysand's state of mind; empathy in this definition is also referred to as the "empathic vantage point." This use follows Kohut's original formulation but has been substantially amplified by the Ornsteins (1985) and Schwaber (1984).

2. A primary bond of communication between caretaker and child, a formulation that Lichtenberg has enlarged to a bidirectional bond between two people; one can think of this bond as an "empathic connection."

3. An imprecise usage to designate the analyst's way of conveying information to the patient, a description of how the information is conveyed; in this usage, empathy becomes a verb as in "I empathized with the patient's need to feel more vital," when what is meant is that the analyst said something like this to the patient and believed in doing so the patient felt understood. This is the most problematic use of empathy. It is unfortunately the one most frequently encountered in case discussions.

The critics of empathy have seized upon Lichtenberg's third usage, the one he himself faulted for its imprecision, and assumed that it reflects *the* self psychological view of empathy. Empathy was never conceived to be a prescription for treatment, as though a therapist only needs to be "immersed" in the subjective life of the patient, make an "empathic connection with the patient," and then communicate that understanding by "empathizing" and all will be well.

Teicholz (1999) has detailed the postmodern criticism of empathy (for example, Mitchell, 1993; Renik, 1993) that has remained unaltered by the clarifications offered by her and the other friends of empathy. The critics have directed their arguments against a faulty understanding of empathy. For example, Aron (2006) expressed concern that an expression of empathy on the part of the analyst can be inauthentic when, in expressing empathy, the analyst betrays his or her own beliefs and values. In this view empathy and authenticity are at opposite ends of a pole. This view raised the question: Can an analyst be empathic about a patient's sadistic fantasies? My answer is, "Of course." Empathy as an investigatory stance certainly has an affective impact on both analyst and patient. But, in this view empathy is erroneously depicted as an action of the analyst that can be at odds with how the analyst feels about the patient and material presented by the patient. The danger that concerns the critics of empathy is that they believe that empathy entails the analyst's acceptance and implicit or explicit endorsement of the patient's subjectivity. Through this expression of empathy, it is argued, the analyst obliterates his or her own subjectivity. On the contrary, the attempt to understand the patient's subjective experience is in no way an endorsement of the patient's fantasies, values, ideals, or even behavior. Seeing the patient's world from within the patient's experience can obliterate the analyst's subjectivity only if the analyst's subjective world is so fragile that even just entertaining an alternate perspective can shatter the analyst's sense of self. In fact, it is precisely when the analyst is confronted with material that goes counter to the analyst's values and beliefs that the analyst's empathy is most crucial. If not then, what's the analyst's personal analysis for?

The gist of the argument of other critics is that the empathic therapist does not provide patients with an opportunity to confront a real person with real feelings. By arguing against an imprecise and incorrect use of empathy, the critics fail to appreciate the role empathy plays in understanding the subjective life of another person. As a consequence, they also fail to appreciate the role of narcissistic rage (Kohut, 1972) in life and psychopathology, the reactive rage of a person with a vulnerable sense of self. Kohut did maintain that empathy can form a positive bond between patient and analyst, but this view does not propose that empathy is all that is needed to treat and to cure. An empathic connection is a necessary but not sufficient basis for therapeutic change. I believe that the erroneous views of the place of empathy in self psychology can best be corrected by articulating the complexities of empathy and doing so in a developmental context. And the fine details can become clearer if we first examine the precursors of empathy.

One place to begin is with a consideration of the development of affective communication. Michael Basch (1983), using the affect theory of Sylvan Tomkins (1962), has proposed a developmental progression that leads from affect to feeling to emotion to empathic understanding.

Each of these steps, according to Basch, adds a new dimension to the complexity of affective communication. Each builds on, encompasses, and integrates what has gone before. Following Tomkins, Basch views empathy as an affective process that enables a person to connect with others by sharing their feelings and thus putting himself or herself in their shoes. However, clearly something more is involved in empathic understanding than simply sharing of affect. As Basch notes, in contrast to its developmental precursors, empathic understanding requires cognition and the ability to take an objective view toward oneself through reflection. According to Basch, affect is necessary in the development of empathy, but cognition is essential for the empathic understanding that is a requisite for therapy.

Virginia Demos (1984) furthered the discussion by distinguishing different components of the child's affective experience and also focusing on the many ways that these components may impact upon and be responded to by the caregivers. She asks us to imagine a pair of scissors lying within the visual range of a young child. The child observes the scissors, approaches it, and reaches for it. Demos argued that "these behaviors indicate *simultaneously* the child's affective state of interest, the focus of that interest on the scissors, and the child's response" (p. 12). The child's response reflects motivations of curiosity, self-assertion, and exploration. But each of these motives, separately or together, may also expose the child to danger: "The parent in an effort to empathize with the child may focus on only one, or on two, or on all three components of the child's experience" (p. 13). Or the parents may see only the danger. Here the parents' vision of the world will inform their response to the child's action and color the overall experience that comes to be shared between them.

Is the parents' vision of the world romantic—a place for adventure and exploration, or tragic—a place of danger requiring constant vigilance? If the tragic vision operates for the parents, the child's implicit conclusion from the experience may be that curiosity and exploration are dangerous; if the romantic vision operates for the parents and the child feels guided and supported, the child may discover new ways of self-assertion and exploration of the environment. Either parental response may be derived "empathically" but they are separated by a world of difference with respect to the parents' vision of reality. What is true for parent and child can be equally true for therapist and patient. Empathy is colored by the vision of reality of the empathizer and the context in which it is generated.

In agreement with Basch (1983), Kohut (1984), and Demos (1984), I also consider empathic understanding as requiring the cognitive, conscious participation of the analyst. In fact, that's what makes empathy open for learning. As Kohut (1984) stated, "Empathy is not God's gift bestowed only on an elect few. For the average individual training and learning make the difference, rather than the fact of endowment.... Via the theories of self psychology, the self psychologist can empathically perceive configurations that would otherwise have escaped his notice" (pp. 83–84).

Empathy, like any skill, can be acquired and enhanced by training and learning. Yet it initially enters via the realm of procedural memory and later emerges as an important dimension in the clinician's repertoire. I follow Basch's distinction between the developmental precursors of empathy and empathic understanding. But, the precursors I propose are derived from various sources, including empirical infant research in which affect is a basic constituent. The precursors of empathy may or may not be conscious. As nonconscious procedures these precursors can be made conscious. In the process of empathic understanding we make conscious much of the information we have gathered through our procedures, reflect on it cognitively, organize it, and shape it into communications to the patient and ourselves. Empirical infant research and studies in social psychology can provide a refinement in our understanding of the precursors of empathy. Specifically, I recruit a number of caretaker–infant interaction studies, cross-modal transfer, vocal rhythm coordination, state sharing, and entering the behavioral, action, affective, and proprioceptive stream of the other. These precursors of empathy eventually jell and provide the base that underlies the cognitive components of empathic understanding. These precursors are, in part, procedural and nonconscious. They are a necessary precondition but are not sufficient for empathic understanding, which also requires explicit, declarative memory.

Contrasting explicit/declarative and implicit/nondeclarative memory can clarify and distinguish between the procedural components of empathic understanding that constitute the precursors and the declarative knowledge that is a prerequisite of empathic understanding. As Joe Lichtenberg, Jim Fosshage, and I (2002; see also Fosshage, 2005) spelled out, "The terms implicit and explicit refer to whether or not memory can be consciously recollected or not" (p. 77). Explicit/declarative memory is the memory system of consciously processed events. There is a semantic subdivision of declarative memory that includes all kinds of facts, such as a patient reporting how old she was when her father stopped drinking, or where she lived as a child. The episodic subdivision of declarative memory refers to specific events such as the family relationships, alliances, and squabbles that typically took place during the Sunday lunch. Episodic declarative memories often lead to the co-creation of model scenes in treatment and invite the analyst's empathy.

By contrast, implicit/procedural nondeclarative memory refers to information acquired when learning a skill through repeated performance. Procedures are organized around actions to attain goals, such as driving a car. Learning skills, such as shifting gears while driving a stick-shift car or learning to self-soothe after having been provoked and enraged, initially demand much attention. With repeated practice and increasing control, performance of such skills becomes smoother and automatic, requiring minimal attention.

Recall the work of Karlen Lyons-Ruth and the Boston Change Process Study Group. They enlarged the realm of procedures to encompass implicit relational knowing. We have come to understand that procedural knowledge not only includes how we do things, such as how to play the violin, but also a range of behaviors that include how to relate to a baby or toddler, how to flirt, how to have fun, how to express frustration, and how to box. To this list I now add "how to enter the subjective experience of another person" and "how to signal one's readiness to respond to another person entering one's private experience." As interpersonal actions, these behavioral responses are *in part* organized on a procedural level. As procedures, they are automatic and nonconscious.

Many of the "how to's" I listed begin as learned skills, but after practice they become automatic and nonconscious. Changes in these procedures can occur directly by turning our attention to them. The procedures involved can then be made conscious, brought under conscious control, and may or may not be available for verbalization. For example, riding a bicycle is nonconscious, but we can make it conscious quite readily by attending to the sequence of moves, placements, and balance of our body, legs, and arms.

But now for another distinction—between these nonconscious procedures and the dynamic unconscious. Declarative knowledge involves symbolization and meaning. It refers to a narrative of experiences and events, to the "what," "why," and "wherefore." Narratives are subjected to all the ways in which we organize, subjectively shape, enhance, and repudiate our experiences and aspects thereof. What one represses or why one defends belongs to the dynamic unconscious and hence to the realm of declarative knowledge. Like all distinctions, this one is easier to maintain at the extremes and more difficult when we approach shades of gray.

With the distinction between declarative knowledge and procedural knowledge, and between the dynamic unconscious and nonconscious in mind, I return to a consideration of empathy by way of a vignette by Robert Emde (1990; Buchsbaum & Emde, 1990). To study affect in maltreated preschool children, the beginning of a story is told to a child using a doll family. The child is then asked to complete the narrative. These "story stems" are designed to elicit specific issues such as empathy or restraint of aggression. In one of the stories, a boy is hungry. His mother warns him not to get too close to the stove, but he cannot wait. He knocks the pot of hot gravy off the stove and burns himself.

Timmy, a 3½-year-old severely neglected boy, completed the story by having the mother doll clean up the mess. She then scolded the boy doll for being too close to the stove. In a painfully plaintive voice, Timmy had the little boy respond: "But the gravy burned me." The mother in the story did not respond, and Timmy then had the boy take it upon himself to step away from the stove. In Timmy's other stories, the parents repeatedly ignored the boy's needs.

Emde notes that Timmy's responses reflect his procedural knowledge of how to cope with a painful situation. Timmy did not depict a mother who empathically entered the distress state of her son. The mess was cleaned up, but the hurt child was left to fend for himself. Evidently, Timmy, as narrator, could respond to the pain of the little burned boy. He could address the actuality of the situation. He did represent the burned child's plaint, but he did not represent the possibility of help. And, in Timmy's story, there is no reference to empathy. Not to expect empathic relatedness may well be coded procedurally rather than as declarative memory. Timmy demonstrated his expectation of how parents behave and how he is likely to behave when he is hurt. But, as

Emde explained, Timmy did not say, "This is how my mommy acts" or "I remember that my mommy didn't help me when I burned myself." He did not recall declarative memories of his experiences and then fashion a response to them, either altering them or rationalizing them. He did not represent the problem declaratively but automatically. He expected his parents to be unresponsive.

Timmy's vignette illustrates the operation of procedural memory without accompanying declarative knowledge. What's to become of Timmy? Well, he could grow up not to expect empathy and help from others and to be highly self-reliant; he might become disillusioned and hopeless about any benefit or pleasure to be derived from relationships—or all or none of the above. However, there might be the circumstances where, if Timmy became a patient in treatment, translating procedures into declarative memories, as Bucci (1997) has proposed as necessary across the board, would indeed be therapeutically necessary.

When I propose that empathic understanding engages therapist and patient in a procedural dyadic system, I am not speaking of the usual explicit/declarative dialogue between therapist and patient wherein the patient "corrects" the therapist's misunderstanding or the therapist's being out of sync. This back and forth between therapist and patient addresses misattunements and disjunctions that can be "negotiated" (Pizer, 1998) until both partners feel that now it's "right." However, on the level of negotiations, only the extent to which empathy is, or has been, part of declarative knowledge is engaged. Now let's consider the possibility that the procedural knowledge of the patient runs counter to the possibility of being empathically understood by the therapist. The field is now set for an enactment that communicates the implicit nonconscious expectations of the patient. For example (now for another series of "what ifs"), what if Timmy, now in therapy, had said, "I remember that my mommy didn't help me when I hurt myself" and his therapist responded "empathically" to Timmy's experience, "Not only did you hurt yourself but you were left all alone in your pain—no one helped"? What if this did not feel right to Timmy and he responded, "I was glad that Mommy didn't help because she gets so upset it makes things worse"? A disruption might then ensue until therapist and patient co-created a narrative that felt right. In this instance exploring the empathic mismatch might touch on the therapist's implicit expectation of being expertly adept at grasping Timmy's experience of neglect via empathy, and Timmy's equally adhered to implicit conviction that handling things on his own is the best way to deal with upsets.

There are clear therapeutic benefits to be derived from investigating the components of an empathic exchange, the precursors of empathy as well as the disruption, impasses, and stalemates in the empathic exchange. We can thereby increase our ability to understand those circumstances in which the therapist's grasp of the patient's experience furthers their therapeutic connection and when it disrupts their connection. The "empathic listening perspective" (P. and A. Ornstein, 1985, p. 43), as Kohut (1982) has indicated, can be more than simply a way of gathering data about the subjective life of another person. It has affective consequence. In most instances this is pleasurably soothing, affirming, comforting, moving, and validating. But to some patients, as I have discussed elsewhere (Lachmann, 2000), expressions of empathy feel toxic, infantilizing, humiliating, patronizing, or demeaning. Can these aversive experiences by patients be attributed solely to failures in empathy and misattunements by the therapist? Is the alternative to ascribe the problem to empathy-resistant patients? My answer to both is "no"!

Beatrice Beebe and I (2002; Beebe et al., 1997) have argued that from early development onward *both* aspects of an interactive sequence are represented and are known to the person. Mother and child will both be familiar with patterns where either one can be a pursuer or pursued, a dodger or a chaser (Beebe & Lachmann, 2002). The inherently dyadic nature of these representations implies that both roles in an interaction are known to both partners: "[I]n adult treatment, the patient knows both roles in the interaction intimately and in some cases may exchange them: for example, masochist–sadist, predator–prey, dodger–chaser, abandoner–abandoned" (p. 118). The same is true with empathy in an interactive sequence; the roles of empathizing and being empathized with are also generally familiar to both participants. However, one or the other side of these representations may be more dominant in organizing a person's experience.

When empathy is understood to be bidirectional—both empathizing and feeling empathized with, both expressing and accepting empathy—it is represented by both participants of the interaction. One side of this duo may overshadow the other. For example, in patients like Timmy as an imagined adult, the therapist's attempt to empathically understand Timmy's experience may not resonate with Timmy, activate his acceptance of being empathized with, or foster his capacity for empathic understanding of himself or of others. In these circumstances the therapist can draw on procedural precursors of empathy and then infer typical organizing patterns such as model scenes, as discussed in greater detail in the treatment of Carla and Nora in the following chapters.

When empathy is understood to emerge in a dyadic framework it potentially constitutes a dimension of the ongoing regulations between therapist and patient; it may contribute to both disruption and repair of their ongoing regulations and may heighten an affective moment for one or both participants. Certainly, an empathic bond may not be present throughout the treatment and at all times. Furthermore, ruptures of the empathic bond and its repair, as well as the other forms of affective engagements such as humor, creativity, and surprise, also contribute toward firming the therapeutic relationship. Both partners bring an array of precursors of empathy to the exchange. However, since the contributions of the one empathized with are an integral contribution to the experience of empathy for both participants, a slew of questions arises: What is contributed by the empathized-with patient? What is the patient able or unable to provide? Once the therapist accesses the patient's experience, does the patient signal cold rejection or a degree of receptivity? Can the patient feel empathized with, feel felt? Can the patient reflect on this experience? These are just some lines of inquiry that follow when empathy is viewed as bidirectional.

Having spelled out what I mean by empathy or empathic understanding as bidirectional feedback and a particular form of connection in a dyadic system, I now turn back to the components of empathy, the precursors, at the level of nonconscious automatic processes. These pave the therapist's path toward understanding the patient's subjective experience. The precursors to be considered include cross-modal transfer, entering the behavioral action stream of the other, entering the affective and proprioceptive stream of the other, transmission of feeling states, and the bidirectional regulation of facial mirroring and vocal rhythm coordination.

The Sharing of Subjective States

Several empirical investigations of cross-modal transfer illustrate the origins of the procedures that are relevant for empathy. Bargh's study of priming of an elderly stereotype in college students included cross-modal transfer as an implicit procedure; that is, the students transferred what had been stimulated in one mode to their behavior in another.

Studies of caretaker–infant interactions offer compelling evidence that the rudimentary capacities of cross-modal transfer that are called upon in adult treatment are present from birth on. Infants as young as 42 minutes can imitate the facial expression of an adult model (Meltzoff, 1985, 1990). In this study, the infant was given a pacifier while he looked at an adult model sticking out her tongue. The pacifier was then taken out of the baby's mouth and the baby had 1 minute to imitate the adult. During that minute the baby could be observed to make successive approximations until he finally stuck out his tongue. Sticking out the tongue is not a reflex. The baby has to work at it until he finally approximates the action. Thus, the infant from birth can already perceive the correspondence between what he sees in the face of the adult, and what he feels proprioceptively in his own face.

Amazingly, the infant can already translate back and forth between environmental models and inner proprioceptive information, and detect matches, from the beginning of life. The infant can bring about a correspondence of an internal state and behavior with the environment. Through cross-modal perception of correspondences, inner and relational processes are coordinated from the beginning of life (Beebe & Lachmann, 2002). Meltzoff argued that cross-modal matching provides a fundamental relatedness between self and other, between inner state and environment. He suggested that it provides the earliest experience of "like me." Later we will see that the search for "like me" experiences is ubiquitous throughout life.

In another study, Meltzoff and Borton (1979) blindfolded infants who were between 3 and 5 months old. Then they placed either a smooth or a nubbed rubber ball into the infant's mouth for a brief period, and then removed the ball. When the blindfold was lifted and the infant was shown the two balls, the infant preferred to look at the one he had had in his mouth. That is, the infant was able to translate information from the tongue, whether the ball was nubbed or smooth, into visual information.

Cross-modal perception allows the infant to abstract a pattern from different modalities. As adults we often rely on this capacity in the infant. When a toddler falls, and we say, "Ohhhhhhh," dropping our voice, we are imitating the fall with the contour of our voice to convey our understanding of the event. At another time, perhaps for a slightly older toddler, we may say "oops" or "oopla," with a lilting surprise and upturn in our voice to convey a somewhat different experience of the fall. Or do we? What we vocalize will depend on with what we have empathized and our vision of reality—whether we lean toward wanting to convey a sense of danger or our confidence in the toddler's ability to get up, whether we want to discourage exploration or to provide support.

In the oops or oopla vocalizations we empathize with the child's ability to recover. Under the best of circumstances, with the best match between toddler and adult, both partners can translate and match the contour of the vocalized affect with the experience of falling down and, in some cases, with subsequent self-righting. It is one way of conveying empathic understanding and of feeling empathized with.

These studies illustrate that the infant is already equipped from the beginning of life with rudimentary capacities crucial for the development of empathy and interactive relatedness that provide access to his own inner state. But, the precursors of empathy in cross-modal transfer can be traced back still further—to a basic human responsiveness to music. In considering the connection between language and music, Daniel Levitin (2006), a psychologist–neuroscientist–musicologist, points to the common neural pathways of music and language. He states:

> The close proximity of music and speech processing in the frontal and temporal lobes, and their partial overlap, suggests that those neural circuits that become recruited for music and language may start out life undifferentiated.... Consider that at a very early age, babies are thought to be synesthetic, unable to differentiate the input from the different senses.... What may have started out as a neuron cluster that responded equally to sights, sounds, taste, touch, and smell becomes a specialized network.... With increasing exposure, the developing infant eventually creates dedicated music pathways and dedicated language pathways. (p. 125)

Patel (2003) has argued that music and language share some common resources. The presence of cross-modal transfer can thus be seen as a residual resource that remains after sense modalities have differentiated through development. Yet even after differentiation of pathways, an ability to link different pathways is retained through cross-modal matching. This capacity for cross-modal transfer can reach almost to a kind of synesthesia, where an experience in one sensory modality can trigger an equally vivid experience in another. Vladimir Nabokov (1989) eloquently describes this phenomenon. He calls it colored hearing: "The long *a* of the English alphabet has for me the tint of weathered wood, but the French *a* evokes polished ivory" (p. 34).

The value of cross-modal transfer was clearly recognized by the great conductor Arturo Toscanini, who asserted that a good conductor hears with his eyes and sees with his ears. He can visualize the score when he hears the music and he can hear the music just by seeing the score. Similarly, when we read a novel or hear a patient describe a compelling scene we also use cross-modal transfer as we depict and imagine the scenes we read or hear about.

Cross-modal transfer can also infuse the kind of self-transformation some artists experience during the creative process. We previously also encountered cross-modal transfer when Stravinsky composed music at the piano and was simultaneously thrilled and transformed by the music he heard himself play. Hearing what he produced affected him and affected what he produced. Stravinsky cross-modally transferred, back and forth, from bodily and proprioceptive experience to sensory modes (auditory, visual) and from sensory modes to bodily and proprioceptive experiences to the hands that pounded out the notes—a continuous circle. But it is not only artists who have this kind of experience. It can happen with patients and therapists who hear or feel themselves saying or doing something different and are affected by it.

Affective Communication

The role of facial expression in affective communication has been given a developmental grounding by the work of Davidson and Fox (1982). These researchers demonstrated that by 10 months the brain is lateralized for positive and negative affect just as it is in adults. They studied 10-month-old infants as the infants watched a video of a laughing actress. EEG recordings of the infants' brains showed the pattern of positive affect as evidenced by EEG activation of the left frontal lobe. As the infants watched a video of a crying actress, their brains showed a pattern of negative affect as evidenced by EEG activation of the right frontal lobe. That is, the mere perception of emotion in the partner creates a resonant emotional state in the perceiver.

Unlike the Meltzoff study, in the Davidson and Fox study, the infant does not have to actually match the partner's behavior, such as sticking out his tongue, to be affected by the partner's facial expression. What the infant perceives on the face of the partner is sufficient to alter his or her internal state. Since the infant's internal state is altered, in effect, the face of the partner remains with the infant even after the partner has gone. These findings are of particular relevance for infants whose partners' faces show predominantly negative affects.

The link between the perception of facial expression and brain activation patterns in the perceiver provides one way of coordinating the emotional state of caretaker and infant. Both mechanisms—those documented by Meltzoff and those by Davidson and Fox—operate at a nonsymbolic, procedural level. These findings demonstrating how one person resonates with the affective state of the other are relevant to our investigation of the precursors of empathizing as well as of feeling empathized with.

Studies by Ekman, Friesen, and Ancoli (1980; also Ekman, Levenson, & Friesen, 1983) offer further clarifications as to the role of implicit nonverbal communication as a precursor of empathy. Ekman and his coworkers first taught an exact set of muscle movements to actors and to scientists who were professionally familiar with the physiology of the face. Both of these groups were instructed to contract a particular forehead muscle and, at the same time, particular eye and cheek muscles. These contractions resulted in a series of facial expressions that were not seen by these subjects and were not verbally labeled. Ekman then gave both groups a second task. He instructed his subjects to relive various emotions, using the Stanislavski method of acting. During each task Ekman measured autonomic indices such as heart rate, temperature, and skin resistance of the subjects.

Here is what Ekman found: Simply producing the facial muscle action patterns resulted in more clear-cut autonomic changes than reliving the emotions. He concluded that just contracting the facial muscles elicits the associated autonomic activity. Various facial movements are associated with different patterns of physiological arousal.

Ekman's experiments shed further light on empathy, the way in which the feeling state of one person can be "transmitted" to and received by another. The onlooker's contraction of the same facial muscles as perceived on another's face enables the onlooker to feel the same autonomic sensations as the other person.

Dimberg, Thunberg, and Elmehed (2000) investigated the findings of Ekman further. Using propositions by "Darwin (1972) that facial expressions of emotion have a biological basis ... [and] are controlled by 'facial affect programs,'" they exposed college student subjects to happy, neutral, and angry faces, tachistoscopically, in a way that could not be perceived consciously. By measuring the facial muscle patterns of these subjects they determined that they reacted with distinct patterns that corresponded to the happy and angry stimulus faces. The researchers concluded that positive and negative emotional reactions can be unconsciously evoked "and form the basis for affecting emotional experience" (p. 88).

Following Dimberg and colleagues' work, Sato and Yoshikawa (2005) found that specific overt facial action patterns were elicited when adult volunteers were shown photographs of angry and happy faces. Reactions occurred within 800–900 milliseconds after exposure to the photographs. The authors suggested that "facial mimicry is not only a form of intra-individual communication but that it also functions as a form of inter-individual communication" (p. 18). They further speculated that mirror neurons might play an important role in this process. Such communication of affective reactions with or without the conscious awareness of the "receiver" would not be possible without cross-model transfer.

We can extrapolate to psychoanalytic treatment. As we speak with patients, our physiological state will naturally match or become similar to that of the patient, and the patient's state will match or become similar to ours. Implicitly, both therapist and patient search for someone "like me." One way of searching is to enter into the behavioral stream of another person. This is one of the precursors to, and components of, empathy. Although the studies cited involve face-to-face communication and some of our patients lie on the couch, these nonverbal, implicit procedures operate through vocal rhythm and other modalities as well.

Vocal Rhythm Coordination: Let's Do Dinner

Numerous studies of self- and interactive regulation involve the visual modality, caretaker–infant face-to-face interactions. Communication that does not rely on a visual connection is clearly applicable in analytic treatment.

In a series of studies, Feldstein and Welkowitz (1978) reported on the use of an automatic vocal transaction analyzer to investigate vocal patterns in college students as they spoke to each other. Electronically, the researchers could determine from segments of the conversational stream when each speaker spoke, when he or she paused, when he or she spoke simultaneously with the other, and when he or she switched. The measure of vocal rhythm coordination was a simple correlation using scores based on the duration of pauses and switching pauses of each speaker. Vocal rhythm coordination can indicate whether one speaker interrupts another, hogs the floor, or matches the duration of pauses of the other speaker and gracefully manages taking turns in a conversation. The content was not recorded.

So, imagine a group of female college students gathered together in a room, each with a special clip-on microphone, paired up so that every student could be monitored with every other student in half-hour conversions. (In asking the reader to "imagine," I am taking advantage of cross-modal transfer.) All the while, their vocal rhythm, but not the content of their dialogue, was monitored. At the end of the study, the subjects were given a questionnaire on which they were asked questions such as, "With whom would you like to go out for dinner?" The experimenters found that those pairs whose vocal rhythms were more coordinated liked each other better and chose each other more often to be dinner companions. Here, I propose, another precursor to empathy can be identified. We might operationalize it as the reciprocal positive interest of the two conversationalists. And, most importantly, this interest is conveyed and received by each partner, nonconsciously, on a procedural level.

Dan Stern Watches a Boxing Match

On September 10, 1966, Muhammad Ali defended his heavyweight world championship title against Karl Mildenberger, the challenger, in a bout in Frankfurt, Germany. In 1977 Dan Stern (2002) reported his frame-by-frame analysis of a video of this boxing match. He analyzed this film to study the complexities of a well-coordinated interaction and came to a rather startling conclusion. A good portion of the time each boxer responded to the other at a speed faster than adult visual reaction time. Stern calculated that Muhammad Ali could throw a left jab in 42 milliseconds. If one were to apply a stimulus–response model, there would need to be an interval of at least 180 milliseconds, the fastest recorded visual reaction time, between the punch of one boxer and the block of the other. That means that in a boxing match, a punch thrown by one boxer could not possibly be the stimulus to which the other boxer responds with a block or a dodge.

I watched this video of the boxing match in slow motion and saw sequences where the two boxers looked as though they were playing patty-cake. The punch of one boxer and the block by the other were simultaneous in that the gloves of the boxers made contact between them at the same time.

Instead of a stimulus–response model, Stern proposed that "we are forced to look beyond a stimulus and a response standing in isolation and must view larger sequences of patterned behavior ... The successful punch reflects one fighter's ability to decode the other fighter's ongoing behavioral sequence so that the other fighter's next move is correctly anticipated in time and space" (p. 109). One boxer enters the behavioral stream of the other boxer and can thereby, nonconsciously, predict the other's behavior on a procedural level.

The boxing match illustrates the most basic stage, on the level of procedures that are necessary but not sufficient to bring about an empathic exchange. It illustrates a complex interactively regulated system, wherein each partner "predicts" sequences of the other's behavioral stream in relation to his own. Only when each boxer is studied in the context of the interaction can the "emergent" behavior be understood as organized by both participants. However, there may indeed be certain behavioral sequences that are better understood from the point of view of the individual boxer. For example, each boxer may be more likely to utilize a particular sequence of jabs and blocks, of approaches and retreats. The specific manner in which a boxer punches is a highly practiced skill that does not alter much from fight to fight. Each boxer's manager will no doubt study the style of the opponent and, through his manager's instructions, each boxer can then learn to anticipate the preference of the other fighter. Training each boxer in a pattern that will begin as a learned skill but will become part of his nonconscious procedures will increase his ability to adjust to and predict the behavior of the other by the time the fight occurs.

The boxing match illustration opens a window to the co-creation of nonconscious behavioral sequences entered into by the two participants. Each boxer must "sense" and translate complex information into a proprioceptive response without any cognitive detour. Being able to enter the behavioral stream of the other is a skill that provides the procedural underpinning for the eventual emergence of empathy in other circumstances.

The improvised entrance of each boxer into the other's behavioral sequences shares overarching organizational principles with the social relations between mother and infant, therapist and patient, and the process of transmitting skills between teacher and student, supervisor and candidate. Whereas the two boxers need go no further than to predict each other's behavioral sequence, the co-creation of empathy requires this and more.

Isaac Stern in China

In the Ali–Mildenberger boxing match, we noted that each boxer felt himself into the behavior stream of the other. I now turn to two musicians who felt themselves into the affective behavioral stream of the other. The interactive procedures and the quality of cognition involved here come closer to analyst and patient in an empathic interchange.

Shortly after China opened its doors to Western influence, in 1979, Isaac Stern toured China and filmed his master classes for young Chinese violinists. The film made of this tour, *From Mao to Mozart*, contains the scene used in this discussion.

Violin playing—as does playing any musical instrument—begins as a learned task and eventually becomes a nonconscious procedure as the player becomes more proficient. Yet, playing a violin or any musical instrument may once again become conscious and require the application of declarative knowledge at any time when the musician focuses her attention on changing technique. However, once the change in technique has been mastered, the necessity for conscious attention and thought diminishes; the nonconscious automaticity of the procedure takes over once more. The performer may then turn toward other musical and interpretive considerations. Thus, how to hold the arm or where to place the fingers on the violin is automatic, felt, and not thought out, but how to phrase a passage is deliberate.

In *From Mao to Mozart* a 10-year-old girl plays a piece technically correctly, but mechanically. Obviously, she had learned her violin lessons well. But in less than 2 minutes Isaac Stern alters her playing in a remarkable way and she learns to play with feeling. A procedure has been altered. The ease with which this occurred suggests that there were no dynamic-unconscious motives or, put differently, that there was no declarative knowledge weighing against a shift from a mechanical to an affective mode. There is, of course, another untestable hypothesis: namely, that the transference authority of Isaac Stern provided such a powerful motivation that it overshadowed all other considerations.

Here is the sequence of the scenes. First, the young girl plays a piece without feelings. Isaac Stern asks her to "sing it." After she does he praises her and suggests she play it like that. But first Stern plays this piece and imitates the charming way in which she sang it. Next he plays it without feeling and maintains a "still face" remarkably like that of the mothers in Tronick et al.'s study (1978). He tells her to listen to herself as she sings it and then to figure out how to hold her fingers on the violin to make it sound beautiful and natural. Stern then plays the piece again with feeling and asks the young girl to play it. She now plays with feeling and he praises her.

Although a Chinese interpreter was present, Isaac Stern connected with this girl to a large extent through the language of music, and through postural and facial expressions, as Stern implicitly invited her to enter his own affective and behavioral stream. He imitated her emotionless playing to demonstrate how he experienced her playing. When he asked her to "sing it," he connected with her, and had her connect with herself, on a more immediate and intimate level. He tapped into aspects of her declarative and procedural knowledge. She sang the piece with feeling and, already as she sings, we see her moving her fingers on the violin strings. Here is cross-modal transfer in action. The young violinist, akin to Toscanini's conductor who translates music into visual symbols, translated the music into a bodily experience, into the proprioceptive procedures required for playing the music with "feeling." Moreover, Stern shifted the context of her experience from a situation in which she had just been criticized by engaging her in a task in which she could succeed. In addition, he had taught her something: how to make use of cross-model transfer, hearing a melody in her mind's ear and translating it into movements. What she learned transformed her violin playing and her facial expressions showed that she knew it.

In this dyad, master and student have entered into each other's behavioral and affective stream, but they did not do so similarly, symmetrically, or equally. In this reciprocal interplay each learned something about the other and about himself or herself. Clearly, each also derived a considerable degree of satisfaction and pleasure from the exchange. This may well have been a heightened affective moment for both participants. The young violinist played for the master, and Isaac Stern creatively and profoundly impacted the young student's musicality, and on a grand scale broke through a massive cultural barrier.

The young violinist, through disruption and repair of self- and interactive regulation and heightened affective moments, began to play with feeling. We don't know to what extent this one event transformed her violin playing and her sense of self since repetition of her new acquisitions would have been needed to increase the likelihood of their becoming stable in her repertoire of accessible resources. But we do know that in the 1990s she became concert master of the Singapore Symphony.

In clinical practice this shift from an impassive, perhaps even obsessive mode to an affective one is often far more difficult to accomplish. Dynamically unconscious, defensive motives for avoiding affectivity often result in our taking more than 2 minutes to accomplish such shifts.

Summary

In this chapter I illustrated the precursors to empathic understanding, referring to infant and adult research, studies of cross-modal transfer, facial mirroring, vocal rhythm coordination, and entering the behavioral and affective stream of another person. These are prerequisites for making affective contact with oneself and another person and for the process of transforming the affective experience of both participants.

The bidirectional influence of empathizer and empathized-with was illustrated in the study of vocal rhythm coordination in the college students and of Isaac Stern and the young violinist. In the work of Meltzoff, Ekman, and Feldstein and Welkowitz, the researcher, like an "empathizer," acquires knowledge of the subjective experience of his or her subjects through procedures that tap into their behavior, as informed by their own sense organs.

I have focused on the precursors of empathy—the procedures that are necessary but not sufficient for empathic understanding. The process by which this empathic connection occurs and the obstacles encountered in its path become important considerations for joint (and self-) analytic investigation. The distinctions among the developmental precursors and procedural components and empathic understanding are useful in delineating the role of empathy in the therapeutic process. In the next chapter, I consider empathic understanding directly.

4 Empathic Understanding

There is some controversy whether to consider empathy a background presence in the analytic relationship or as one dimension (albeit a major one) in the analytic engagement. In the latter instance, it occupies the foreground of the analyst's attention in listening to and communicating with the patient. Support for both positions can be found in Kohut's (1959, 1982) writings. I have been arguing that empathy is best considered to be one of several contributors to the analytic dialogue, along with humor, creativity, and recognition of one's transience. In addition, we can also accord a place for factors like intuition and common sense. I do not want to give empathy a privileged place and thereby downgrade the other dimensions of the analytic engagement. Therefore, I believe it is better to consider empathy as present only when it occupies the foreground of the therapist–patient engagement. My dialogue with Judith Teicholz illustrates these two views of empathy.

Teicholz (2006) considers empathy to be an essential background dimension of the analytic relationship. Other analytic activities such as interpretation and confrontation can be foreground but, even so, she argues, they must be encompassed by empathy. In contrast to Basch (1983), Demos (1984), and the more circumscribed definition of empathy that I offer, Teicholz, along with some views of Kohut's, proposes a broader role for empathy. Whereas I emphasize the extent to which empathic understanding relies on cognition and the analyst's conscious participation, Teicholz emphasizes the extent to which empathy serves as an underlying, possibly unconscious guide. She identifies empathy as a background contributor not just to the analyst's listening but also to how the analyst selects among a range of choices with respect to what psychic content to address, how best to modulate various modes of interaction, and maintaining the quality of engagement.

In a clinical vignette, Teicholz describes her supervision of the treatment of a young woman, a recent college graduate. The patient complained about a man whom she dated and who was not treating her well. She then went on to muse about what kind of birth control she would use on their upcoming weekend trip together. The therapist whom Teicholz supervised said to her patient, "What's this? You're saying you don't like him, he's not treating you well, but you're wondering what kind of birth control?" (2006, p. 57). Teicholz's supervisee understood her intervention to be a confrontation. That is, she drew the patient's attention to the implications of what she was saying, implications that had apparently been denied or rationalized. Teicholz considered the therapist's comment an "expression of profound empathy" (p. 57) and spelled out many of the implicit communications contained therein—for example, "I won't sit by quietly while you put yourself at risk" (p. 57).

However, did this therapist enter the patient's subjective world and articulate what she saw, felt, or sensed from within the patient's perspective or did she voice her own vision of the world, bring her patient into it, and then "confront" the patient with what she would have thought or done if she were the patient? In this instance empathy may not have been absent. But can we credit empathy with a decisive role? What guided the treatment at that moment seemed more likely to have been the analyst's alarm about the patient opening herself to an external danger as well as concern about the patient's comfort and safety, so this therapist voiced a common-sense-based reaction: I believe that when we credit empathy as a guide for this intervention we are stretching it too far. Empathy then loses its specific contribution to analytic treatment and thereby shortchanges other avenues of analyst–patient engagement.

From my circumscribed definition, an analytic intervention conveying empathic understanding would require the analyst to access the patient's experience. It would entail the analyst's sense that the patient's behavior was organized by a fear of being abandoned or by a concern about being hurtful and rejecting. Cognition would make its appearance when the analyst then connects the patient's plan to buy birth control to her insecure attachment. The therapist might then articulate the patient's fears and concerns and the price these exact with respect to her well-being, self-respect, and safety. If this formulation captures the patient's circumstances, then the patient's loss of subjective awareness of her self-interest and the imbalance between self-interest and attention to the other would need to be addressed.

Consonant with the proposals outlined in these chapters, empathic understanding could be conveyed through interpretations to the patient that addressed her fear of being left alone or of injuring her boyfriend's feelings by letting him know how ambivalently she felt toward him. The therapist would address the patient's anxiety and acknowledge that buying birth control might provide some reassurance. Being ready for sex could ensure her having a weekend with him, but only so long as she did not reveal how she felt. I offer this illustration of an *approximation* of empathic understanding to argue that this interpretation, although it captures the patient's anxiety and ways she reassures herself, would probably have been *affectively* off the mark. I believe it would probably have been therapeutically far less effective than the treating therapist's confrontation.

What was required was a heightened affective moment, based on a departure from the usual ways this analyst and patient talked to each other, and thus a violation of the patient's expectations. The treating therapist drew the patient's attention, whereas my suggested affectively accurate but verbose interpretation might have evoked interest but not action on the part of the patient. It might therefore have been far less effective. As I will discuss later, what may have contributed to the patient's attention was a violation of what the patient had come to expect in the course of the therapeutic dialogue. It was most likely a surprising, but not hurtful violation of her expectations. In this clinical example, was "empathy" in the background, serving as a guide? Perhaps, but so were "tact" and "common sense," an ironic view of reality in contrast with the patient's comic view, as well as a degree of "alarm" and "reality testing."

Recall Kohut's (1984) example of the psychiatric resident who was given a ticket for speeding as he drove to his analytic appointment, and to whom Kohut said, "You are a complete idiot" (p. 74). This "interpretation" was not justified by Kohut as an illustration of empathy. Rather, it argued for the judicious application of an evocative and perhaps even provocative approach, when appropriate. Was there empathy in the background? Perhaps, but certainly irony was in the foreground.

I want to reserve empathy for those instances in the treatment when it is in the foreground and provides the substance of the analyst's intervention. The door is then left open to acknowledge other equally powerful paths of engagement that promote transformation and therapeutic action. Thus, while I hold to Kohut's view of empathy as a mode of observation, I believe it is useful to be more circumspect about what we label "empathic." Furthermore, I have been advocating that empathic interventions are invariably co-created but they are also part of a complex event that involves cognition and imagination on one hand and a variety of implicit relational procedures on the other. I discussed the latter in the previous chapter and referred to them as the precursors of empathy. Unless there is interference from either participant, the precursors of empathy are a major participant in accessing one's own affectivity and communicating with the affective life of another person. But the former—the cognitive and imaginative components—are no less important. I now turn to them.

Robert McKee at the Movies

So far, many of the illustrations in this book have focused on interactions between actual people. I now ask, how can we "empathize" with the experience of a person who is not physically present in the consulting room? This question addresses a range of possibilities from empathy toward a character in a film or book to empathy toward a patient's parent, partner, spouse, or someone who is spoken about in treatment but not present in the flesh. Asking these questions recognizes that indeed empathy can arise in such situations. Then a key component of empathic understanding would involve imagination. In these instances we as readers, listeners, and therapists must endow absent or fictitious characters with qualities that enable us to connect empathically with them. And, the author, actor, or patient must endow them with qualities that "speak" to us and invite us to enter their personal world. In this empathic process, our consciousness and nonconsciousness are no doubt expanded. Let's take a closer look at this process.

Screenwriter Robert McKee (1997) has discussed the empathic connection that a successful film establishes with its audience. Echoing Meltzoff, McKee says, "Empathy means 'like me'" (p. 141). The audience must find some quality in the protagonist that can be recognized as "like me" as embodying even a shred of humanity. Something about the character must strike a resonant chord in us. That moment of recognition is essential, says McKee, so that the audience will want the protagonist to achieve whatever he is after; otherwise, the bond between the audience and the story is broken.

McKee holds that "the audience's emotional involvement is held by the glue of empathy.... We empathize for very personal, if not egocentric reasons.... Through empathy, the vicarious linking of ourselves to a fictional human being, we test and stretch our humanity" (pp. 141–142). Here McKee joins Kohut (1959) in arguing that through empathy, by entering the subject world of another person, we are able to transcend our egocentricity and to stretch our connections with humanity. McKee also recruits cognition and imagination in his discussion of empathy.

Interestingly, when we sense a character is "like me" it does not necessarily mean that we like him or her. McKee depicts Macbeth as a monstrous figure who "in Shakespeare's hands becomes a tragic, empathic hero" because Shakespeare has given Macbeth a conscience. The audience can then connect with Macbeth because "he is guilt-ridden just like me. He is a human being, he has a conscience like mine" (p. 143). Depicting Macbeth as an "empathic hero" is McKee's shorthand for two interconnected processes: One refers to an aspect of humanity in the character and the second to the pull this exerts on the audience that promotes a connection with that character. Macbeth, although a heinous character, is able to evoke the audience's empathy. He can be compared to Shakespeare's Othello (A. Lachmann, 2001). Unlike the villain Macbeth, Othello is a victim. But, as with Macbeth's guilt, we can recognize Othello's vulnerability and torturous doubts as human qualities we all share. That makes Othello's murderous rage all the more tragic, moving, and, finally, frightening.

There are further complexities here. That we feel empathy for characters does not guarantee that they feel empathy for themselves or for others. Othello, for example, manifestly lacks empathic understanding in that he is unable to sense himself into the world of Iago. He does not grasp Iago's vulnerability and his rage at having been passed over and not appointed to be Othello's lieutenant. Nor can Othello sense Desdemona's simple devotion, fidelity, honesty, and love for him. But although we in the audience can empathize with Othello because of his "human qualities," he is not capable of empathic understanding and cannot sense what others are experiencing.

And then there is Iago, who brilliantly illustrates the point that empathy is not the same as compassion. Like Macbeth, Iago is a treacherous villain, but the two differ in that Iago *can* enter the subjectivity of others and easily manipulates Cassio, Othello, and Desdemona. He grasps their inner world with uncanny precision and aims his unscrupulous behaviors precisely at their soft spots. His uncanny ability to read his victims makes him so fascinating. Some of us may even see in Iago someone who does what we might imagine or desire to do on occasion. Iago thereby stays within the radar screen of our empathy even as his malevolence seems to move him off that screen totally.

The combination of empathy and villainy in the same person has wide ranging clinical and conceptual implications. For Kohut (1971) and Goldberg (1995), such possibility was encompassed by the "vertical split." The therapeutic transgressions of Masud Khan (A.-M. Sandler, 2004) provide a chilling illustration of unsavory uses of empathy. Apparently, in Khan empathy and grandiose self-centeredness, extraordinary perception of human nature and arrogant exploitativeness resided side by side.

Wynne Godley (2001), an analysand of Khan, published the story of his analysis with Khan. He stated that his encounter with Khan severely blemished his adult life and repeated his disastrous childhood years. From the first session on, Khan intruded himself into Godley's treatment and life. Godley reports that initially Khan was interested in him but, as he soon discovered, this interest was based on Godley being married to the daughter of the world-renowned sculptor, Jacob Epstein. Khan's anti-Semitism then got the better of him and he tried to break up the marriage, even as Khan and his wife and Godley and his wife socialized and went out for dinner together. Khan even tried to pair Godley with a patient of his, an unmarried woman who had just had a baby. The two did meet but they were really not interested in each other.

Rather than exploring and analyzing Godley's transference reactions, Khan responded sadistically, stating that, unlike some of his colleagues, he believed in paying back aggression from his patients in kind. Khan invited himself to Godley and his wife's home and whispered to him in a venomous tone that he lived like a pig. "My bad experience resided mainly in the fact that Khan's characteristic response was indignation and withering sarcasm. Yet he sponsored the notion that not only he himself but also his patients were well-bred geniuses" (Godley, 2004, p. 43).

In his writings, Masud Khan (1960) presented a very different view of how he worked. He stated that he would not reveal his conflictual unconscious transference to his patients but that he valued the analyst's transference to the patient in its entirety as it contained and reflected his human appreciation and responses to the patient's realistic needs. Khan described a moving moment in his treatment of a suicidal, depressed woman. Three days before she was to go on vacation she told Khan that she had impulsively stolen two books. After she told Khan what she had done, he responded:

> "Should you wish me to return the books I'll do so." She got up and meekly handed me the books. I decide not to make an issue of it then. It was an important point, I felt, and had to be handled with tact. The next day she reported that she had had a dream the previous night which she had forgotten; but her first waking thought after the dream was: "If I had been caught stealing I would have had to commit suicide. I couldn't have survived that humiliation." She was very grateful that I had not bullied and humiliated her with interpretations, but had helped her to resolve the fix she had got into. (p. 136)

Khan asserted that his role in the analytic situation was basically and dynamically this: "to be there, alive, alert, embodied, and vital, but not to impinge with any personal need to translate her affective experiences into their mental correlates." This was how he managed the empathic connection—that is, not through verbal interpretation but through his "alert" and "vital" presence. "If I was not all there in my body-attention she would register it straight away. I could never quite find out how she registered it, but I could always sense it had happened by the change in the affective rhythm or a new slant of material emerging next day" (p. 141).

What a striking contrast between Khan's description of how he worked and Godley's experience of how it felt to be Khan's analysand. Godley (2004) wrote: "Patients, like infants, may be unable to identify abuse;

they may even suppose that the perverted process which is destroying them is veritably building them up into something special" (p. 42). I thought of my consultation with Judy, the young college student who needed to be "tough," when I read this. In her case the analysis promised to fulfill her "curative" fantasy of becoming "tough." Both cases argue for the necessity for the analyst to monitor more than the process of treatment and its transference–countertransference dimension. They argue that more than empathy is required. Khan wrote eloquently and sensitively about the need for his patient to experience his embodied sympathy, through his body attention. "In such states I felt this patient needed and borrowed my flesh and bone to hang on to" (p. 142). Yet as Demos (1984) has illustrated with the child reaching for the scissors, empathy does not ensure that the response it generates will be the only valid one possible. The link between empathic understanding and therapeutic action will be mediated by the therapist's worldview, by the therapist's sense of the moment, by whatever creativity the therapist may possess, and lots more, including the therapist's decency.

An Empathic Rupture and Repair

We generally assume that to be understood and responded to empathically will translate into being able to feel empathically understood and to empathically understand others. However, that may not always occur. Anna Ornstein (discussed in Lachmann, 1990) described a pertinent instance in her analysis of Mr. S, a rigid, humorless man who controlled his feelings so that he would not betray any affective responses. He was hypercritical and rationalized his hostility behind logic and reality. For the first 2 years of the treatment, Ornstein attempted to maintain a continuous attunement on the patient's affective experience with some success. After about 2 years Mr. S had better contact with his feelings but more often than not still avoided potentially disruptive affects. She questioned whether or not she needed to address the isolation of affect more directly, but still chose at that point to maintain her empathic immersion in the patient's subjective experience. Progress continued so that ruptures and repair of the selfobject transference led to important genetic reconstructions with respect to Mr. S's inability to attract his mother's attention and also with respect to his response to his father's need to be "right."

Ornstein's treatment thus continued to be based on her empathic immersion in the patient's experience and maintaining her focus on the fluctuations of the selfobject tie. Mr. S thus felt safe enough not to withdraw into angry silence when he felt hurt or humiliated and he was able to experience and express anger directly. Nevertheless, Ornstein noted that an aspect of his character pathology remained untouched. Specifically, his transference to his wife—his expectation that she would provide him with the affirmation and approval that he had failed to receive from his mother—continued unabated.

Ornstein speculated that the empathic understanding that a patient receives in analysis may not be forthcoming in extra-analytic relationships. Of course, that is true but raises the thorny question: Why doesn't the experience of feeling empathically understood lead to an affective transformation that would then find expression in other relationships? Why doesn't the experience of feeling empathically understood increase one's ability to be self-reflective? When this shift has not occurred, is a shift required in the analyst's responsivity?

Ornstein did shift to a position of an "outside observer" and made the following extra-analytic transference interpretation. The incident that provoked this exchange in interpretative stance was a domestic tit-for-tat that was so covert it could easily have slipped under anyone's radar: Mr. S returned an article to a neighbor that Mrs. S. had borrowed without first checking with his wife to see if she was finished using it. Ornstein asked Mr. S "whether he thought that his returning the borrowed article without asking [his wife] was related to his anger and disappointment over her having once again not fixed his breakfast for him" (Lachmann, 1990, p. 64). Mr. S became severely distraught, angry, and defensive. It took him a week to explicate all the facets of his reaction to this interpretation. But, he was able to repair the rupture based on the prior years of analytic work. In a second, similar incident related to his wife, Ornstein was able to maintain her empathic immersion in the patient's experience and he was able to become more self-reflective on his own.

If Ornstein had not shifted her earlier perspective to that of an "outside observer," as she did in the first incident, could the second, more benignly resolved one have occurred? In the case of Mr. S, the shift in analytic perspective in the first incident, I believe, was essential because his self-reflection and therefore his capacity for empathy for others were severely impaired. They were suffused with the self-hatred that he had been defending against and that he had expressed toward his wife.

Ornstein's interventions raised the question of whether more than an empathic interpretive stance may be required to foster a patient's developing empathy for other people. I don't believe we can reduce this issue to a technical matter because people vary in terms of how empathy for others ranks in their overall scale of values. Some patients develop empathy for others in the course of their treatment; some are more concerned with developing and making full use of their skills and talents, sometimes at the expense of empathy for others. The "technical" issue raised by Ornstein's case can, however, be considered in its own right.

Ornstein's Mr. S and the patient about whom Teicholz wrote ("you're wondering about birth control?") illustrate the analyst's flexibility in accessing how best to engage the patient from a perspective that takes the analyst out of the subjective life of the patient and into the life events of the patient. In these instances analyst and patient are in a vis-à-vis position at the very least. Does empathy dictate the perspective to which the analyst shifts? Perhaps, but the shift can also be prompted by alarm, frustration, a therapeutic assessment, or other affective signals experienced by the analyst.

In imagining ourselves in a play, film, or story, we come close to the process of treatment where we also enter, imaginatively, into the narratives of patients and important people in their lives, as they recount their experience. Yet, there are patients who resemble the character of Othello in that they are able to engage our empathy while they themselves lack empathy either for themselves or for others. In those instances our empathic understanding may be based on our sensing their humanity in spite of their overt actions and their guilt. Our empathy may also derive from our wish for reciprocity or our disbelief in their capacity for villainy; it may also be responsive to their wish to be "understood." And some patients, like Timmy, are able to enter the subjective experience of others but do not expect to be the recipient of empathic understanding by others. Finally, there are patients for whom unbridled entitlement and empathy may even enjoy life alongside each other.

Can we expect patients to be "empathic" toward therapists? A therapist in supervision with Lew Aron (1996) talked about his conflict and discomfort when one of his patients spoke about wanting to hear him present a paper at a conference. At some point later in the exploration of this topic, Aron suggested to the therapist that he ask his patient how he imagined the therapist would feel seeing him in the audience, looking up at him as he delivered his paper. The point of Aron's question was to address the discomfort of the therapist and the ability of the patient to sense or anticipate the therapist's discomfort. Aron's intent was similar to Ornstein's treatment of Mr. S—that is, how to evoke a patient's empathy for another person, the patient's therapist, or mate? An attempt to enable the patient to recognize the effect he or she has on another person is also a central concern of Jim Fosshage (2003). He proposed an other-centered perspective wherein the analyst speaks to the patient not from within the patient's subjectivity but from the subjective perspective of another person—for example, how the analyst experienced the patient at a particular moment. I see all of these as attempts to further a patient's ability to enter the subjective experience of another person, to develop an empathic vantage point. When are these steps necessary and when can we rely on the ordinary process of treatment to bring about a shift toward an empathic vantage point?

These are tricky questions since many of the patients who present with self-pathology have been "parentified" children, very attuned to a parent who required them to be intimately connected with the nuances of their parent's affective states at the expense of their own subjective self-awareness. They were trained to be "empathic." Some of these children complied but other rebelled. Analysis affords these patients an opportunity to focus on their own experience and the care and comfort of their own sense of self. At certain points in their lives and their treatment the balance can shift for these patients to an extreme of not caring about their effect on others. Such lack of concern about their impact on others can be a statement of a patient's progress in analysis—part of the process of extricating oneself from the "parentified" child role. There is an important distinction between the patient's concern for the feelings and comfort of the analyst and for the feelings of comfort of his or her mate or child. Nor does it serve the patient well if the analyst equates the patient's lack of concern for the analyst with a lack of concern for other significant people in the patient's life. Ultimately, this issue, like so many in psychoanalytic treatment, is best looked at with respect to the balance between self-interest and attention to the others and on a case-by-case basis.

Clinical Illustration: Precursors to Empathy and Empathic Understanding

The vignette that follows illustrates the co-creation of an empathic exchange and both the conscious and imaginative components and the procedural nonconscious components that entered into empathic under-standing. Carla sought analysis in her mid-40s because she had spent her life as a workaholic. She held a position of great responsibility, but was always so consumed by her work that her social life suffered. She had many close but no intimate relationships, and she had had a number of affairs that ended without much regret on her part. Her chronically overwhelmed state and her wish to lead a less burdened, more balanced life brought her into treatment. Furthermore, she also felt responsible, throughout her life, for compensating her parents, especially her father, for the failures they perceived in themselves and for their disappoint-ment in their son.

At the end of 1 year of analysis, Carla was enjoying the eighth month of her first sustained relationship, with Alan. She had actually known him for almost 20 years since they traveled in the same social and pro-fessional circles. During that time he had been married, but was now in the process of divorcing. There was passion and mutual adoration between them and she could not be happier. However, as she noted, he did drink a bit too much. Until now her hair-trigger-like eruptive rage, about which she had spoken, had not made an appearance in her daily life or in her treatment.

One evening both Carla and Alan had a bit too much to drink. When Carla asked Alan about the progress of his divorce and the custody battle with his wife over their child, he made some vague dilatory remarks. She became somewhat critical and disappointed in his vagueness and passivity. He sensed her pulling away and began to "pick" at her, want-ing a commitment from her not to leave. It was not clear whether this referred to leaving him or just leaving the apartment to return to her own place.

Carla became enraged. Alan countered. Now Carla was really ready to leave and threatened as much, a typical response on her part as she recounted these events. They settled the matter, seemingly amicably, and went to sleep. The next morning Carla awoke in a rage. She did not know why except that she felt she had been brooding all night. She was beside herself, both angry and unclear as to why she still felt so angry. In her session Carla recalled that Alan had admitted that he had been unresponsive to her and shouldn't have picked at her. If she would only just point that out to him when he did it, he had told her, it would all go easier. As she recalled his comment in the session, it was then that her rage rekindled: "Why should I always be the one with all the responsibility?" I inquired about her rage and she described some familiar and some new material about her family.

When Carla was about 11, her father, a heavy drinker, gave up drinking, he said, for her. Indeed he did not drink again ever after. She felt resentful for the responsibility and the burden this enormous, unsolicited "gift" placed on her. She then recalled the Sunday lunches with her mother and father and her 8-years-older brother. The whole family, but apparently especially her father, was afraid of being bored. We had spoken extensively about this fear on her part in past sessions. Now it came up again as the centerpiece in her account of the usual Sunday family lunch. Her father would ask her mother what activities or entertainments she had planned for the day. The mother, not having planned anything, would become defensive. Her father would then pick at and needle her mother. A fight would ensue and eventually both parents would turn to Carla and ask her to judge who was right. Carla's description of the Sunday family lunch put me there.

To escape the fights Carla would go upstairs to her room and, as I listened, I climbed up with her. In silence she would brood and feel angry and overwhelmed about the demands being made on her. She felt trapped and screamed in her room. But there was no place to which to escape. She thought that her rages came from those experiences.

I knew Carla to have been a precocious and extraordinarily articulate child. The scene and the rages she described just did not match how I had imagined her. So, at that point, I said to her that I thought those frustrated rages came from an inarticulate little child, from a much earlier time. For the first time in her analysis, she cried. My comment was derived from my empathic understanding of Carla, and more. It included not only my affective resonance with her description, but also inferences about her cognitive and affective development, and more.

Carla now recalled being in her room as a young child, about 3 or 4 years old, when her father was still coming home drunk at all hours. She heard her parents fight and the sounds of their fighting came through the walls of her bedroom. Even then they had expected her to take sides, to be the parent to them. She now told me, also for the first time, that neither of her parents had much experience feeling cared for by their parents. In fact, her father was adamant about not wanting to be in a marriage and warned both of his children not to get married. "Why don't you run off and join the circus?" he would say to Carla.

If my clinical illustration were to end here it would be similar to the magician explaining that he made the elephant disappear by putting it into a black box and drawing a curtain. I have described how and when I entered Carla's experience and the effect of my intervention in bringing to light relevant material. I was aware of imagining myself into her room, feeling alone with her, feeling angry and frustrated—and sensing, to my surprise, that this was happening and at an age when she could not yet articulate in words all the resentment she felt. But even then I would still be omitting what went on "behind the curtain" in me and in her that contributed to this interaction. In retrospect I realized that Carla and I had co-created a younger version of Carla. I sensed myself into the experience of this "imagined" little girl. My intervention turned out to capture, precisely, experiences that Carla had not articulated.

Carla's session occurred at a time when I had just finished teaching Kohut's (1968) paper on Miss F. I had spent some time with the class discussing Kohut's attention to Miss F's high-pitched voice as valuable clinical data that pointed to the legitimate cry of a young girl whose mother could not show the appropriate gleam for her daughter but, instead, kept deflecting her daughter's attention onto herself. I thought of Kohut's case during the session as I juxtaposed Carla's extraordinarily facile verbal ability with her inability to make sense out of her brooding rage in the morning after her fight with Alan. After the session I recalled that in my own analysis, many years ago, during a time when I was experiencing enormous frustrations in a relationship, I recovered a memory from a time when I was not yet articulate and could not verbalize my discomfort. I had had a boil, a painful infection that needed to be lanced. The memory came from a time when I, too, had been frightened and could not yet comprehend what was happening to me.

When I was with Carla and made my intervention, this memory did not occur to me. It did afterward, as I thought about the session. In my intervention, describing Carla's rages as sounding like an inarticulate little child, I linked my recollection of Miss F with myself. The intervention utilized procedural knowledge, matching the pattern of my unarticulated childhood experience with Carla's description of her experience. Of course, the intervention also reflected my knowledge of early development, as well as my sense of the powerful affective charge of the moment. All of these informed my empathic understanding and the model scene that Carla and I co-created.

Before continuing the treatment of Carla, a word about model scenes (Lachmann & Lichtenberg, 1992; Lichtenberg, Lachmann, & Fosshage, 1992). Co-created by analyst and patient, they depict and extend images—metaphorical descriptions of the patient that can be used to illuminate and explore aspects of the therapeutic relationship, of enactments, and of other puzzling occurrences in the treatment. Often model scenes can provide a safe entrance into potentially shame-ridden "confessions" that would not be so available in other ways.

Once a model scene is evoked, described, or identified and becomes a focus of further inquiry, patient and analyst imagine themselves into the context of the scene. Placing oneself and others in a scene brings that experience to life with greater affectivity than often results from ordinary discourse. Model scenes and their metaphoric relationship to the experiences in which they take shape, whether triggered by words, phrases, stories, or memories, can be powerful sources of affectively intense forward movements in exploratory therapies (Lichtenberg, in press).

Thus, we co-created a model scene derived from Carla's descriptions of her childhood experiences: a little girl, alone in her room, enraged, frustrated, wanting to get her parents' attention, and hopeless about getting it. She was given the responsibility to take care of her parents, wished to escape, felt trapped, and was as yet too little to articulate the complexity and enormity of these feelings. We captured these experiences on several levels. Implicitly, my intervention acknowledged that it was beyond her, as a little girl, to articulate the complexity of her feelings and experience.

I entered Carla's childhood world on both a nonconscious, procedural level through my own early experience and on a declarative level through recalling Kohut's recognition of the important "truth" contained in Miss F's high-pitched voice. Through implicit cross-modal transfer I linked Carla's description of her continuing rage, her proprioceptive memory, raging in her room at age 11, with my own procedural memory of inarticulate rage and my declarative memory of Miss F. The procedural, implicit, cross-modal transfer of what I sensed about Carla's experience enabled me to explicate what I had gathered procedurally and declaratively. This constituted empathic understanding, a process that is usually summarized as vicarious introspection.

Carla's contribution to this experience was complex as well. When I articulated what I had surmised to be Carla's experience, she could now imagine herself as a little child, hear her own desperate screams, and now feel heard. Prompted by my use of "inarticulate" and the further description of her as a "little child," Carla could now empathize with her own childhood experience and recognize her parents' limitations, as well as receive my empathic accompaniment.

Why I used the word "inarticulate" was not clear to me at the time. Even as I said it, I do recall giving it a second thought. It is not something I usually say. But, I think, guided by Miss F's and my own experience of inarticulate frustration, I thought that her depiction warranted it. It followed that her rage belonged to a time prior to the emergence of her verbal facility. I felt very gratified by Carla's reaction to my intervention. I, too, felt understood. When Carla cried, I was also very moved.

Yes, I sensed myself into Carla's experience—as in the original meaning of the German word *einfühllung*—but the whole clinical encounter went much further than that. I suspected that her rage was a procedure, automatically triggered, that predated the acquisition of her elaborate fund of declarative abilities and memories. As the session continued, I suggested to her that such rage was an alternative to being able to express herself as articulately as she does now. I later said that I thought she was repeating her dread of being trapped in a situation from which she desperately wanted to escape. She couldn't escape then, but she certainly could now. A recurring theme in her life had been replaying this scene, feeling trapped, and escaping from it. Her tears were a signal that she felt understood and relieved and that she had found some perspective on this troubling pattern. She commented about her tears that she rarely cried and it was the first time she had cried in a session. She thought it was a good thing.

The next time I saw Carla she told me how shaken she felt by the previous session, in particular by my comment about her rage as that of an inarticulate little child. She said, "I've been in a rage since my childhood, at least since I was 3 or 4. When I went up to my room, I used to bang my head on the pillow, and rock and sing. But it wasn't singing, it was screaming. I've been in a rage, embattled, forever. When you said, 'inarticulate little child' it made me want to cry." As Carla now spoke of banging her head, she repeatedly demonstrated this by banging her head on the pillow as she lay on the couch. In doing so, I believe she brought this automatic procedure into a connection with the narrative of her early experience and our current dialogue.

Carla had begun to empathize with her own childhood. She cried and banged her head and felt frustrated as she had in her childhood. But now, in the session, she was not alone.

As Carla narrated her ongoing childhood experience of feeling alone, burdened, and enraged, she had made room for me at the Sunday family lunch. I sat there with her, and then accompanied her up the stairs in her frustrated, trapped rage to her bedroom. We co-created a model scene that captured ongoing aspects of her childhood relationships with both parents, as well as with current reverberations with Alan. The exploration of these experiences gave words to previously unarticulated pain, and integrated the head-banging procedures ("This is how I deal with the frustrated rage I cannot express.") into her fund of declarative knowledge. Carla could now recognize how her automatic arousal of frustrated, head-banging rage was evoked in contexts in which she felt trapped by, overwhelmed by, and resentful about responsibilities assigned to her.

When Carla invited me for Sunday lunch with her family, I no doubt amplified her experience by punctuating it with analytic noises as I accompanied her with my vocal rhythm in the course of her description. However, not until I reflected on her, my, and our experience and had made my intervention did we co-construct an empathic exchange. Then we could both reflect on our experience. I did so privately, after the session, and Carla did so as well and in our subsequent dialogue. Carla and I reflected on her view of her parents and their emotionally barren childhoods, as well as on her own dilemma of being the precocious caretaker of her parents, and on the loss of her childhood that this entailed.

Notably, Carla had developed empathy for her parents. She spoke about their not having enjoyed good parenting when they were children. So far as I was able to tell, I did nothing to foster this surprising development of empathy for her parents. It emerged and was co-created in our work together.

In subsequent sessions we understood her rages as an attempt to communicate to her parents that she existed and that she was trapped in an unbearable role. She had felt ignored during their fights and overwhelmed with responsibilities when they turned to her to take sides. "I could never be an inarticulate little child. I was afraid they would forget about me." To show me why she felt she was so forgettable, Carla told me, "I used to be called 'the cyst.' When my mother became pregnant with me she went to a doctor who said that she had a cyst and it should be removed. Since my brother was sick at the time, she put it off and then it turned out that it wasn't a cyst." So there we were, the "boil" and the "cyst." Carla's analysis continued.

Summary

Empathic understanding and being empathized with are bidirectional and co-created. As the analyst senses into the behavioral/emotional, procedural, and, eventually, declarative knowledge of the patient, the patient may invite, resonate with, or obstruct such a "visit." Viewed in this way, impasses and derailments of empathic understanding are the joint property of analyst and patient. Analysts cannot rely solely on their "empathic" ability to enable them to connect with patients or to enter into the patient's experience. The process by which this empathic connection occurs and the obstacles encountered in its path become important considerations for joint and self-analytic investigation. The distinctions among the developmental precursors, procedural components, and empathic understanding are useful in delineating the role of empathy in the therapeutic process. Entering the private world of the patient is a co-created event that draws all the sense modalities and imagination at the disposal of both therapist and patient. Finally, I have argued for a definition of empathy that recognizes its specificity and distinguishes it from "just being nice."

5 Through the Lens of Humor

Whether explicitly acknowledged or implicitly applied, empathy has been given the most prominent place as a vehicle for therapeutic change. In fact, we have tended to privilege the transformation of self-pathology through empathy with some neglect of the other transformative path such as humor. In this chapter apart from seeing humor as a transformation of self-pathology, I consider humor as one central aspect of the process of transformation.

To some extent, empathy can be acquired, mimicked, pretended, and even "taught" in analytic training. In fact, as I quoted in the prior chapter, Kohut held that in self psychological training, the analyst becomes aware of configurations that might otherwise go unnoticed. Hence, empathy is furthered. But he did not translate empathy into interventions that sound "empathic." There are therapists who have learned to express sincerity, compassion, and caring when they say, "How did you feel about that?" or "That must have been terribly painful." They may not do damage and their intentions certainly are to be helpful. These analysts can probably get along for some time with ersatz empathy, but not ersatz humor. Unlike empathy, humor, spontaneity, and creativity can't be taught, although they can be liberated through life experience or in therapy.

It's not only that some analysts just are not gifted in humor and therefore don't practice it within their usual therapeutic repertoire. It's more than that. The use of humor, either by the patient or the analyst, has received a bad rap in analysis, although the reverse is not true. Humorists and cartoonists have had a barrel of fun skewering psychoanalysis.

In psychoanalytic treatment, a sense of humor has been questioned for patients and analysts alike. As did Kohut, Warren Poland (1990) linked humor and wisdom and considered it "... one of the special delights of clinical analysis [to see] the liberation and development of ... humor in the course of a patient's analytic work" (p. 197). Nevertheless, although humor is an intrinsic part of social communication and for Kohut one of the transformations of archaic narcissism, it is sad but true that playfulness and humor have often been pathologized, if not totally excluded, from the therapeutic process. This pervasive and pathologizing analytic stance toward humor was summarized by Poland, who bemoaned this trend in psychoanalysis. He boldly stated that "... the principle of abstinence constricts the appropriateness of the analyst's own direct expression of humor" (p. 219).

For Freud (1927a) and the papers by generations of analysts who followed in his footsteps, humor was reduced to its unconscious meaning, thereby throwing a wet blanket over the inclusion of humor and playfulness in the treatment process. But when it comes to humor, Freud did write about the way in which humor can enable us to transcend our limitations.

At times, the analytic community has put Freud's ideas to chilling use. For example, Ron Bodansky (2004) described his reanalysis of a man whom he considered to be the possessor of a great sense of humor. This man reported that in his previous analysis, his analyst never laughed. So, the patient said, he gave up on humor only to feel empty and depleted. But, at the end of his analysis he did speak to his analyst about the absence of humor in his analysis. She told him that she often had to pinch herself not to laugh because laughter, according to her, did not belong in analytic treatment.

I encountered a similar analyst, many years ago, at the beginning of my analytic training (Lachmann, 2004). I arranged a consultation for my personal analysis with a well-respected and well-liked analyst. It was during the heyday of ego psychology and I had already completed my graduate work in clinical psychology. In our consultation I made what I thought were some pretty humorous observations, to which he responded with straight-faced literal-mindedness. The analyst asked me why I wanted to be analyzed. I gave him my reasons. When I finished, he asked me, "Anything else?" I said, "What else is there besides sex and aggression?" He did not even smile. After the consultation I decided not to see him. I could not imagine trusting someone with whom I could not share what to me was precious, my sense of humor.

Some Sources for a Sense of Humor

In describing the origins and basis of empathy, I focused on implicit verbal and nonverbal communications as developmental and procedural precursors of empathic understanding. But what about the origins of humor? I believe that they, too, can be found in early development in general and in family life and its shared culture in particular.

Dan Stern (2005) described the universality of a game played by parents with their infants. "I'm gonna getcha, I'm gonna getcha, I'm gonna getcha ... gotcha" will get a joyful laugh from a baby if the timing between the third "I'm gonna getcha" and the "gotcha" is about 3 seconds. The game evokes a joyful violation of expectations and is predicated on the infant's ability to tolerate and enjoy mild surprises. A longer or shorter time interval will either produce no response or be frightening to the child. The game is based on the importance of timing, a salient dimension of much humor.

Fonagy and Target (1998) argue that the inclusion of irony, humor, and skepticism provides a balance when the mother mirrors her baby's distress. The inclusion of irony, humor, and skepticism, they argue, "ensures that the infant recognizes [the mother's] emotion as analogous, but not equivalent, to their experience" (p. 94). Without such useful "contaminants" of the mother's perspective within her mirroring of the child's anxiety or distress, the mother's response might simply reinforce the child's anxious state.

The examples by Stern, Fonagy, and Target argue that humor and its variants are a natural part of communication between adults and infants. In fact, their inclusion is necessary in that they provide a developmental spur. Implicitly, they also underscore the role of surprise and timing as important dimensions of affect in the delivery of mirroring responses.

In adult treatment, mirroring with a touch of irony can shift affect directly, as is illustrated in a response by a supervisee. Her patient said to her, "My self-esteem is at zero." The therapist, keeping in mind previous sessions, commented, "Well, that's up from minus ten." In her comment, the therapist had in mind how the patient had described herself in the prior session. In offering her response, she placed the patient's comment into a temporal perspective, recognizing her patient's current despairing state but adding a "contaminant" of irony gently perturbing her. The patient smiled with relief and during the course of the session regained a broader perspective. She could continue to speak about her current despair without feeling as totally enveloped by it as had been true of her in the past.

I can vouch from personal experience that familial and cultural factors also contribute to the presence of humor in everyday life and in psychotherapeutic treatment. My mother and her brother, my uncle, were well known in our family and among their friends for their humor and spontaneous wit. Furthermore, in addition to the ever present humor in our family, having grown up in Nazi Germany in the 1930s tapped into the survival value of humor. While numerous analysts over the years have stressed the aggressive (Grotjahn, 1957), masochistic, and paranoid bases for Jewish humor (Reik, 1962), Schlesinger (1979) has argued that Jewish humor is in the service of mastery, a view that is consistent with Kohut's understanding of humor and the one that I hold.

I grew up amidst the custom that when two Middle European Jews met they would first exchange the latest jokes. They would either poke fun at the stupid authorities or mock with sarcasm and irony some potentially tragic aspect of the daily life of the Jews that was no doubt going to get worse. For example, jokes I recall from my childhood went like this: The Nazis had just taken over a town and lined up all the Jews against a wall to be shot. One Jew says to another, "Before I die I would like to have one cigarette. I'm going to ask the commandant for a cigarette." The other Jew says, "Don't make trouble." Or, two Jews are assigned to kill Hitler. They are given guns, knives, bombs, and hand grenades and wait in a dark alley for his motorcade to pass by at 12:00. At 12:15, no Hitler. At 12:30, no Hitler. At 12:45, still no Hitler. Finally, one Jew turns to the other and says, "I hope nothing happened to him." Or: "A toast to Hitler, Himmler, Göbbels, and Göring! May they live to be 120—in total." Humor could mock feelings of helplessness or temporarily transcend daily horrors by providing immediate intimacy between fellow sufferers or even fellow renegades.

After Freud (1905b) located jokes in the psychopathology of everyday life, no therapist, male or female, could really feel safe when veering off the prescribed, nonhumorous (if not antihumorous) analytic path. The analyst who used humor risked facing charges of phallic exhibitionism, wanton disclosure of personal qualities, and being too revealing, seductive, judgmental, self-indulgent, or even too gratifying to his or her patients. Owen Renik (1993), in the spirit of self-disclosure, advocated that we "play our cards face up in analysis." But even he did not advocate that we include humor—the joker in that deck. Alas, much therapeutic treatment is conducted not only in a state of abstinence, but also in an atmosphere of humorlessness. Too often a patient's foray into humor is pathologized as a "resistance," or as hidden hostility, or as a denial of anxiety, or as a masking of depression. Of course, this should come as no surprise because psychoanalysis was invented by obsessionals to treat hysterics. Obsessionals take themselves very seriously and generally have trouble seeing absurdities in themselves and in life. However, hysterics, having sexualized their experiences, are quite capable of fooling around.

Boundaries of Humor

It's actually not quite true that humor has been kept out of psychoanalytic treatment. Therapists have used jokes as a way of conveying attitudes or moral points. Some therapists also revert to humor when they feel challenged or threatened or when they are confronted by a provocative patient. In these situations the therapist is tempted to put down, parry, or "one-up" the patient. Any of these tactics may aid the therapist and may even be an adequate response for engaging the patient, but humor can also be a vehicle for defensive retaliation by the threatened therapist. If the patient is anxious and deadly serious, humor can misfire.

Here are three examples of analysts responding to patients who have put them on the spot. A feminist patient said to her male analyst in an initial session, "I'm into consciousness raising. What are you into?" And the analyst responded, "Unconsciousness raising" (Jacobs, 2001).

Then there is the candidate analyst about whom Grey (1992) has written. With admiration he described this young colleague's ability to get out of a tight spot. As his patient, this candidate had an attractive and seductive young woman who "arranged her enticing self on the couch and then turned suddenly to confront the candidate-analyst with the accusation that 'You're looking at my legs!'" (pp. 22–23). The analyst's response was, "Shouldn't I look at your legs?" (p. 23).

The third illustration comes from an initial session during the same era in which Jacob's vignette took place. My patient was a member of a radical feminist group and asked me whether I believed in penis envy. Somewhat seasoned by then, I was not taken aback. I said to her that I thought she was worried I would be more loyal to Freud than to her in working with her. The content of the question did not need to be addressed.

Let's leave aside the female patient–male analyst issue in all three illustrations and just focus on the analytic dyad. In the first two cases a patient is experienced as provocative by an analyst and the analyst's response can be placed on a range of defensiveness from clever (Jacobs) to coy, sarcastic, or perhaps even belligerent (Grey's candidate-colleague). In both instances the reader is implicitly asked to see the situation from the point of view of the challenged analyst and to empathize with the analyst's ability to get out of a tight situation. But, what about an anxious patient struggling to deal with a threatening situation, as was the case in the third illustration? Would humor have been an adequate response to her? There are probably any number of humorous comebacks to that question. Offering one to the patient may have established a competitive banter as the mode of therapeutic relating at best or a failed connection at worst. Here, humor would have been at the expense of the patient rather than in the service of furthering the treatment.

In neither of the first two cases were the implicit concerns of the patient recognized. To assess the role of humor in these instances, further information about the ambience before and after the interchanges in the session would be required. In these first two examples, a variant of humor was used by the therapist to regulate discomfort and as a therapeutic tactic. From the presentations it is clear that in both instances the analyst felt better and the treatment even survived. In both instances the presenting analysts also described a subsequent widening of the field of analytic inquiry. However, my point is that in neither case was there a positive affective experience shared by therapist and patient.

In my third illustration, humor was not involved. But the patient's concern behind her "challenging" question was inferred. Her question, however, was not experienced by me as a treatment challenge.

The point of including humor as a means for transforming affect in the therapist–patient interaction is not to use it as a tactic to help an embattled therapist turn the tables on the patient, but rather to further the implicit relational knowing of both partners. Humor can provide a positive affective experience for both participants. Only in that sense can humor share the analytic stage with empathy.

The context and affect surrounding the first two vignettes described is crucial in considering the role of humor in the treatment process. Certainly the responses of the first two therapists may have done no harm, but they risked perpetuating a tilted pattern of relatedness between therapist and patient. The therapist would be reinforcing his more dominant authoritarian role with implicit challenges and retaliating rather than submitting to the patient. Of course, in both instances the therapists succeeded in extricating themselves out of tight spots and, used in this way, humor can even open the door to a moment of intimacy. All this is to say that when humor is used in analysis, it can certainly have a complicated impact on both partners, but when it is eliminated, what remains is dry, flat, and bloodless. The effect of eliminating humor from psychoanalytic treatment is to transform the patient into a cadaver, like his humor-avoidant therapist. But, when applied appropriately, judiciously, and sparingly, humor is a social lubricant and equalizer. In addition, through humor, we can circumvent anxiety or express a challenge or reply to one that we might not get away with had we been more direct. Whether or not this benefits the patient and the treatment can only be assessed on a case-by-case basis. Most important, however, through humor and spontaneity we can also achieve an incomparable degree of intimacy that is hard to match through other avenues.

There are two points about humor in analysis that require further elaboration. First, humor is an aspect of human relatedness. It is not necessarily an obstacle or resistance to engaging in the process of treatment. We can connect with patients through humor as well as through other paths that contribute to the transformation of self-pathology. This is particularly true when a patient has a highly developed sense of humor, when humor is an everyday component of conversations. Humor then becomes a valuable resource, as it is for Eric, whose treatment I will soon describe.

Second, humor can enable patient and therapist to speak about aspects of the patient's character and experience that may feel shame ridden but are being revealed by the patient because the therapeutic ambience feels safe and noncritical. The analyst's capacity to include humor in the analytic dialogue can thus be crucial to the treatment process, as in the case of Nora, to be discussed later in this chapter.

The Treatment of Eric

Following the death of his father, Eric had seen an analyst in another city for several years, with substantial benefit. He moved to New York to pursue his career as a writer. When I began to see him, soon after his move to New York, he had already planned his first book and proceeded to write it at a rather rapid clip. His achievements with respect to work and intellectual pursuits were high, but were not matched by comparable successes with women. A central focus of our initial sessions had been his plan to sleep with a thousand women before he got married. I asked him if sleeping with one woman a thousand times would do, but he did not think so.

This brief interchange contains the gist of my contention that there is a legitimate therapeutic use of humor. I know, and Eric knows that I know, that he did not literally mean "a thousand women," but we also implicitly knew that he conveyed an important and somewhat shame-ridden "truth" about himself. That he longed for more sexual experiences was obvious. But, implicitly, he longed for acceptance and to be thought of as attractive by women—and that is why quantity counted. Perhaps a thousand endorsements would put those doubts to rest.

In my response I certainly did not address the "grandiosity" implicit in the "thousand" but only teased him about the difference between "need gratification" and "object constancy." Furthermore, I implied that there might be a woman who would want to sleep with him a thousand times. And I joined Eric on the level of adolescent banter in which we joked about women as providers of "sexual services." Should Eric's plan have been explored further? After all, his humor covered underlying feelings of inadequacy. How much of this interaction should be "analyzed?"

This question brings us back to one of the open questions raised in previous chapters: What is the long-range effect of therapeutic communications that remain implicit? Would translating Eric's implicit communication into an explicit one enhance the therapeutic process? Stern (2004) stated, "I see intersubjective exchanges as occurring largely in the implicit domain and not requiring verbalization to have their therapeutic effect" (p. 185). Perhaps there are instances when translating an experience into words just satisfies our obsessional natures and throws cold water on the exquisite novelty of an experience. Generalizations such as "one should never ..." or "one should always explore and make explicit what is implicit" can hamstring the analyst. In one instance, human, humorous, and intimate contact with the patient may be lost or in the other issues that are vital to the treatment may remain unexplored.

Eric and I did not articulate his longings directly at the time. Furthermore, I don't believe it was necessary or even therapeutically advisable to do so. I think it would have scratched our evolving intimate connection and perhaps even have left a scar. Moreover, not analyzing the issue at the moment enabled us to address it tangentially and consistently as we went along. More of this later.

Eric's first book was accepted by a publisher within a week after he sent it to an agent. It turned out to become a critical and moderate financial success. I thought it was very funny and well written. He immediately embarked on a second book, a "fictionalized" autobiography. He disguised some of the players, changed locales, altered events to increase their humor, and even appropriated experiences of others to round out the character of his narrator. His literary agent was enthusiastic but made numerous suggestions that would require considerable reorganization, revisions, and even the changing of the voice of the narrator. I will be quoting from an early version of his book. There is no likelihood of it being published in that form and I have edited it further, tweaking the style but not altering the content. I also have his permission to present the following excerpts. I told him that I wanted to include them in a book I am writing. His comment was, "I hope I don't get my writing turned down a second time."

Eric's book is in several parts that cover the same time period of his life but highlight different relationships. In one section he wrote about his broken engagement. He described the girl he was going to marry as having been a lot like his father, whom he loved very much. Eric wrote:

She was a lot like him [father], smart, smart as hell, intellectual, loving, beautiful. So the whole replacement factor. God, the two of them got along so well. He should have fucking married her. For me, it just wasn't right. On hundreds of levels. I mean, first of all I'm a clown. I joke, that's what I do. She wasn't. Not that she didn't have a sense of humor. She did. But it wasn't my sense of humor. So she always kinda made me feel bad. Like I was a kid, which isn't hard to do. I do kid around a lot. So I was feeling ashamed of like my best quality. That's the best thing about me. So that wasn't going to work out. More than anything though, it's just, no one was the right person for me then.

In this passage Eric depicts his "voice" and his self-effacing humor— but it's not really so self-effacing. After all, he has considerable hope and expectations and the passage conveys as well his struggle and self-awareness—and it's all packaged in humor. In my comment about the "one woman a thousand times," I tried not to throw cold water on his style and to respect what I could sense early on, and later had confirmed, that he considered his sense of humor to be the "best thing about me."

The last section of the book deals with his two analyses and thus also provides a commentary on the other sections. At the time he wrote this section of the book, we had been meeting, once a week, for about 4 years. Here is an abbreviated excerpt from the section of his therapy with me. Keeping in mind that Eric wrote a "fictionalized autobiography," he creatively referred to topics that came up in the sessions and turned them into events. In so doing, he put them under a magnifying glass and revealed the complexity, the upside and downside of his humor and mine. Furthermore, he gave voice to the intersection of his comic view and his tragic view of life.

My new shrink actually is pretty fucking funny. We think the same shit's funny. One time, I was like, he made some joke that wasn't funny and I didn't want to be compelled to laugh. To give the courtesy laugh. So I sat there sorta grimly. Probably a weird little smile on my face. And he's like, "What's making you so uncomfortable?" Here we go, not knowing what to do when he or anybody makes a bad joke. Do I laugh? Do I pretend it's funny? Help them avoid a potentially uncomfortable situation of making a bad joke by pretending it's funny? I do that. Back to taking care of other people's feelings who don't even want you to. We decide, for our purposes, to go joke free for a while in therapy, as a test. We both suck at it but we get better and for a few sessions there was this new mood which I liked for about 15 seconds. I liked getting into that space. But the truth was I sucked at it. I like processing my experiences through humor. And I didn't want him sitting there quiet like while I made jokes. I use a humor lens. So what? I'm deadly fucking serious too. The two go well together for me. My friend, David, makes dead father jokes. I like that. It's intimate. That we both know it's okay to laugh at that. But when it's unfunny, I'll call him on that now. The world's pretty fucken [*sic*] funny to me.

Me and my shrink have a good laugh, a good cry, we're in it together then. By the time I got to him I could let him in. I liked to dig together in therapy. Seeing things, observing things about me that I didn't come right out with. We worked more consciously with the unconscious stuff happening and it would rise up to the surface and we'd grab it. Like when I talked about this girl at the register at the coffee shop I go to. I make no time with her. I don't even try. "Thank you, here's your change." "Thanks." Even less rap than I usually have. Usually I can muster something and I was talking about this in therapy. I mean this must have happened to me a million times in my life but now, emboldened by this whole idea of change, "Oh you can change this, let's change this." So I bring up this girl, and he's like, "Why didn't you ask her out?" I was like, well, she's too young for me. She was probably 20 or 18, maybe 22. You couldn't tell. I was 27. I got a skeptical look for that one. Eyebrows up. He was like, "I think you underestimate the extent to which young women are attracted to older men." He had me there. So we start deconstructing the whole thing. Of course what comes out is that I can't imagine she'd possibly like me. This beautiful young girl at a coffee shop. So he like, "Why not?" You feel stupid suddenly with an assumption like that. There's no real reason to simply presume anyone won't like you. So that was more or less proven to me here with a reverse, just working backwards from my behavior. I didn't expect anyone to be attracted to me. So, of course we are going to joke. At least I was and he too if he wanted to because a lot of this shit is funny.

Implicitly, in his treatment, Eric described his vision of the world through his lens of humor, a lens we share. Beyond our joking, we share a comic view of the absurdities of even tragic aspects of the world. As I believe is clear from my discussion of Eric, humor can be the conveyance and the packaging of much of what is included in the comic vision of the world.

When Eric spoke about his enjoyment of "digging into his experience" with references to "me and my shrink" he was giving voice to what I described earlier as a romantic vision of the world. The presence of a tragic view is seen in his underlying dread of never feeling that he is loved. Furthermore, Eric was deeply affected by the loss of his father, yet, as he said 6 years after his death, he and his friend can laugh at "dead father jokes." Both in content and style, Eric's writing is also laced with irony. Any one of the visions of reality at any moment in the session can occupy a backdrop or become a central theme. My point is that, contrary to the claims of some analytic perspectives, the ability to see the world through the lens of humor does not reflect either a denial of reality or an inability to feel pain and reflect upon one's feelings and experience.

Eric's first analysis had focused on the devastating loss of his father just as he was entering adulthood. In our work we were thus able to concentrate on "adult" issues such as work and his relationships with women that had remained as problematic in his life. By the time we terminated treatment, Eric had married a woman who appreciated his sense of humor and he had also become a father. During much of his writing career, although he worked well, he was still partially supported by his mother, a condition that could not continue into his marriage. Thus, getting married also entailed a change from devoting full time to writing to taking a full-time job that would enable him to write as well. When we last spoke he had not returned to rewriting his fictionalized autobiography, but had written another book that was quickly acquired by a publisher.

So far I have illustrated humor as a dimension of the therapeutic engagement—neither to pathologize it nor to diminish it as a resource from which a patient might derive considerable pride and success. The language of humor can be spoken in therapy without translations into psychoanalytic English.

The Treatment of Nora

I turn now to the use of humor in the treatment of Nora, who might be described as grandiose and with an inflated view of herself. She is on her third marriage and it is not working out well. That's what first brought her into couples' treatment with another therapist, who thought that both Nora and her husband would do better if they were seen individually at this time. Then, for many years Nora had been seen in an individual treatment in which she said she never felt fully engaged and from which she felt she did not derive any benefit. She also had her own reasons for seeking individual therapy, now, with me. In spite of considerable competence in her work, she consistently found herself to be ostracized, unappreciated, unrecognized, and criticized. She wanted to be in individual therapy to figure out what to do about her marriage and what kept going wrong in her work situation.

"What is this about?" she finally asked herself, puzzled by this repetitive experience of being on the periphery of social groups in her work, rather than at their center where, she believed, her competence, efficiency, charm, humor, conscientiousness, reliability, intelligence, and social skills should place her. After a number of sessions in which I got to know her better, I thought that her self-assessment, presented implicitly and explicitly, was quite accurate.

In the first months of our weekly sessions, Nora brought in a series of dreams. In them she depicted her desire to be taken care of and pampered. She was willing and able to pamper and take care of her husband, but she said he did not reciprocate. "He is passive–aggressive," she said. A dream followed in which a man with whom she had had a brief affair tried to put his arms around her. She tried not to be attracted to him but he put his hands on her breasts. Another man said, "I saw what you did." We understood the dream as expressing her fear of being found out, that she was not as innocent as she liked to appear to be, and that she contributed to the impression people had of her. The nature of this "contribution," it turned out, was how crucial it was to her to be seen and treated as special. The extent to which she "showed off" and flirted was barely concealed in her need to be the star. Additionally, she tended to close her eyes and ears to maintain her "innocence," so much so that she wouldn't see or hear problems that, if she were to note them, would actually help her avert pitfalls. Simultaneously, she was also quite

outspoken and came on quite strong; she was more than a bit opinion-
ated and could even be tactless in telling others what she thought and
how things should be done.

This character analysis was engaged in quite fervently by her in
the first months of our work together and was conducted amid tears,
laughter, and surprise at what she was discovering about herself.
Historical material was interspersed among these personal explorations and revelations. Nora's father left her mother when Nora was an
infant and she and her two older brothers and a sister were raised by her
maternal grandmother. Her mother worked and at night went to stay
with her boyfriend. Nora recalled entreating her mother to stay home
with her. She pleaded, begged, and demanded that she stay home, and
even had her grandmother's backing, but to no avail. Her having been
abandoned by both her parents, we inferred, led to her life pattern of
seeking unavailable people and trying to convince them to stay with her.
Her attractiveness and resourcefulness enabled her to bounce back after
her string of failed relationships.

Nora viewed the problems in her life as a consequence of having been "arrogant, mean, and dismissive of people in a former life."
Therefore, she must accept, gracefully, being disregarded and treated
badly in her present life. I said to her, "We are not going to use this
'former life' explanation. I think what you have been describing has to
do with your not expecting very much and covering this feeling with
bravado." She cried and spoke about wanting a one-night fling with a
coworker. He wanted a relationship and she never got her fling. By way
of corroborating her "not expecting very much," she said that just today
she had taken another look at this man. She could not understand what
possessed her to want to have a fling with him, even for one night.

In a following session, Nora announced that she felt like a swan
surrounded by ducks, by which she meant limited people who didn't
appreciate her and didn't understand her. She was forever trying to
enlighten them. She was reasonable and logical and they were critical
of her and incompetent and didn't realize how efficient and hardwork-
ing she was. This description applied to her marriage as well as her job.
Her husband told her that he wanted to have a baby. Since they were
both in their early 40s, she suggested that he have his sperm tested. She
had already been tested but he had not. This had been "dragging on"
for some time and he had not done anything about it. Furthermore, she

complained that he was always too tired for sex. "What is this?" she asked. "At work similar things occur. I am a swan and all those around me are ducks." I said to her, "I now understand why there is no ballet called Duck Lake." We both laughed, equally heartily.

And now a few words about this intervention. It illustrates the inclusion of humor in the therapeutic dialogue as a crucial aspect of the transformative process. I responded to Nora's grandiosity humorously, rather than confronting it, which could have shamed her further. Nor did I spell out the immediate interpersonal and transferential implications of her comment that she was a swan surrounded by ducks. When I presented this material at a psychoanalytic conference, it was suggested that if she was the swan here, I was being depicted as another one of those ducks who did not sufficiently celebrate her. In pointing this out further, I could have made it clear that people would resent being looked down upon by someone who considers herself so superior. From here, the suggestions went to direct confrontation. Who wants to be with such a conceited person?

Such interventions take Nora's comment quite literally, and assume the therapeutically relevant issue here is her concealed or disguised haughty attitude toward me. In reflecting such an impression back to her, I would certainly have shaped a very different session from the one that followed my actual intervention. In fact I might well have co-created a session with Nora in which the issue of not being understood would have been central, but with the further implication that these other people understood her only too well. But, most importantly, it would have indicated that I, too, did not understand her, that I took her too literally, and that I stood ready to shatter her evolving idealizing selfobject transference to boot.

I sensed that Nora's self-depiction as a swan was somewhat "tongue in cheek." Her comment emerged in a dawning recognition of her feeling safe in that she felt we were both swans. We were talking one swan to another. She revealed to me that she and her husband gave people they know titles, not always flattering ones. But in my case they referred to me as the "chairman," a la Frank Sinatra, because she felt that I was very much in charge. The assumption that behind every idealization lurks a devaluation does not always hold. However, in depicting herself as a swan, there was a degree of exaggeration that did indeed conceal Nora's feelings of shame. In playing with Nora's grandiosity, I assumed that I would enable her to feel that the qualities she described, which were unappreciated by her coworkers, could turn out to be a source of strength and pride, and a resource for her, in spite of the current detrimental effect they had on relationships with others.

After our laughter died down sufficiently, she proceeded to describe a variety of circumstances to illustrate how she was misunderstood by the ducks. Just the other day, she and her coworkers had gone out for lunch and the talk turned to wines. Nora had made a study of wines and was quite expert at it. She expected her expertise to be of interest to the others. Certainly, if the situation were reversed she would be very interested in learning more from them. So, when someone said that they liked California wines, Nora stated that she didn't like California wines because they were aged in oak barrels. That gave the wine a certain flavor that she didn't like. Apparently, her lesson was not welcomed.

Another time, one of her coworkers, apparently in an attempt to find a way of connecting with her, to speak her language, told her, with some excitement, that she recently had had foie gras. "Oh," said Nora, "you should have had a sauterne with it." That coworker had been avoiding her since then.

Just yesterday, the staff of her office had decided to take an important guest out for lunch. They chose Gino's Restaurant. "What?" said Nora, "that's a pizza parlor. What are we going to do? Eat pizza and drink Gallo wine?"

In each of these instances Nora was appalled by the limited taste and lack of sophistication of her coworkers. But more to the point, she could not understand their reaction to her: withdrawing from her and considering her to be difficult and high maintenance. "What is wrong with all these ducks?" she asked. She had changed jobs numerous times and husbands three times to try to address this problem but to no avail.

Nora's tone in recounting these experiences was one of bemused astonishment. She was quite serious but spoke in a light, somewhat playful manner. So when she described the incidents with her coworkers and their reaction to her attempts to enlighten them, I felt that she was on the cusp of being ready to investigate these incidents. I also had in mind the findings from the empirical infant research that Beatrice Beebe and I (2002) have described in an earlier volume. Recall that what is initially represented is a self in relation to an object. To the list of such pairs that includes abandoner and abandoned, seducer and seduced, and so forth, in Nora's case I would add "swan and duck." Thus, I tried to capture in imagistic and metaphoric form, as a model scene, what Nora described with her coworkers and what she recalled about her childhood. So I said to her, "Imagine a 5-year-old little girl who, on Mother's Day, draws a Mother's Day card and gives it to her mother. The mother looks at the card and says, 'You call that a Mother's Day card? It's a bunch of scribbles with crayons.'" Nora said, "That's exactly my mother. No matter what I did, she was critical and she would reject it."

But now Nora could see that she was on both sides of that scene. She was the little girl, the duck, who wanted recognition and praise from her critical, rejecting mother, the swan. And she recognized her similarity to her mother when she, the swan, treated her coworkers, the ducks, with arrogance and contempt when they may have been trying to curry some favor with her. Through her own associations and self-reflections, Nora could now begin to address the issues that were so troublesome in her relationships. I believe that what enabled her to do so without feeling shamed or that her sense of self had been shattered was my enjoyment of her "swanness." In turn, this enabled her to deal with both aspects of the model scene simultaneously and alternately.

In summary, I have described an interaction between Nora and me in which a comic vision of reality was implicitly engaged by both of us, although not to the exclusion of others. Nora illustrated her comic vision through her frequent changes of jobs and husbands. The essence of the comic vision is found in her hope and in seeking happiness in new beginnings. She improved her lot in life through genuine hard work, working her way up from an environment in which her brothers had become drug pushers, one having been imprisoned twice already. She had worked her way through college, and now held an executive position.

Nora and I implicitly shared a comic vision of reality but different from the one I shared with Eric. Although play and humor may not be essential to the establishment of a comic vision, they promoted the therapeutic ambiance in which Nora could access increasingly more shame-ridden experiences in her life. The extent to which feelings of shame prompted her to appear arrogant and "show off" had cost her dearly in her work and love relationships.

Nora brought up the characteristic patterns of her relationships, initially not to illustrate them but to bolster her claim that she was misunderstood and ill treated. Yet, the spirit in which she opened them up made them available for therapeutic exploration. By responding in a playful manner to her perplexity and outrage at being so poorly treated and rejected, I resonated with Nora's feelings. My humor and playfulness, I believe, offered a slightly askew and surprising perspective, like a fun-house mirror, and she could begin to reflect upon herself as well.

This material spanned just the first 5 months of Nora's treatment. Through humor her expectation that she would be misunderstood and rejected if she did not come down off her high "swan" was disconfirmed. In describing the process of this session with specific emphasis on the co-creation of a model scene, I have proposed that the role of spontaneity and humor in the therapeutic process, like a spice, when sparingly used, heightens the flavors. In Nora's treatment, the role of play and humor served to establish an atmosphere in which she would feel both understood and able to bring up, self-reflectively, aspects of her way of relating to the world.

As her treatment continued, Nora began a subsequent session with the following account: "My husband came home at five o'clock in the morning. He called from his office and said he was still working, so I star 69ed him because I didn't know if he was in his office or hanging out with friends. But, he was there. I got bored waiting for him and so I called directory assist to try to locate an old boyfriend, but he wasn't there." She liked to imagine that this boyfriend would now regret the way he treated her. He had lied to her that she was the only one. She continued, "I was going to drag this out but I decided to drop it. Being bored is a big problem. I go for excitement and that gets me into trouble." I said, "It's like the swan inviting a vulture for dinner." Well," she said, "that would make it exciting." I said, "Yes, but the feathers would fly. But, I guess that's better than being bored."

The "vulture" was my imaginative expansion of Nora's aviary. In introducing it I expanded on Nora's metaphor and engaged her in imaginative play. Throughout the treatment her use of imagery and metaphor set us up to play again and again on an implicit level of communication. For both of us, communicating implicitly added to the richness of the therapeutic experience. Rather than this quality of communication contributing to overlooking or neglecting transference–countertransference and characterological issues, the opposite was true. It had enabled us to address shame-filled aspects of her life—for example, her three marriages and her affairs into which, she said, she "jumped."

Following my comment, Nora thought about what it is like for her to feel so bored and why she tried so hard to avoid that state. Her thoughts went to being at home when her mother would leave. Although her grandmother was kind, she was fiercely overprotective with all the children. They were not allowed to go out of the house, even at times during the day when the sun was shining. "We weren't allowed to cross the street. I did not cross the street by myself until I was 10 years old. I did try to cross once by myself and almost got hit by a car. The school guard told my grandmother and then we were picked up each morning by a taxi, and picked up from school also. It sent the wrong message—that we were very rich. But, it made me a good passenger."

Two important themes emerged from these recollections. They opened areas for investigation that those analysts who see humor as a diversion would argue would not be reached unless one confronts narcissistic character traits like arrogance and exhibitionism. Nora first described the extent to which self-regulation of arousal, stimulation, interest, curiosity, and exploration were required without benefit of a context of interactive regulation and, second, how she became an imperious "passenger."

"When I went to college, I wanted to have fun. I wanted to be friends with the prettiest girls and go out with the prettiest guys. I wanted to go into acting. My acting teacher asked me why I wanted to be an actress and I said I wanted to have lots of affairs with married men. I thought I could do that on the stage in plays and that would be easier." Nora's acting career never took off because, she said, she could not play the game. She could neither be nice to people who were just secretaries nor become the mistress of an influential man. She continued, "So, instead, I got married three times doing what I wanted to do on the stage. I had offers from married men who wanted to set me up, but I just couldn't do it." She returned to the theme of wanting her husband to come home and be with her. Then she doesn't think about how to stir up trouble. I said, "It seems that you assigned your husband the role of grandmother. He keeps you at home and that's good, but it also gives him a bad name: 'boring.' It's as though when you were kept at home you decided, 'When I grow up and go to college, I am going to go out and have fun.' And you did." She then connected her hope that in her three marriages she would find someone with the adventuresomeness of her mother but that she would be able to keep him interested in her. She would not find him boring and he would not find her boring. Ultimately, she did find her husbands boring. They turned out to be her kind, but restrictive, grand-mother and so she left them.

As her therapy continued, Nora and I addressed her long-standing dread that her hopes and expectations would be deflated, that she would become bored, that she would be condemned to a lifelong search for new exciting objects, but that she would be haunted by the criticism and withdrawal by others. In the portion of the treatment described, Nora moved in the direction of increased self-reflection with self-appreciation. Her grandiosity moved toward acquisition of a sense of perspective.

When I presented the treatment of Nora at a psychoanalytic con-ference, some colleagues pointed out that swans are vicious and that that factor should be addressed in working with Nora. My response was criticized as remaining on too superficial a level in that I failed to address her aggression. Other colleagues brought up the story of the ugly duckling. Leaving aside whether or not these ways of understand-ing Nora were accurate, in both instances the therapist would have been reenacting with Nora the childhood experiences that I tried to capture in the "Mother's Day card" model scene. I would have been dismissing her own strivings toward upward mobility and elevating the unsophisti-cated ducks to swanhood with little benefit to Nora. I believe that stay-ing with Nora's experience enabled her to reflect on herself in ways that might not otherwise have come about.

Humor and Spontaneity Gone Awry

I have been emphasizing the benefits of including humor and sponta-neity in the analytic process: The patient's perspective may be broadened, self-reflection may be increased, and a feeling of intimacy between ana-lyst and patient can be promoted. But there are also risks and potential disasters. A risk is that the patient may feel shamed and hurt. More often than not, humor emerges spontaneously, without premeditation, making it unlikely that humor, irony, or a spontaneous gesture can be planned. However, we can be cognizant of the tone and atmosphere that pervade the session. That's probably the best indication that the therapist may relax sufficiently to "play" a bit in the session. But, the best intentions can also go awry.

One of Helen's goals when she began her lengthy analysis was to be able to form a satisfying relationship with a man. By the age of 31, when I first saw her, she had had several long-term relationships that morphed into friendships and then finally ended. What she was looking for was a man with similar interests, fun, brilliant, imaginative, sensual, and professionally accomplished. Early in the treatment she commented, "I think I have too small a window. Perhaps I reject too many possible men because my expectations are too high." What she wanted from treatment was to "enlarge my window."

As I reflected on Helen's comment at even this early point in her treatment, I was somewhat surprised. She struck me as a very bright, accomplished, attractive young woman. I thought that her expectations, though high, were not at all out of line. I said to her, "I don't do windows."

Eventually Helen came to understand what I meant and how I meant it, but at the time she was enraged by my flip comment. A rupture continued to haunt her analysis for a considerable time. I could see that my comment indicated to her not only that I did not share her view of herself, but also that I did not want to help her. My intention may have been good, but my "humor" was abrasive and my timing was way off. Her treatment continued with a focus on her professional struggles and relationship disappointments.

Privately, I considered my comment and that in making it I violated her reasonable expectations of finding a helpful response from her therapist. I also wondered if I had felt intimidated by her considerable professional and intellectual accomplishments. The fact that 10 years later, on the heels of a significant professional achievement, she did meet and later marry the man who really was perfect for her in every respect—who did fit into that small window—does not mitigate my chagrin over the insensitivity of my comment. I agree with Taerk (2002) that "moments of spontaneity … set the stage for analyst and analysand to experience surprise and experiment with new ways of being" (p. 738). Yes, but, not always.

Here is another illustration, not about humor but about spontaneity. Carrie grew up in the shadow of a brother who had died several years before she was born. The story of the death of the brother had been shrouded in secrecy in her family. Eventually, she uncovered that he strangled to death when he slipped out of his infant seat after her parents had momentarily left him alone. The meaning of this event was sometimes in the background, other times in the foreground of sessions for several years. As she began one session Carrie cried and was visibly distraught. She began to speak about a work-related setback that was linked to an important and shaky relationship. As she spoke, sitting opposite me in a chair, I noticed a cockroach crawling along the handbag that she had placed on the floor next to her chair. I continued to listen to her but kept one eye on the cockroach. Then the cockroach crawled onto my carpet and with my hand raised I jumped out of my chair and killed it. She said, "Killing the cockroach was more important to you than listening to me. You know, that moment when you took your attention away from me, that was how long it took for my brother to strangle." Although she said that had she been in my chair she might have done the same, she felt utterly abandoned.

My point in these two vignettes is that although both treatments continued and although it may be "all grist for the mill," does the mill need all that much grist? These spontaneous moments were not fatal; they were gratuitous. Variations of these moments are ever present; avoiding them, if possible, promotes better treatment. I don't believe that either instance helped the process of treatment or that either facilitated getting to something that would have been inaccessible otherwise. In accessing humor and spontaneity there is always a balance: Does one hit the patient's funny bone or jugular?

More Thoughts on Humor and Spontaneity

In my work with Eric and Nora, I was ever cognizant of a necessary "discipline" to my interventions. I kept in mind the concept of spontaneous disciplined engagement that Joe Lichtenberg, Jim Fosshage, and I (1994) have written about as a principle of therapeutic technique. I did not want either to "upstage" Eric or Nora or to turn their treatment into a showcase for my humor. But, neither would I want to be party to a dry, pedantic exercise. Many of my interventions were thought about prior to my offering them, but my playfulness and humor were spontaneous and on the level of my procedures.

The way in which Eric and I, and Nora and I, spoke and listened to each other illustrated the inseparability of self- and interactive regulation. Clearly, we both had preformed modes of communication, unique and personal like our fingerprints, that we brought to the analysis. But, in addition, we each learned how to adapt to each other's tone, rhythm, and style. In this process we developed as a unique dyad, like no other.

At its best, humor is not imposed on the patient for the benefit of the therapist or used only as a stopgap device to enable the therapist to extricate himself or herself from a transference–countertransference impasse. Both participants—therapist and patient—co-create the emerging content and the context of their interaction. My comments to Sally (who hated New York [chapter 2]), Eric, and Nora were all preceded by "invitations" from them in the form of exaggerations and metaphors indicating some openness to a more playful interaction. The therapeutic experiences could only have come about through this particular therapist–patient combination at this particular moment in time. Once a particular, apt interchange has occurred, it cannot be transported to any other therapeutic dyad. Humor is thus a good illustration of the emergent quality in the therapeutic dyad when viewed as a system. The interventions by Jacobs ("unconsciousness raising") and Grey's colleague ("Why shouldn't I look at your legs?"), although they were in response to questions by the patients, did not reflect interactions co-created over time. Like the patient who questioned me about penis envy, those patients sounded scared, seemed to be anticipating some threat, or were issuing a challenge for some other reason. They did not indicate a readiness on their part to fool around. Under those circumstances humor and spontaneity are far more risky.

The essence of humor lies in timing and surprise. Timing involves a pleasurable experience of delay and anticipation. It requires patience and a willing suspension of disbelief to subordinate oneself to the acceptance of the world as contained in the setup before the punch line. Surprise entails a violation of one's expectations, as I discuss in the chapter that follows.

A final word about humor in psychoanalysis: When the analyst departs from the traditional "patient-talks-analyst-listens-and-interprets" model, the therapeutic ambiance can be refreshed. However, we must bear in mind that when the windows of the analytic consulting room are opened to fresh air, sometimes a moth or mosquito can fly in, or a cockroach can crawl in.

PART 2

Expectations

6 Expectations
Affirmed and Violated

This chapter and the two following are built around the concept of violations of expectations. Violations of expectations can transform positive affect into fear and frustration, as illustrated in the "still face" study. In contrast, empathy and humor, especially when timed just right, can provide pleasurable and exciting violation of expectations. Therapeutic action can be furthered or impeded as analyst and patient affirm or violate each other's transference expectations.

Revisiting Violations of Expectations in the Treatment of Sally, Nora, and Carla

My comment, "assuming I have grown up," to Sally (chapter 2) was unanticipated, a surprising violation of expectations for both Sally and me. Momentarily it destabilized Sally's tragic worldview, and enabled us to move toward greater intimacy. Similarly my "duck lake" comment was unanticipated by Nora (chapter 5). It tweaked her pattern of defending herself through superiority and contempt against the unresponsive and invalidating world of her coworkers.

In these instances my interventions grew out of the implicit relational knowledge that each patient and I had acquired over time. I challenged Nora's and Sally's long-established expectations of living in an affectively unresponsive or dangerous world. Both patients were surprised and, in addition, felt their playfulness was recognized and appreciated. In both instances a therapeutic process was furthered. Nora could join me in investigating her participation in her exclusion by her coworkers. The Mother's Day–card model scene in Nora's treatment was particularly relevant as a depiction of a little girl's violation of expectations. It explicitly depicted a vulnerable, "innocent" child who wants an affective, affirming response and a rejecting mother who shatters that expectation. In Carla's case characterizing her rage as that of an inarticulate little girl was also unexpected by her. To a greater extent than I had anticipated, I met and exceeded her implicit expectations of affective responsivity.

In each of these illustrations, violations of expectations were an emergent property of the therapist–patient interaction. They emerged out of the implicit procedures of the therapeutic process and utilized content of the sessions that was manifest at the moment. They were affectively grabbed by both the patients and me, as we co-created an intimate "now" moment (Stern et al., 1998) that moved along in the flow of the treatment. This process changed the analytic ambience toward an affectively more positive tone.

In this and the two chapters that follow, expectations met, affirmed, and violated are given their proper due in transforming affect. Furthermore, in the subsequent discussions, violations of expectations are recognized as residing in implicit, procedural, nonconscious interactions, as well as in explicit declarative communications.

Empirical Studies of Violations of Expectations

The terms I have been using—"expectations" and "violation of expectations"—are drawn from empirical studies of infants. Infants have already developed expectations as to how interactions with significant caregivers will go by the end of their first year of life. Each partner's communicative behavior will conform to and meet or not meet the other's expectations. Infants can notice and predict what is expectable in their environments (Beebe & Lachmann, 2002; Stern, 1985). For example, in a study by Singer and Fagan (1992) 2-month-old infants had a ribbon tied to one of their legs with the other end tied to a mobile. The infants learned that kicking their leg moved the mobile. In this phase of the study infants were found to detect contingencies between what they did and what the environment did immediately following their actions. Moreover, the infants' repeated use of this contingency and the obvious pleasure they took in it shows that it had an affective meaning for them. In the second phase of the study, when the ribbon was disconnected, they reacted with surprise and distress when their kicking failed to bring about the expected response from the mobile. Detection of contingency facilitates the development of a sense of agency or effectance.

Neurophysiological evidence also suggests that familiarity, repetition, and expectancy constitute the most powerful organizing principles of neural functioning (Cormier, 1981; Gazzaniga & LeDoux, 1978; Hadley 1983, 1989). As expectations become established, breaches or violations of expectations also exercise a powerful organizing effect on infants. But expectancies do not develop only in regard to the inanimate world. Infants can use this ability to develop expectancies about how social interactions will go, which is crucial for the organization of early representations.

Let's revisit the effects of violations of expectations as shown in the "still face" study (Tronick et al., 1978) to which I referred in chapter 1. The instructions to the mothers to assume a "still face" initiated a violation of the infants' expectations of affective responsivity. The infants at first tried to elicit such a responsive reaction from their mothers in line with their expectations and then, failing to do so, they withdrew.

In a subsequent study, Cohen and Tronick (1983) instructed normal mothers to simulate a *depressed* facial expression, with flat affect and lowered activity, as they interacted with their infants. At first the infants smiled and cooed. The infants then made repeated efforts to elicit a response from their mothers. They showed surprise expressions when the mothers failed to respond, and then cycled through disengagement and repeated efforts to elicit a response. Eventually, the infants became overtly distressed and disturbed, and about half of the babies cried. Even after the mothers resumed their habitual manner of relating to their infants, with their usual affect and behavior, the babies remained in their distressed state. For the infants of "normal"—that is, nondepressed—mothers, both the "still face" situation and the simulation of depressed affect violate expectations of maternal affective responsivity. The infants reacted accordingly—with manifest distress.

From these studies we can infer that early patterns of mother–infant interactions, when repetitive and characteristic, organize evolving pre-symbolic representations, referred to as "expectancies," over the first year (Beebe & Lachmann, 2002). Infants expect an affective response to their communicative efforts. Furthermore, expectations go beyond simply preferring expressive faces to still ones or happy faces to sad ones. What the infant seeks and eventually comes to expect is a contingent response from the caretaker as demonstrated in experiments in which contingency was tampered with independently of affective cues (Murray, 1991; Murray & Trevarthen, 1985). In the experiment, mothers and infants first learned how to interact successfully over closed circuit TV while in separate rooms. Then each infant was shown a portion of a video of his mother responding to him in an interaction that had taken place several minutes earlier. The infant, of course, had no way of understanding that his or her mother was not live but a videotaped replay. So, the infant treated her as though "live" and tried to interact as he had done before. But, the resulting interaction between infant and mother was now "out of sync" with what each partner was doing. The replay disturbed the infant's expectation of contingent responsivity and thus their ability to interact. The infants expected a *contingently* affective, responsive partner and were distressed when this expectation was violated.

Enter Tiffany Field and her coworkers (1988). They raised a quite different question about the "still face" studies: Would infants of naturally depressed mothers have become accustomed to their mothers' depression over time and therefore, having established a different set of expectations, would they not be so distressed by this still face behavior? To investigate this question Field compared infants of naturally depressed mothers with infants of nondepressed mothers in two situations: in the still face situation and during spontaneous play. In the still face situation the infants of nondepressed mothers showed more distress than the infants of depressed mothers. The behavior of naturally depressed mothers and their infants was not affected by the still face situation. For these infants a still face had come to be the expected. To clarify the distress reaction in the nondepressed mothers and their infants in the still face situation, Field studied the activity levels and heart rates of both the mothers and infants and found that both of these measures were elevated in the mothers and their infants. She concluded that the still face situation might have been anxiety arousing for both the nondepressed mothers and their infants. But these elevations in activity level and heart rate were not found in the depressed mothers and their infants. These infants seemingly had become accustomed to their mothers' depressions.

Another critical question grew out of Field's findings: Is the depressed behavior of the unresponsive infants specific to interactions with their depressed mothers or does it generalize to interactions with other, nondepressed adults? You can see that this question goes to the heart of several issues. Most immediately it touches on what we might think of as an early form of transference, in which a given set of expectations leads to a generalization of reactions—in this case, depressive reactions when a new person is encountered.

In their further investigations, Field and her colleagues studied mothers and infants in a spontaneous play situation in which there would be many opportunities for infants to engage with an interested stranger. Field's sample in the spontaneous play situation consisted of 40 depressed mothers and 34 nondepressed mothers and their 3- to 6-month-old infants. Numerous demographic, ethnic, environmental, and stress factors were found either to be equally distributed in the two groups or to be not significant in differentiating them.

The novel and significant findings of this study were that "the infants of depressed mothers performed more poorly than the infants of nondepressed mothers when interacting with the stranger and the behavior of the infants "did not differ as a function of interacting with their mother or the stranger.... The infant's depressed style of interacting generalized from interactions with their mothers to those with nondepressed adults except that the infants of depressed mothers showed more head and gaze aversion with their mothers than with the stranger" (p. 1575).

Head and gaze aversion is typically found in infants with depressed mothers. Tronick and Gianino (1986) suggest that such aversive behavior may be "self-regulatory" and serve "to reduce the negative affect engendered by unresponsive maternal behavior" (p. 1575). The self-regulatory function of aversive behavior also has important implications for adult treatment. Aversion and other variations of avoidant behavior are often viewed only with respect to the person being avoided. The function of this behavior, to regulate one's own affect and stimulation, can thereby be missed.

One further finding is of particular interest. The infants of depressed mothers had a negative effect on the nondepressed stranger. Although the strangers were "blind" as to whether the infants with whom they were interacting had a depressed mother or not, the stranger performed less optimally when interacting with the child of a depressed mother. Field et al. (1988) concluded that "the infants' depressed style of inter-acting not only generalized to their interactions with nondepressed strangers but also seemed to elicit depressed-like behavior in the non-depressed adult" (p. 1577).

Recall now that Davidson and Fox (1982) were able to demonstrate lateralization of the infant's brain for positive and negative affect. That is, they were able to show elevated EEG recordings for the left and right frontal lobes, respectively, in their infants as they were watching a laughing or crying actress. The study, as was discussed in chapter 3, constituted an important early demonstration of a necessary but not sufficient precursor to empathy. This methodology can be extended in that lateralization provides an important entrée into emotional state. Dawson (1992) applied the Davidson–Fox methodology to the study of depressed mothers and their infants compared to a control group. First the infants were shown cascading bubbles of water to determine a baseline frontal EEG. Both groups were then observed with mother and infant engaged in face-to-face play. The mothers then left, a stranger played with the infant, and the mothers then returned. For the non-depressed control group, the EEGs of the infants showed positive affect with the mother, negative affect when the mother left, and positive affect when she returned. The findings for the infants of depressed mothers were the reverse. These infants showed negative affect with the mother, positive affect when the mother left and with the stranger, and negative affect when the mother returned.

Dawson thus demonstrated that by 10 months of age, the emotional responsivity of infants of depressed mothers is already organized differently from that of normal infants. The same event that activated positive affect and the associated EEG pattern in normal infants—for example, the mother playing peek-a-boo—elicited negative behavior and the associated EEG pattern of activation in infants of depressed mothers. Again, the findings confirm that for these infants interactive events and inner state were coordinated, but the infants of the depressed mothers show a reversal of the usual organization.

The work of Tiffany Field demonstrated the unique impact of the depressed mother on her child. The work of Dawson demonstrated that this impact could also be detected in the infant's response to a stranger. Further studies of infants responding to their depressed mothers reveal a wide range of responses manifested in different ways. Based on both observational reports by infant researchers and reconstructions by analysts who treated patients whose mothers were "dead" (Green, 1983)—that is physically present but psychically absent—Stern (1994) has elaborated, extrapolated, and synopsized a variety of coping mechanisms of the infants of depressed mothers. In what follows I restate and reframe these coping mechanisms with respect to the way in which the infant's violation of expectations of affective responsivity can be transformed in the infant–mother dyad.

In studies of depressed mothers, depression is usually assessed through the mother's self-reports on a questionnaire. The mothers typically report having symptoms such as feeling depressed, listlessness, having gloomy thoughts, sleep disturbances, and so on. The self-reported "depression" does not differentiate among sources for the depression— that is, whether their depression is due to the recent loss of a loved one, a postpartum depression, or a long-standing mood disorder. Nor are "empty" depressions differentiated from "angry" depressions.

Stern recognized that these depressed mothers are not continually depressed. In fact they make heroic efforts to be with their baby and to stimulate their baby. Since it is reasonable to assume that all depressions are not alike, different coping styles of infants may be associated with different forms of maternal depression. But, each mother–infant pair establishes its own set of expectations and how violations of these expectations are handled. The different patterns that Stern described are not mutually exclusive and babies will cope with their depressed mothers using several of them.

Some infants imitate their mother's affect in order to be with her. Thus, they seek relatedness through their own repeated "microdepressions." They thus convert what other babies might experience as a violation of affective responsiveness into their own "expectation."

Some babies make it their job to reanimate their mothers, to try to get their mothers to be livelier. These babies tend not to give up hope of getting their depressed mothers to respond. But for this to occur they must at least experience some success in their endeavors to enliven their mothers. These babies retain a hope for affective responsiveness. They try to minimize violations of these expectations by engaging their mothers through charm, coaxing, or by "seducing" them to join in an affective interaction.

When these babies don't experience some success, if they consistently fail, they may lose interest in the mothers and become curious and fascinated with the inanimate world. These babies shift from having their experiences violated to finding experiences in which their expectations of stable responsiveness, albeit nonhuman responsiveness, are met.

The valiant attempts by the mother to relate to her infant are perceived quite early by some infants as inauthentic. Both mother and infant may then develop what Winnicott (1960) has called "false self" organizations. The distinction between a violation of expectations and expectations being fulfilled is lost here. The infants respond to the "forced" affectivity of the mother as though it's the real thing. Mother and baby engage in a conspiracy and pretend that there is affective responsivity in their interaction.

Under some circumstances, to escape from the negative experience, the infant may get overinvolved with self-regulation, self-stimulation, and self-manipulation, as Tronick and Gianino (1986) described. That is, the infant may avert head and gaze, suck on his or her cheek, rock back and forth, or seek solitary self-regulation in the face of deadening or aversive maternal stimulation. The most soothing response is then drawn from oneself, and the disappointment of not finding others to be emotionally responsive is avoided.

I do *not* suggest that the patterns of infancy are continued without change into adulthood. However, sometimes these patterns persist or may reappear in adulthood, fulfilling self-regulatory functions at physiological, affective, or symbolic levels. In general, these patterns evolve throughout development and most are likely captured in the dialectic tension between transformation and temporal continuity (F. Lachmann, 2001).

To summarize at this juncture: The "still face," the "out-of-sync," and similar studies demonstrate the early establishment of expectations of affective responsivity and the disorganizing effect of violations of expectations of predictability, contingency, and reliability—that is, of expectations of living in an affectively responsive and familiar world.

These studies provide a basis for inferring that expectancies accrue and are organized across the first year of life. By 6 months the infant's way of relating dyadically becomes stable and characteristic. When repetitive and characteristic, these early interactions, involving patterns of self- and interactive regulation, organize evolving expectancies over the first year. However, these early interaction patterns will be subject to developmental reorganizations and transformations as well as reinforcement through repetition, after the first year.

Expectancy and violations of expectancy are powerful conceptual tools for viewing development, both in normal and in less than optimal mother–infant dyads. These concepts also hold promise in clarifying transactions in the therapist–patient dyad.

There are two levels at which the concepts of expectancy, or expectation, and its violation become relevant therapeutically. The first involves broad stretches of time and is concerned with not only how a person's expectations may have been violated but also, in turn, how he or she may have become habituated to violating the expectations of others. A second level involves a shorter span of time: the moment-to-moment regulation of self and other in the dyadic interaction. My point is that in the violations of co-created expectancies of each partner lie opportunities for heightened affective engagement that can be transformative.

As in the priming study mentioned earlier, any negative aftereffects of experimental studies of violation of expectation in infants are short lived. Otherwise, the experiments would be unethical. In life circumstances, however, violations of expectations of affective responsivity are generally repeated over and over, and they become the substance of strain trauma. However, matters are different in the surprising positive violations of expectation I already described in several treatments. There, the continuing therapeutic relationship reinforces a positive experience for both partners. A firmer bond, greater intimacy, and increased self-regard by both participants may evolve.

Violators and the Violated

I now turn to life circumstances that range from grave to traumatic and their effect on expectations. Mayes and Cohen (1996) have summarized the literature on infants' expectancies and disruptions in expectancies in social interaction in the background of children exposed to early traumatization or who were otherwise considered to be at risk. "Out of the daily routines of being cared for, infants develop expectations for their parents' behaviors—the familiar touch, sound of the voice." Against this background, what is unexpected gets attention. "Children, growing up in chaotic, inconsistent homes sometimes marred by violence and regularly by neglect, may be indiscriminate and unpredictable in their social relatedness" (p. 136). These observations have led Mayes and Cohen to hypothesize that the violations of expectations in early life may curtail and interfere with these children's "ability to feel safe and secure with others or when alone, to enjoy reciprocity, or to be able to endure normal frustrations, in short, to anticipate familiar scenes and tolerate the unexpected" (p. 136).

I will refer to these findings again when I discuss the early life of children who grew up to be violent. The fate of children for whom early distress reached extreme proportions was tragic. They lacked ordinary resources to deal with deprivations, frustrations, and injuries to their sense of self. Aggression "erupted" from them rather than serving as a reaction to their circumstances (Lachmann, 2000). For these children, the possibilities were restricted. Their inability to deal with early, repeated experiences of violations of expectations led to profound social withdrawal and massive outbreaks of eruptive aggression. But there is more. It can also eventuate in their determination to violate the expectations of affective responsivity of others, to shatter others' feelings of living in a safe, predictable world. In chapter 7 I elaborate this hypothesis further: To be the recipient of early and continuous neglect and aggressive, abusive, cruel, or sadistic violation of expectations can emerge in the developing child as a propensity to violate expectations.

The hypothesis that a shift can occur from being the target of violations to becoming a violator of expectations is based on the work Beatrice Beebe and I (2002) reported that what is initially acquired by the infant and by the partner are presymbolic representations of the interactions themselves. That is, violations of expectations are co-created and thus organize experiences in *both* partners simultaneously as to what it is like to be a "violator of expectations" and what it is like to have one's expectations violated (Beebe & Lachmann, 2002). Each partner gets to know and expect and eventually to represent what it is like to be on either side of this interaction. Thus, both sides of the interaction get to be known by each partner. For any person, one or the other side of this interactive representation may be more dominant.

Not all violations of expectations are disorganizing to infants or to adults. To a child a "jack-in-the-box," or to an adult a surprise party can be a joyful, nonthreatening violation of expectations. Of course, some children may become terrified, shocked, by the sudden eruption of the figure from the box, and some adults may become painfully embarrassed by a surprise party for them. Violations of expectations evoke a range of reactions and their effect is determined by the meaning, context, and interaction involved in the surprise.

Before continuing, another quick summary and some inferences: Violations of expectations are co-created. That is, expectations are violated in circumstances where one partner anticipates familiarity and affective responsivity and thereby provides a willing if unwitting "foil" or "dupe" for the other partner. For the other partner, the violator, violations of expectations may be a long-standing organizer of experience and motivation. Sensing expectations of safety, the violator may set out, deliberately, to violate those expectations, perhaps as his or her own expectations had previously been precipitously violated. On the other hand, the violator of expectations may be motivated by grandiose fantasies and revenge for previous narcissistic injuries. Violations of expectation are an emergent experience, co-created and transforming, and may be distressful or joyful, traumatic or therapeutic.

A Range of Violations of Expectations

In presenting this set of concepts to friends and friendly critics, I am often asked if I cannot find a better term than "violation" to describe the various ways in which expectation can be challenged. I like the term "violation of expectations" because it links experiences along the developmental continuum, and is evocative, somewhat "shocking," and itself a violation of expectations. I also prefer to talk about a range that is differentiated from one extreme to the other by the various "violations" I listed before. On various points along the middle of this range of violations, I place phenomena with both positive and negative valences: defying conventions, shattering traditions, ridiculing customs, mocking institutions, transgressing taboos, betraying trust, breaking rules, and telling lies. Further along toward the more problematic end of this range, I place destructively invading the privacy of another person or traumatizing him or her through assault or rape. And toward the more pleasurable end of the range, I place discovering and displaying the fact that one is the possessor of extraordinary gifts, skills, or talents that may come as a shocking surprise.

The theme of "violations of expectations" straddles implicit procedures and explicit declarative communication. Even when only present as implicit procedures, they are important and at times central organizers of a person's experience. Therefore, they lend themselves to the construction of model scenes, especially in instances of perversion and in instances of creativity, as I discuss in the next two chapters. Violations of expectations are clearly not the only motivation or organizer of perversions and creativity, but they provide a significant thread that connects a variety of phenomena that, on the surface, share little in common. I focus on this theme because I believe it has generally been neglected and can illuminate procedures of self- and interactive regulation, especially of procedures regulating heightened affect that are implicated in perversions of sexuality and aggression and in creativity.

Closely related to these phenomena and to pathologies in the sense of self generally is the sense of specialness, or of being exceptional. Having one's expectations violated and being the violator of the expectations of others are both routes that can eventuate in feeling "exceptional." Discovering that one has extraordinary talents, whether as musician, artist, scientist, or chess player, can meet one's grandiose self-expectations, as was the case with composer Richard Wagner, or it can affirm a long-held sense of "specialness." In either instance the person's sense of self may be profoundly affected. In other people this quality, this "specialness," can evoke feelings of admiration, awe, and envy, reinforcing grandiose self-expectations further. The response does not need to be positive to be reinforcing. For example, Nora's officemates responded to her "specialness" by rejecting her, and she in turn responded by firming up her sense of being a "swan," special and superior.

The range of violations of expectations can transform affect by coloring a person's expectations of the future, thereby heightening fears, pessimism, and distrust or promoting grandiosity, arrogance, and a conviction of one's specialness or leading to creativity, inventiveness, and adventuresomeness. The heightened affect that accompanies violations of expectations potentially organizes these experiences far beyond the brief time they take up in a person's life.

Sex, Lies, and the Internet

Here is a case to illustrate a paradox embedded in the concept of violations of expectations—namely, that such violations are co-created. This may appear unreasonable since, clearly, one person does the violating to another person. But, the phenomenon does involve two parties; in this case the violations of expectations came to the fore in the form of lying. Both partners, whether in telling lies or being told lies, potentially experience a violation of expectations. These expectations are not merely cognitive in nature for the person who tells the lies or for the person to whom the lie is told. That is, to tell lies or to be told lies can shatter one's trust as well as one's sense of safety and stability in the world.

Both Ferenczi (1933) and Balint (1969) considered the traumatic effect on the child when the child seeks confirmation or validation of events that occurred and the parents or other adults "gaslight" (i.e., they lie, deny, or pretend that what happened, or what the child saw or felt, did not happen). In the other direction, Kohut (1966) drew attention to the rupture of the selfobject tie that occurs when the child's need for the omniscience of his parents is disturbed by their *failing* to catch their child in a lie. Herein resides a subtle violation of expectations, the consequences of which, according to Kohut (1968), would be noted in the person's failure to transform the idealizing selfobject tie into a set of guiding ideals.

The treatment of Doug illustrates not only the failure of his parents to catch him in lies, but also their explicit and implicit encouragement of his lying. It was difficult to determine what specific effect his long-standing pattern of having gotten away with lying had in forming his subdued, taciturn character style, but it certainly became an issue in his marriage. By lying, Doug violated his wife's expectations of being able to trust him and to rely on his integrity. As a matter of fact, whether Doug's pornography watching on the Internet, which he concealed from his wife, is considered a "perversion," "sexual compulsion," or just a creative hobby, its function was primarily for self-regulation of affect and had less to do with his wife than she thought. By lying, he not only tried to conceal his pornographic interest, but by this time lying had become an automatic, nonconscious procedure.

When Doug's wife, Adrienne, caught him watching pornography on the Internet, she did take it very personally. Perhaps as a consequence of her long therapy with an analyst who apparently equated the effect on her with the intent of her husband, perhaps based on her own background, or perhaps as any wife might who found her husband watching pornography on the Internet, Adrienne became enraged. She took his behavior as an action directed against her. She equated her hurt and anger as indicative of Doug's intent and accused him of betraying her, being deceitful, untrustworthy, insulting, and not finding her sexually attractive.

Adrienne then brought up a list of Doug's behaviors that she found objectionable: He had a smirk on his face when he spoke to her; he checked up on her when he asked her to do something for their home; he treated her as though she was an idiot; and he consistently micromanaged her. But this pornography watching was the last straw, and she packed him off to therapy.

Doug agreed with most of Adrienne's complaints. He was particularly cognizant of his micromanagement. But, he explained, she sometimes forgot and then got angry with him for not reminding her.

When I first saw Doug, he and Adrienne had been married for 11 years. Early in their marriage, Doug's firm had sent them on a remote overseas assignment for several years. Adrienne found this life very difficult, and had a "breakdown" in the form of a manic episode. They came back to the States for several weeks, and when Adrienne was stabilized on medications they returned overseas. Several years later Adrienne gave birth to their son, and they again returned to the States. Things went well for the next 3 years. It was upon their return to the States that Doug began to watch pornography on the Internet. At that time Adrienne was not interested in having sex with him.

The relationship between Doug's parents and between Doug and his mother established a long-standing pattern that included lying. At one time, so a family story goes, Doug's father bought a boat and did not tell his wife, fearing she would have objected to the expense. He also counseled Doug not to tell things to his mother that would upset her, to maintain an appearance of propriety, and always to do the right thing. Doug believed in avoiding confrontations with his wife even if it involved lying or at least concealing important information and certainly if it entailed potentially upsetting news for her.

Doug described his mother as "anxious, angry, frantic, critical, and yelling in a high-pitched voice." No slight flaw would escape her attention and she would explode. He handled her by stepping back, being detached, just observing, and letting pass whatever was upsetting her at the moment. Doug's account resembled a case report by Lemma (2005), who described lying as co-created by a person protecting himself in the only available way against an intrusive omniscient other.

Doug recalled his parents' fights. When Doug was 3½ his father left the home. When he was 8, his parents divorced. Both remarried but his mother subsequently divorced her second husband while his father remained married to a woman Doug "despises."

During his teen years, Doug's mother was often asked how her divorce had affected Doug. She responded, "Oh not at all. He's doing very well." Doug said to me, "Can you imagine the kind of pressure that puts on you? What you have to live up to? I felt a pressure to hide problems, an obligation to fix things. My mother was convinced that I wasn't affected by the divorce, so outside pressure came from that. There was no room for my problems and there was a pressure to make things seem to be okay. I wanted to be a better person than my father, more responsible, not cause pain to my mother." Doug attributed the basis for his parents' divorce to his mother's "high standards" and his father's "less than honesty."

During early adolescence Doug would sneak out of his house to meet his friends. They smoked pot, snorted cocaine, and engaged in other questionable adolescent behaviors. When questioned by his mother about where he went at night, with whom, and so forth, Doug would lie. He was amazed that, although he thought his lies were rather transparent, his mother never challenged him. He realized she preferred to be lied to rather than have to face "real" issues and problems. Doug's lying began as a learned response to his mother's questions and to avoid her emotional explosions and his feelings of shame. It eventually became automatic. Ironically, in lying he met her expectations.

From 10th grade on Doug went to a boarding school where he did very well. Added to the theme of "concealing" his feelings and behavior, a new theme emerged that organized his life: "If you want something done, do it yourself." Getting little personal support from his family,

Doug learned not to rely on having others meet his expectations and to rely only on his own resources and decisions. He made good choices with respect to work and became quite successful. It was in his marriage that the problems of his past surfaced most clearly. He married a woman who, unlike his mother, did not prefer a lie to "the truth."

Based on our exploration of his history and his way of relating to Adrienne and me, I told Doug about how I understood his pornography watching and his concealment of his thoughts and behaviors. I focused on his long-standing determination to do things on his own, to avoid distressing others by telling them things that they might not be able to handle and would really prefer not to know. Specifically, I understood, based on his early life and his experiences in school, that he needed to regulate his anxieties and affect states on his own. I thus offered a contrasting perspective from his accustomed self-accusations and criticism. We investigated his anticipation of being shamed, criticized, and seen as imperfect. His automatic lying and concealing of information was designed to keep others from having to deal with potentially distressful information. Its effect was, of course, just the opposite. He not only caused Adrienne distress, but also was seen by her (and by himself) as a liar.

As we explored Doug's relationship with Adrienne, what struck us both was the extent to which he concealed even inconsequential news from her and lied about matters that were of little importance. His underlying motive became apparent to him: to avoid being questioned, potentially opening a Pandora's Box in the form of his mother's "hysteria," and then being shamed. Lies would tumble out of his mouth before he even had a chance to consider whether the story he was spinning could hold up under scrutiny. An everyday lie might come about as follows: His mother would call to tell him that she would go with Adrienne to watch their son in a school play. He might not give the message to Adrienne, thinking that because his mother did this every year, Adrienne would know that she would come along, so there would be no need for him to relay the information. When his mother would call again and tell Adrienne that she had spoken with Doug, Adrienne would confront Doug, and he would make up an elaborate "explanation."

In the course of exploring these issues, especially his propensity to anticipate being shamed and the self-regulation required to keep his feelings under control, Doug attempted to reveal more about his work life and private thought to both me and Adrienne. Once, Adrienne's father came to visit. As he was leaving, for some reason, he grabbed Adrienne angrily and hurt her. Later, Adrienne was angry with Doug, who was not present, for not having said anything comforting to her when she told him the story. She felt Doug should have offered to take some action toward her parents. Doug told me, "I had a whole list of things I wanted to say to her, but I didn't say any of it. I kept it all to myself." We were able to clarify that it was not as though Doug was unaware of his feelings; he was just unable to articulate them. Doug felt that Adrienne should know that he was on her side, that there should be no need to make this explicit.

After his pornography watching was discovered, Adrienne restricted Doug's Internet privileges on his home computer. She was not worried that he would jeopardize his career by using his office computer for anything other than work. But Doug had a small hand-held computer on which he kept addresses, notes, and appointments. One day he discovered that through this small computer he could access the Internet. Doug and Adrienne had decided to make a purchase on eBay and he was to put in the bid. When he was unable to do so through his home computer, he entered the bid through his hand-held computer. He told Adrienne that he had put in the bid, and she asked him how. Doug was aware of a fleeting fear that if he revealed that he did have unrestricted Internet access, Adrienne would question him further and further. He feared that she would not believe that he had just discovered this feature on his hand-held computer, that he had not used it previously to watch pornography. He feared she would accuse him of concealing Internet activities from her. Before he knew it, out of his mouth came an elaborate story about having gone to a nearby Internet café to place the bid. But Adrienne knew that that place had been closed for more than 2 weeks. What was even worse, Doug knew it, too. And so in the second year of treatment we increased our sessions from once a week to twice a week.

Initially in our sessions, Doug would recount events in his life in what I described to him as "newspaper headlines." They were accurate and succinct descriptions of his experiences, but the details that contain the devil were missing. I linked his style of talking with me to his dread of revealing more than he thought I, or he, could handle. In that case I might become overwhelmed and angry. I then encouraged him to report the story and to editorialize, which he was increasingly able to do. Since his more detailed reports were quite accurate, they were also self-revealing, and shame arousing. He was ashamed of the extent to which he fell short of the standards he set for himself as well as for not tolerating this shortfall well. He said, "My behavior doesn't meet my ideals."

Through our exploratory work Doug was able to understand how desperately he had been trying to keep his mother and others from becoming "hysterical." To maintain the appearance of living up to his "ideals" he had to keep his life private. In addition, I encouraged Doug quite directly to tell Adrienne what we had been discussing: specifically, that his lying and concealing had more than anything to do with his feelings of shame about not living up to his standards. Furthermore, his "micromanagement" had been his way of life since at least high school. Although her reaction to these aspects of Doug was understandable, his behavior was not designed, either directly or indirectly, to denigrate her, criticize her, or to express hostility, contempt, or a lack of concern toward her. They were ways of organizing his life that had been relatively successful, and had stood him well from an early age on. They had provided him with a sense of comfort, safety, and familiarity as to who he was in relation to the world in which he lived. I felt these suggestions were necessary since Adrienne, although increasingly distressed and troubled herself, would not return to her therapist (with whom she seemed to have had an acrimonious parting), see another therapist on her own, or agree to couples' therapy, all of which Doug (with my encouragement) had been proposing. "These are your problems," she told him.

In tandem with our sessions, Doug had been more open with Adrienne, telling her what he was thinking as much as he could. Although there have been no more lies on Doug's part, there has continued to be considerable miscommunication and misunderstanding in their relationship. Adrienne has become increasingly anxious, unable to sleep, angry, impatient, and suspicious. As Doug and I continued to explore his dread of being shamed, dread of being the trigger that could set off his mother, and dread of being less than upright, he became more self-reflective, and able to see himself in a more complex way. With some success I have helped Doug not to be defensive or critical of Adrienne.

She subsequently has said to him that she would try not to take everything so personally.

Watching pornography actually had not played a large role in his life earlier, but became part of the theme of regulating his own states, tensions, anxiety, and excitement. It became prominent when Adrienne expressed a lack of interest in their sexual life, although the pattern did not start then. In exploring the themes contained in his pornography watching, Doug came to grasp the extent to which it provided him with a way to control and regulate his shame and anxiety. He was shielding others from having to deal with his demands since he feared that expressing them would lead to people becoming critical of, angry at, or rejecting of him. And then he would feel ashamed.

Beginning with his mother, who was easily disturbed and who needed to feel in control of herself, Doug kept his inner life to himself and lied about his outer life, his behavior. This self-control had been required in the context of his maintaining as harmonious a relationship as possible with his mother. His mother contributed to their interactive regulation by believing and not questioning his lies. Thus, Doug developed the conviction: I have to manage my own feelings and decisions by myself. I can do this best by revealing as little of myself to others as possible. Lying, concealing, and his "headline" way of speaking about himself illustrated these convictions.

Telling lies entails a complicated interactive scenario. Whereas telling lies had clearly been characteristic of Doug in his earlier life, Adrienne's critical, often judgmental reactions, similar to his mother's, contributed to the continuation of his lying. The question of violation of expectations is complicated here. Adrienne was both surprised and enraged at Doug's lies, but she also expected to be demeaned and badly treated. Doug's lying confirmed her long-held fears and expectations. However, once lies are told, being lied to becomes an expectation by the partner, and feelings of doubt then pervade the relationship. In the face of not being believed even when he was telling the truth, the circumstances are ripe for co-creating a web of lies.

Under these circumstances I told Doug that since his wife would not participate in couples' therapy, he would have to do it alone, and I would help him. I suggested that it was important to enable her to feel safe and that he best try to be neither defensive nor retaliatory when she questioned him. We had seen from past experience that such responses on his part escalated into full-blown fights in which Adrienne's convictions about herself and Doug were only strengthened. That is, I suggested to Doug, or perhaps I may have tried to "teach" him, to respond empathically to Adrienne. The benefits of this suggestion were that it reduced the acrimonious atmosphere that had been pervading their life, their marriage, and their relationship to their son.

Doug's expectations of himself and of Adrienne shifted in the course of our work. Able to access how more readily he feels as well as what he expects of himself, he has eliminated his propensity for "eruptive" lying. Although that tendency had characterized much of his relationship with Adrienne, it was not present in his work life. There, his "honesty" and "rationality" were prized since there was no danger of evoking shrill hysterical screams from his mother or her later stand-ins.

Doug's lying and Adrienne's fragility co-created a system in which each partner pushed the other toward a more extreme position. The telling of lies, the violation of expectations of cognitive and affective responsivity, reverberated between them. The lies of Doug transformed the doubts of Adrienne into rigid suspicions, which, in turn, increased the likelihood of Doug lying. Here the process of transformation moved in the direction of increasing the rigidity of each partner's affective pattern.

Framing my interventions to Doug along a leading edge helped him avoid the shame he invariably anticipated but also enabled him to bring in embarrassing—that is, shame-ridden—experiences. For example, at his work he evaluated his subordinates and they evaluated him. He was described as "smug" and "arrogant" by several of his subordinates. He had not told Adrienne about this but was curious about how he could be seen in this way. He was receptive in our exploration of this distressing news. Importantly, he initiated an investigation of his character style, one that he had found essential to his functioning and had defended vociferously in the past. Our discussions extended to his relationship with Adrienne, where he could see his part in perpetuating the tension between them. One typical source of conflict had been putting their son to bed. Adrienne would read to him for what Doug considered to be too long a time. He would criticize her for this behavior, which led to her becoming more adamant. He was able to concede that this was what Adrienne wanted to do; it was not harming their son irrevocably. Even though he believed he was right in his objections he was able to step back and let her be in charge of the going-to-bed ritual. He would spend time with his son in other ways. In this process past expectations were recontextualized. Doug's expectations that, unless he retained control of all that transpired, his world would explode or implode were absorbed in a new context. He gained a better understanding of Adrienne's reaction, her sensitivity to being dominated, and the potential benefits to their son of not having his parents struggle over him. Doug could see how his criticism of her undermined her shaky sense of herself and prompted her to become more stubborn, and he could see how the benefit to their relationship that accrued from his ceasing the criticism far outweighed the control he would be relinquishing. The atmosphere in his home lightened.

Through empathic understanding the therapist can touch, meet, and even surpass a patient's longings to be understood. Therein lies the therapeutic action of empathy. In working with Doug, I tried to "teach" him to violate or "disconfirm" (Weiss & Sampson, 1986) Adrienne's expectations of being belittled, insulted, and found to be unattractive. Hostilities did diminish between them to a level that was more tolerable.

Perversion and Creativity

In this chapter findings from early childhood have laid the groundwork for considering how expectations and their violation can serve as prime agents for transforming affect. To have expectations of affective responsivity met and to be able to tolerate violations of expectations are basic to establishing a sense of presence in the world. Otherwise, the constant violations of everyday expectations would be continuously destabilizing. As that world becomes increasingly familiar to the developing child, trust in its safety and predictability is increasingly established. Then, disbelief can be safely suspended, as in humor, play, and the use of metaphors. Surprises can then be enjoyed.

Meeting and violating expectations occupies a central role in connecting therapist and patient affectively along a range usually experienced as pleasurable. In therapy, expectations—met, surpassed, or violated—are found along a range that is tilted toward the pleasurable end, whereas in life this is not necessarily so. In life this range extends much farther into the painful direction that includes trauma and having one's expectations violated through assaults of one kind or another.

Violations of expectations evoke strong affect and contribute crucially to both creativity and perversion. I came to this view as I thought about Kohut's inclusion of creativity as a transformation of archaic narcissism. I thought of creative works of the late 19th and 20th centuries as containing a strong element of defiance of traditions. Before that time artists painted and composed for God and patrons. Violating what was expected of them would have put them out of work. J. S. Bach, I believe, was great because in his music he not only met but also surpassed the expectations of his patrons and his audiences for the last 350 years. But as later generations of artists began to exhibit and sell their work to the public, they could challenge and educate, tease and provoke. They began to work in an artistic context in which shocking the audience was one way of engaging them. A new sensibility entered the artistic world, of which Stravinsky's *Rite of Spring* is a prime example. And many shocking new works of art were criticized at the time as "perverse." Once a door opened for the creative artist to violate the expectations of a tradition-bound public, then other ways of violating expectations could enter through that door as well. As I reflected on these shocking premiers in the world of art and music I wondered whether perversion and creativity shared some common thread. I began to consider that in both the essential element might be violations of expectation.

Both creativity and perversion have long presented psychoanalysts with an array of challenges, wonder, and probably even some envy. After all, Freud (1927b) said that "before the problem of the creative artist analysis must, alas, lay down its arms" (p. 177). In the same vein, he also said, "Whence the artist derives his creative capacity is not a question for psychology" (1913, p. 187). Freud did not express the same sense of awe or admiration about perversion. About perversion, Freud (1905a) asserted that it was the negative of neurosis. The pervert does what the neurotic might wish to do, but out of guilt, fear, and reality considerations, the neurotic confines these desires to the realm of fantasy and conflicted wishes.

A moralistic tone hovers over psychoanalytic discussions of these topics. Creativity is idealized; perversion is condemned. Given these extremes, it may be difficult to conceive of a common thread between perversion and creativity, but there is already some literature that addresses this link. Chasseguet-Smirgel (1984) links perversion and creativity in that in both there is an aim to restore the lost primary narcissism of infancy.

In both she asserts there is a desire to escape from reality constriction into a world in which our wishes would be satisfied. Rather than labeling an early developmental stage as "primary narcissism," I hold that both perversion and creativity are co-created through early experience and continue to be reinforced throughout the person's development.

The dictionary (Webster, 1976) defines creativity as "artistic or intellectual inventiveness," and perversion as "deviating from what is considered right or acceptable, stubbornly contrary, obstinately disobedient, any of various sexual acts or practices deviating from what is considered normal." As traditionally defined, both are seen as residing in one person who displays or inflicts these acts or practices upon himself or on others. The diagnosis "perversion" is thus clearly a pronouncement by a judgmental observer. Yet, times change and what previously may have been considered perverted may now just be considered private or only "kinky."

Chasseguet-Smirgel did avoid the pejorative, moralizing tone often found in discussions of perversion, but she remained within an instinct–defense–sublimation model for creativity. In such a framework, pathologizing is just around the corner for both perversion and creativity. Rotenberg (1992), whose views are close to mine, succeeded in steering clear of pathologizing in coining the term "optimal operative perversity" to describe the artist's tendency to deviate from and to contradict a "previously held principle of organization" (p. 171). In his use of the term "perversity," Rotenberg emphasized a somewhat sly, quirky, and defiant quality. Perversity is thus eminently applicable to certain creative artists.

In the two chapters to follow I take a parallel line of thought in pursuing the theme of violations of expectations in creativity and perversions. Some creative artists' expectations of being acclaimed, of being "special," I connect to a family myth in which they triumphed in a close call with death. This "event" took on mythical proportions, and remained as a story that accompanied them throughout their lives. That is, for these artists, just being alive violated their family's expectation that they would not survive an early life-threatening illness or some other brush with death. For some perverted persons, on the other hand, early experiences of traumatic abuse and neglect led to feelings of self-negation that were reinforced throughout their lives, leading them to destroy the lives of others.

Perversions and creative works are also linked in that both are co-created by a violator of expectations and one whose expectations are violated. Violations may be directed against a person—for example, an "innocent" child or an unsuspecting jogger in a park, or a group—for example, those who willingly suspend their disbelief, such as the members of an audience at a concert, in a theater, or at a museum or the unsuspecting students in a school. The appearance of "innocence" or of being "unsuspecting" can be the unwitting contribution of the "innocent" bystander or the "theater-going public" to having their expectations violated. In the instances to be described, creative productions and perverse acts have at their root violations of expectations, from mild departures from the commonplace or from an average expectable environment, to playful teasing, stimulating thrilling surprises, to—at an extreme—traumatic, shocking, terrifying, or vicious assaults that involve inflicting pain and murder.

7 Perversions of
Sexuality and Aggression

As Sylvan Tomkins (1962) said, affect makes good things better and bad things worse. In the prior chapters the role of affect in fostering transformations has been viewed predominantly from the vantage point of making things better. In addition, I have also been discussing how violations of expectations can be experienced pleasurably, contributing to arousal of positive affect and thus to developmental transformations. In this chapter I explore the reverse direction: violation of expectations in which sexuality and aggression are recruited and can spiral into betrayals of trust, invasions of privacy in the form of exhibitionism and voyeurism, and even assaults and murder.

In reflecting on the "dark side" of violations of expectation, the domain of perversions is opened for exploration. In so doing, I propose that the concept of violations of expectations provides a unique handle for understanding the organization and treatment of perverse behavior therapeutically. Specifically, I propose that close attention to how expectations are generated and co-created in a dyad can clarify the process through which perverse behavior comes about and simultaneously avoid a moralistic tinge that can seep into treatment. As Kohut demonstrated for the topic of "narcissism," avoiding the trap of moralistic judgments places us on firmer clinical ground. The same can be the case for "perversion."

I am certainly not alone in trying to get moral judgments out of clinical discussions of perversion. Numerous authors have voiced their dissatisfaction with the morality-tinged discussions of perversion in the psychoanalytic literature and have offered different solutions. Their emphasis has recently turned toward the question of whether each partner considers the other to be a "whole object" and treats him or her as an independent center of initiative, recognizing his or her separate subjectivity. But this emphasis on whole object relationships has itself become a new morality, justly criticized by Muriel Dimen (2001). That is, she criticized the expectation that a "whole-object" love relationship is used as the deciding factor as to whether the term perversion is applicable. Similarly, Steven Purcell (2006), although recognizing the destructive aims, or masturbatory qualities, or antirelatedness aspects of perverse sexuality, also observed that the sexual pleasure of perverse patients had important positive functions. Furthermore, the perverse behavior of patients pointed to their need for complementary responses from their partners. And, if among some analysts a new morality judgment has replaced the prior one so that objectifying or dehumanizing another person in the sexual act has come to constitute sexual perversion, Purcell points out that dehumanization of one partner by the other does not always violate that partner's expectations, thereby raising the question of whether the term "perversion" is applicable in this instance. Do consenting partners in a sadomasochistic relationship fulfill the requirement for practicing a "perversion?" Even more important, what's the difference whether they do or do not?

Arnold Goldberg (1995) looked at the structure of perversion from a self psychological perspective and defined it in terms of the individual psychodynamics of the person, the use of sexualization, and, most important for my purposes, the split in the person's sense of reality. Such a person lives in two realities—for example, one in which there are real consequences for one's actions and the other reality in which consequences do not apply. In this instance, engaging someone and bringing him or her into the world of real consequences is then followed by violating his or her expectations. It is here, in the negotiation around expectations and their violations, both of which are co-created in any dyad, that clinical explorations can be most productive.

Ruth Stein (2005) also emphasized the relational, dynamic structure of perversion in her treatment of a woman whose partner violated her expectation that he would adhere to their "perverse pact." The patient was "intensely involved with a man with whom she shared many professional interests. Their special relationship consisted of ways in which they would excite each other, sexually and otherwise, with minimal physical contact and in a manner that was never tender. Mostly, she would arouse him to masturbate himself while talking to him through the door of men's restrooms or over the phone" (p. 784). These interactions constituted their perverse behaviors.

But these sexualized interactions had a context, a relation-based expectation—and a violation of expectations—of a different kind. The patient had a severe writing block that interfered with her professional advancement. Her "perverse pact" with her partner was that he would hold himself back to keep apace with her. Rather than honoring their pact he pursued his own professional advancement, arousing the patient's rage, envy, and determination to punish him. From the perspective presented here, this man betrayed the perverse pact to which he and the patient had agreed. He violated her expectation that they shared a bond of trust.

According to my understanding of perversion, the pact of this couple consisted of mutually agreed-upon expectations of each other. Labeling it "perverse" adds an unnecessary judgmental dimension to the behavior of both participants. It was the man's violation of the terms of their pact, a betrayal of trust, that constituted his perversity. Based on this formulation, the patient's treatment would focus on her continued adherence to a pact that was being broken, while she expected that it would be fulfilled. This would be her contribution to the maintenance and subsequent violation of the pact.

If we don't hold to the "whole-object" love criterion for sexuality, then the patient's sexual behavior would only be of therapeutic interest to the extent that it interfered with or precluded other aspects of her life, for example, as related to her writing block or her social and sexual isolation. Implicit in the clinical material is that the man would have to constrain himself consciously to adhere to the pact, whereas the patient was already constrained by her writing block. She was unable to do otherwise and yet expected the man to sacrifice his ambitions.

Whether my reformulation of this case conforms to other material of this case is not at issue. Rather, my point is that terms like "perversion" can draw undue attention to dramatic aspects of a patient's life and behavior at the expense of attention to expectations, how they have been met, how they have been violated, and how they engage and repeat early interaction patterns as well as how they attempted to or failed to transform them.

Some time ago the editors of *Psychoanalytic Dialogues* invited me to contribute to an issue on supervision in psychoanalytic training and education (Lachmann, 2003). I was asked to discuss the treatment of a man as though I was supervising the therapist. The patient, Frank, treated by Shari Eliot (2003), sought treatment when a hotel receipt he had left in his jacket pocket revealed to his wife that he was having an affair. In the course of the sessions he told Eliot that since his teenage years he had been "making obscene phone-calls ... to women he knew—his aunts, mothers of friends, and later even his mother-in-law" (p. 314). Or he would go to a newsstand and make sure a woman was watching him as he examined pornographic magazines.

Frank told Eliot about a recurring teenage scene: Each day his mother would come to his bedroom in the basement of their house to use the only shower in the house. "He would lie on his bed, naked with an erection that was partially revealed so that his mother could see" (p. 314). As he lay there he would excitedly rearrange his position. Eliot asked him what he hoped would happen when he did this. He replied that he hoped his mother would notice him. But she never did.

At other times, for reasons never clear to Frank, his mother would come to his room to watch television. Sometimes he would arrange to have a pornographic movie on the screen. He and his mother would then sit silently watching the film until he began to feel frightened and would shut it off. What was frightening was his fantasy that his mother would touch his penis. She never did, nor did she ever say anything to him about these encounters.

Twice before, Frank had sought treatment. During the first treatment, when Frank was deeply disturbed by having made anonymous obscene calls to his wife's mother, his therapist suggested that he channel his energies toward masturbation and toward his pornographic tapes so as not to act them out. Dissatisfied, he ended that treatment. In a second treatment he conveyed his sexual life in detail and felt excited by doing so in the presence of his therapist. But, Eliot reported, the therapist just let him go on and did not say much. He told her he felt like he was masturbating in front of her. In a firm and scolding tone she told him, "You will not!" Her tone made him feel like a dangerous pervert.

There was very little communication in Frank's home. His father was a golf pro and away a great deal. His mother became a cook for the local priest. When he came home from school he would find his mother sitting in front of the television set, smoking, and not even acknowledging his arrival. There was always a pile of *Playboy* magazines lying around, face down, which both his mother and the paternal grandfather read. While rummaging through his father's closet, he discovered a scrapbook of pornographic pictures collected by his father. By the age of 16 his parents let him have girls sleep over in his bed. When the mothers of these girls called, Frank's mother told them that their daughter was sleeping in Frank's sister's room.

A dominant theme in Frank's life centered on having his expectations of acknowledgment consistently violated. The violations in this case were not overtly malicious but consisted of passive nonrecognition. It is easy to imagine that under these circumstances his need to be "seen" and "touched" escalated. Sexuality was the *lingua franca* of the family and that fact presumably contributed to the role sexuality began to play in Frank's life. His first and second therapists were apparently intent on containing his "perverse" behavior. The second therapist also obviously did not understand the co-created aspect of her patient's behavior. Neither therapist recognized the pressure of his need to be noticed and its concrete expression as exhibitionism.

The experiences revealed by Frank in relation to his mother when he was 12 and 13—that is, her obliviousness to his return from school and while they were watching television together in the basement—led to my formulating of a model scene: Frank with mounting excitement hoping and fearing that his mother would notice him. His wish to be seen escalates in proportion to the extent to which his mother fails to recognize, acknowledge, or respond to his presence. The model scene can be understood as providing a blueprint for much of his "perversity."

Frank's violation of the expectations of privacy of the women he telephoned repeated his hope that his withdrawn, detached, silent mother could be rousted. He communicated in the one language that he expected her to understand and, even then, he did not succeed. He kept trying, even as he was afraid of increasing his cries to be seen since they had the potential to get him into realistic difficulties. He asserted his sexuality as a continuing need to demonstrate his presence and aliveness. Looked at from this perspective, Frank's "perverted" behavior was not aimed at denigrating or seducing the women he called, but rather at regulating his sense of isolation by finding some affirming, responsive chord of recognition. Redressing the consistent, massive way in which his expectations of affective responsivity were unmet became his dominant motivation.

In "supervising" this case I suggested that two concepts, "model scenes" and "leading edge interpretations," might be particularly helpful in furthering the treatment. The model scene centered on his exhibiting his sexuality and being ignored by his mother. Leading edge interpretations would address his strivings, what he is attempting to attain or maintain through behavior that, on the surface, looks hostile, destructive, or "perverted." The "leading edge interpretations" would be particularly useful in working with the obscene telephone calls. The therapist would recognize that the calls were made to redress feelings of invalidation associated with present-day repetitions of the model scene.

Four years after publishing the case discussion I spoke with Shari Eliot to find out what happened in this patient's treatment. She told me that Frank had stopped treatment about 1½ years earlier (personal communication, February 2007). His work life had become more successful, his marriage had lasted, he had had another child, and there had been a significant decrease in his obscene phone calls. His use of the Internet and pornographic movies in conjunction with his masturbation had decreased significantly as well. The quality of his marriage had improved. There had been no more affairs.

Prior to termination, Frank spoke in his therapy about not being heard or feeling understood by his wife. In contrast he felt Eliot understood him well. The treatment then focused on increasing his ability to express himself to his wife. His relationship with his wife improved and so did the quality of their lives. Simultaneously, his need to express himself through the obscene phone calls diminished. But, as he ceased to make phone calls to strangers, he began to leave obscene telephone messages on Eliot's office answering machine. Here is where a leading edge formulation paid off. Eliot interpreted these calls as Frank feeling safe enough to make them to her in the hope that she could welcome them into the treatment. Further exploration of the context of the calls revealed that they occurred when Frank was home alone and felt isolated. Whereas much of the treatment had been addressing the calls as regulators of Frank's overarousal, the other side—Frank's sense of depletion—could now be addressed as well.

The treatment of Frank illustrates how expectations and their violations can provide a useful interpretive window on perverse behaviors. Frank's expectations of being sexually recognized in his sexually hypercharged family were constantly disappointed. His "perversion" was a direct translation of that experience. He violated the expectations of innocent, "unaware" women that they were living in a safe predictable world by invading their privacy and shocking them through his sexual exhibitionism. The "perverse" sexual behavior both decreased his intolerable sexual excitement and dispelled his states of isolation and aloneness. That is, his sexual intensity was down-regulated while his sense of isolation and aloneness was up-regulated, and affectivity was increased. Similarly, down- or up-regulation of painful affect states can be found in "perversions" of aggression, whether against oneself or against others.

In placing the co-creation of violations of expectations at the center of my discussions of perversions of sexuality and aggression, the question of whether a person by himself or herself can be engaged in a perverse act becomes relevant. With respect to perversion, whether in the form of sexuality or aggression, does there have to be a literal other person involved? For example, in the case of Frank there were literally two people required to enact his violation of expectations. However, can acts of self-mutilation, doing something damaging to oneself (without involving another person), be a violation of one's own expectations? Yes. The presence of a fantasied other during the perverse act would be of clinical relevance. Like Stravinsky playing the piano by himself, there can be a kind of co-creation even without another person.

When self-mutilation dispels feelings of nonexistence, despair, or ways of dealing with guilt and disappointment, it can be in the service of regulating one's unbearable affect and level of arousal. When people self-mutilate to defy a parent and to "violate" parental expectations by holding a mirror up that reflects to them how they have been experienced by their child, the self-mutilator, the behavior is clearly co-created. My point is that perversions of aggression engage powerful violation of expectations in the form of harm, destruction, shock, and pain to make an affective impact on another person, indirectly or directly.

As I indicated earlier (chapter 1), I view eruptive aggression, a perversion of aggression, as exemplified by the "inexplicable" acts of violence and murder committed by serial killers and mass murderers. Eruptive aggression organized early in childhood through repeated trauma, deprivation, or abuse can break forth in a barely triggering context. I contend that here, too, focusing on the perversity through the lens of expectations and violations of expectations can shed some new light on these behaviors.

Serial killers are men who have killed three or more strangers, for no obvious reason. Even the usual surface motives for murder, such as monetary gain, revenge, or sexual jealousy, are not evident in this group. In *Transforming Aggression* I presented the lives of three men who became serial killers and I now return to these serial killers to examine their lives from a different angle: the place that violations of expectations played in shaping their murderousness. In their serial killings these men recreated their own experiences of betrayed trust, shattered self-confidence, and the violation of all expectations of feeling safe in a predictable world.

In discussing serial killers we are forced to rely on inference and indirect data in assessing the quality of their early years. Independent reliable data are usually lacking, and as informants who might themselves provide some information, serial killers are not much help. Still it is not unreasonable to suppose that at the very least their childhoods were comparable to those of traumatized and at-risk children summarized by Mayes and Cohen (1996). Recall that such children failed to develop coherent expectations of social interactions in many social situations and lacked the resources for responding when the expectations they did have were violated.

Consider the childhood of Henry Lee Lucas (Newton, 1992; Norris, 1988). He was the youngest son in a dysfunctional family. His father had been a severe alcoholic who lost both legs in an accident. His mother, a prostitute, beat Henry and killed his pet animals. When he attended primary school, she dressed him as a girl and kept him in girls' clothing. A kind teacher found boys' clothing for him to wear. Both he and his father were subjected to watching his mother have sex with various men. His earliest memory was of his mother finishing up with a customer, then pulling out a shotgun and shooting the man in the leg. Young Henry observed the man's blood spatter all over the room. To argue that in his early life Lucas was the victim of repetitive betrayals of trust and violations of expectation of living in a safe, predictable world would be to presume that such expectations of safety and reliability had ever been established. In fact, what becomes apparent is that even the most bizarre expectation—of the mother having sex with a stranger in full view—comes to be violated by her shooting the man.

From his earliest age, Lucas would have been aware of both his experience of being abused and the reciprocal experience of his abuser. Through his mother's manner, tone, and facial expressions he may have sensed the power, thrill, or generally heightened positive affect his mother derived from her abusive rages.

As a teenager, Lucas embarked on his pattern of defying societal norms by being cruel to animals and having sex with their corpses. In his 30s he began his killing spree. He explained his pattern of serial killings of women by stating that he killed in order to be sexually potent. Given his background, for Lucas aliveness may have been associated with abuse and danger, and a "still face," to borrow Tronick and Gianino's imagery (1986), with safety. These two factors—recreating the excitement that he saw in the face of his mother, the abuser, and then finding comparative safety in affectless, deadened faces—provided a fertile pattern in which violent behavior can emerge.

For example, as I indicate later, in the case of mass-murderer Kip Kinkel there is some anecdotal evidence that in his first 3 years he was affectionately cared for and nurtured. But, for most serial killers comparable direct evidence is not available. Keeping in mind that both sides of an interaction are represented—the violator of expectations and the one having his expectations violated, there is ample indirect evidence of early trauma, victimization, deception, abuse, and neglect.

The victim also plays a role in the co-creation of perverse violence. Using "co-creation" with respect to violence is, I agree, potentially problematic. But keeping in mind that neither similarity, symmetry, nor equality of contribution is implied, then the issue of blame or responsibility is averted. Thus, simply looking "innocent" or being in the wrong place at the wrong time can be one partner's co-creation to assault or abuse.

The most frequent victims are young children, runaways, prostitutes, and men and women in isolated places. They are typically innocent appearing, vulnerable, and unsuspecting, sometimes alone, and often in need of help. These are the very qualities and circumstances that make them ideal targets for the killer, their "innocence" provoking the killer's violence, inciting him to violate expectations of safety and trust. A devilish variation of this pattern is that the killer himself may feign helplessness. By feigning helplessness, the serial killer frequently lulls his victim into trusting him. He encourages the victim to feel safe only to turn on and kill him or her. A case in point is Ted Bundy (Newton, 1992; Rule, 1989; Sears, 1991).

Ted Bundy

In his early 20s, Bundy wanted a serious relationship with a woman, felt ashamed of his poor background, and believed he had nothing to offer the kind of woman he wanted. He met the daughter of a wealthy family who was "everything he wanted" and strikingly beautiful. She had long dark hair parted in the middle. Bundy was infatuated with her, but she lost interest in him. He was devastated when she finally broke off with him.

Some time later, when Bundy was more self-assured and articulate, he tried to rekindle his first love. He courted her with expensive gifts and luxurious dinners. After 2 months, he ended their relationship. She was shocked and hurt. He had succeeded in wooing her, leading her to expect that he was interested in her, winning her interest, affection, and trust only precipitously to shatter these expectations by abandoning her. She concluded that Bundy's courtship had been deliberately planned. He seduced her to fall in love with him and trust him. Then he rejected her just as she had rejected him. This pattern of establishing a feeling of trust and an expectation of reciprocal affective responsivity, just to violate this expectation, constitutes the essence of perversion.

In subsequent serial killings Bundy continued to enact a pattern of seduction and establishment of trust followed by betrayal in order to violate the expectation that he was trustworthy. Some sketchy information about his early life suggests that this pattern may have been a repetition of his early experience of having been the victim first of his mother's abandonment and then of her deception. Ted Bundy was born in a group home for unwed mothers where he was left for 3 months. His grandparents then raised him as their adopted son. His mother was called his "sister" and there was some suspicion that she had been the victim of incest, his grandfather being the real father. The grandfather was intolerant, tyrannical, volatile, sadistic to animals, and the possessor of a large pornography collection.

Bundy's first girlfriend had violated his expectation of acceptance. He had let down his guard only to be reminded by her how dangerous such a move was. His later victims bore a striking resemblance to her. They, too, had long black hair parted in the middle. Alongside his serial killings, Bundy led another life as a respectable law student and volunteer counselor in a rape victim clinic. To entrap his victims, he would feign helplessness—for example, putting one arm in a sling. Who would have expected this nice, caring young law student to commit such crimes? He established a clear pattern of expectations in his victims that he was a "safe" person and could be trusted, only to betray that trust.

Kip Kinkel

I turn to a more detailed description of a young boy, Kip Kinkel (Woodruff, 1998; see also K. Newman, 2004), who, at the age of 15, shot and killed both of his parents and then opened fire in his high school, where he killed two of his classmates, wounded 25 more, and wounded a policeman as well. Since home movies made by his parents, his diary, and a report from a psychologist who treated him briefly are available, there is considerable information about this boy's traumatic development. Kip was born outside Eugene, Oregon, in a bucolic setting, in a house that his parents had named *Shangri-La*. His parents, Bill and Faith, were high school teachers. Bill taught languages and was fluent in Spanish and Faith taught English. Their daughter, Kirsten, who was 6 at the time Kip was born, lived up to and even exceeded the academic, social, and athletic expectations of the family.

Faith Kinkel was 41 and her husband was a few years older when, unexpectedly, she became pregnant. Bill Kinkel looked forward to sharing his interest in books, languages, sports, and travel with his son. But, more precisely, I think, he had an unshakable expectation that his son would share these interests with him. Parental expectations shadowed Kip's developing years. Kip's inability to meet these standards disappointed his father again and again, and eventually his father came to expect the worst of him, or so Kip told the therapist he saw when he was 15.

Kip's parents were decent middle-class people who were well meaning and caring, but apparently rigidly demanding. Theirs was not a depriving or abusive home, but rather one that quietly screamed: succeed! Subtly and consistently Kip's increasing sense of inadequacy was mirrored. Meeting even average-expectable standards was beyond Kip from an early age on.

When Kip was 3, after he had mastered some ability to speak English, the family went on a 1-year sabbatical to Spain. Everyone but Kip loved learning Spanish. He was placed into a non-English speaking school, but never learned to speak Spanish. Here may have been an early and dramatic violation of Kip's expectations. After he finally succeeded in learning English and communicating with his playmates in school, in Spain he was back to square one. He had a continuous experience of inadequacy, and as recalled by his sister, was bullied in his class. It was downhill for Kip from that time on.

When the family returned to the United States Kip entered first grade, but it was discovered that he had learning difficulties and his parents decided to keep him in first grade for another year. Once again, he was isolated in school. Furthermore, to help Kip overcome his learning disability, his parents, being teachers, tutored him. They studied with him after school for many hours. According to a neighbor, their tutoring program only increased Kip's frustration and constant sense of failure. From a description given by this neighbor, these tutoring sessions were a continuous back and forth of violation of expectations: Kip could not give his parents what they expected and they could not give him the approval he craved.

In home movies filmed by Bill, and included in the *Frontline* TV broadcast (Woodruff, 1998), we see Kip playing Frisbee and trying to do headstands and cartwheels. However, the other members of his family, parents and sister, seemed to be standing too far away from Kip for him to throw or catch the Frisbee. And, as he tried to do the gymnastics his sister performed expertly, he again failed. Bill comments that Kip needs more work as his mother watches him struggle and fail. As I watched the video, I had an urge to run up to Kip and hold his legs steady so that he could gradually learn to do a headstand. Apparently his parents did not feel similarly.

The Kinkels' home movie provides a model scene depicting an organizing theme of the Kinkel family in relation to Kip. The family held to rigid expectations of what constituted a successful performance. As Kip failed to live up to their expectations, they seemed to retaliate by subtly and directly violating Kip's expectation of being accepted as a member of the family. In essence this theme, "I am a failure," came to define Kip's sense of himself.

Between the time of his early school difficulties and his final homicidal rage Kip became increasingly alienated from his family and schoolmates. Like some children of depressed mothers, Kip turned increasingly to the inanimate world: He came to use Internet pornography, rock music, and guns to regulate his chaotic feelings and to find some area of expertise for himself. After Kip was apprehended, the police found an extensive collection of guns and knives, several instruction books on making explosives, chemicals, and a sawed-off shotgun. On a picture of the Thurston High football team he had circled one member's face and had written the word "kill" beside it. Bomb squad members found explosive materials and partially assembled bombs in the crawl space under the Kinkel house.

Kip's ambivalence toward his schoolmates led him to resent their social exclusion of him, but at the same time he tried to elicit their interest. He tried to change his social position by becoming class clown. But, here again he failed. He behaved too outrageously and his antics fell flat, leading to his being ostracized further. In fact, his schoolmates voted him "Most Likely to Start World War III" (K. Newman, 2004). He escalated to bragging about torturing animals, decapitating cats, dissecting live squirrels, and blowing up cows. His fascination with guns and his quick temper resulted in two expulsions from school in one week.

For a school essay Kip wrote: "R I P You Must Die, I will hunt you down and put a hole in your head. With explosives. You hear me.... You must DIE." His teacher's response to the essay was to write, "I'm concerned??"

The teacher's consternation reflects the subtle ways in which this boy's expectations, and those of the people around him, were becoming more and more disconnected. Clearly, no one knew just what to do with him. And with the exception of one girl in his class, a girl who was clearly ambivalent about dating him, Kip could not find any way of creating expectations that he could meet.

Kip's interest in guns finally sent an alarm to his parents. According to Kirsten, Faith had pushed for Kip to be seen by a therapist but Bill was opposed for the entire period of time that Kip was seen by Dr. Jeffrey Hicks, a child psychologist. He met with Kip nine times. At Kip's trial he testified that Faith had brought Kip to see him because she had been concerned about his fascination with guns, knives, and explosives and his "antisocial acting out." During his treatment of Kip, Hicks found him to be depressed and angry. In his notes from their first session, Hicks said Kip reported that he often felt angry, without knowing why, and that he set off explosives to vent those feelings. His work with Kip focused on strategies to help Kip manage his anger without resorting to explosives, and on improving Kip's strained relationship with his father.

To "connect" with Kip, Hicks, a gun collector himself, spoke with Kip about guns. Hicks had several Lugers with which he said he was very satisfied, but he opposed giving Kip a gun. In his talks with the psychologist, Kip apparently felt heard. At one point, Hicks said, he recommended that Kip try an antidepressant, so Faith took Kip to their family physician, who prescribed Prozac for him. Soon after he began taking the drug, Kip's mood seemed to improve substantially and he no longer appeared to be depressed. At that time Bill and Faith decided to end Kip's treatment. The psychologist felt that Kip had made progress in his ability to manage his anger and communicate with family members and that his depression had lifted.

After the therapy was discontinued, Kip asked his father for a Luger. To try to find common ground with Kip, he was given the gun, which he added to his growing secret arsenal. It was one of the guns Kip brought to school for his shooting rampage. Hicks testified at Kip's trial that he was not consulted about the decision to buy the Luger for Kip.

The relationship between Kip and his parents illustrates Lyons-Ruth's (2003) finding that it is the quieter, subtler behaviors on the part of the parent that are associated with later dissociative symptomotology. Although Lyons-Ruth's findings refer to infant–mother behavior, such as mocking or teasing or being subtly, affectively out of tune with the infant, for Kip, it appears that the father–son relationship was the more crucial and decisive. The father's condescending tone in his cold observation on the family home movie that Kip, as he fails in his efforts to do a headstand, needs more work, conveyed volumes about his disappointment in his son. Contradictory behaviors on the part of the mother were also implicated in Lyons-Ruth's study. But it may have been the father's contradictory behavior toward Kip with respect to aggressive play that functioned similarly. In the televised interview, Kirsten described how adamantly the family prohibited toy guns in the house as Kip was growing up (Woodruff, 1998). Yet later, in his desperation to find a common ground with his alienated son, Bill gave Kip guns and eventually the Luger that was implicated in the multiple murders.

Being 6 years older, Kirsten went to college when Kip was about 11. On balance her presence in the family had been of benefit to Kip. Although he was consistently, explicitly and implicitly, compared to her and found lacking, she mediated between Kip and her parents and provided a buffer for him. She tried to negotiate the gap between the parents' expectations of Kip and the level of competence Kip had in meeting them. When Kirsten left the home, Kip no longer had an ally in the house.

Kip kept a journal that I quote at length. In his own words, Kip details the story of his decline into increasing rage, despair, and isolation. In an entry made about a year before his killing spree he wrote:

> I sit here all alone. I am always alone. I don't know who I am. I want to be something I can never be. I try so hard every day. But in the end, I hate myself for what I've become.
>
> Every single person I know means nothing to me. I hate every person on this earth. I wish they could all go away. You all make me sick. I wish I was dead. The only reason I stay alive is because of hope. Even though I am repulsive and few people know who I am, I still feel that things might, maybe, just a little bit, get better. I don't understand any fucking person on this earth. Some of you are so weak, mainly, that a four year old could push you down. I am strong, but my head just doesn't work right. I know I should be happy with what I have, but I hate living.
>
> Every time I talk to her [referring to the girl he wanted to date but who teased him, occasionally, going out with him but retreating when he wanted to become more involved] I have a small amount of hope. But then she will tear it right down. It feels like my heart is breaking. But is that possible. I am so consumed with hate all of the time. Could I ever love anyone? I have feelings, but

do I have a heart that's not black and full of animosity? I know everyone thinks this way sometimes, but I am so full of rage that I feel I could snap at any moment. I think about it everyday. Blowing the school up or just taking the easy way out, and walk into a pep assembly with guns. In either case, people that are breathing will stop breathing. That is how I will repay all you mother fuckers for all you put me through.

Killers start sad and crazy. Oh fuck. I sound so pitiful. People would laugh at this if they read it. I hate being laughed at. But they won't laugh after they're scraping parts of their parents, sisters, brothers, and friends from the wall of my hate. Please. Someone, help me. All I want is something small. Nothing big. I just want to be happy.

Today of all days, I ask her [still referring to the same girl] to help me. I was shot down. I feel like my heart has been ripped open and ripped apart. Right now, I'm drunk, so I don't know what the hell is happening to me. It is clear that no one will help me. Oh God, I am so close to killing people. So close.

I gave her all I have, and she just threw it away. Why? Why did God just want me to be in complete misery? I need to find more weapons. My parents are trying to take away some of my guns! My guns are the only things that haven't stabbed me in the back.

My eyes hurt. They hurt so bad. They feel like they are trying to crawl out of my head. Why aren't I normal? Help me. No one will. I will kill every last mother fucking one of you. The thought of you is still racing in my head. I am too drunk to make sense.

Every time I see your face, my heart is shot with an arrow. I think she will say yes, but she doesn't, does she? She says, "I don't know." The three most fucked up words in the English language.

I want you to feel this, be this, taste this, kill this. Kill me. Oh God, I don't want to live. Will I see it to the end? What kind of dad would I make? All humans are evil. I just want to end the world of evil.

I don't want to see, hear, speak or feel evil, but I can't help it. I am evil. I want to kill and give pain without a cost. And there is no such thing. We killed him a long time ago. Anyone that believes in God is a fucking sheep.

If there was a God, he wouldn't let me feel the way I do. Love isn't real, only hate remains. Only hate. Love Sucks. No, I don't believe in love at first sight because love is an evil plot to make people buy alcohol and firearms. When you love someone or something it is always taken away from you. I also would like to add that I hate each and every one of you. Because everything I touch turns to shit.

The repetitive theme in Kip's diary is hope leading to disappointment leading to self-hatred leading to violence against others and then over and over again. This sequence has the girl he loves as the central character, but no anger or violence is directed against her. It is almost as though he realizes that she stands for his parents.

Kip's expectations of acceptance and recognition from this girl are transparently the expectations that were continually thwarted in relation to his parents. The only mention of anything like reactive anger is when his father threatens to take away his guns, "the only things that haven't stabbed me in the back." He directs his rage against his schoolmates with a special emphasis on the surprise and shock that will accompany its expression. Yet, Kip speculates about another solution, of embracing evil and becoming dead to the world. He enacted this solution by taping two bullets to his chest when he went on his killing spree. When cornered by the police, he taunted them into trying to kill him. They did not.

Kip's solution, akin to what I inferred about the serial killers, also entailed changing live faces into still, dead ones. He did not embrace it as wholeheartedly as did the serial killers. Somewhere, sometime, Kip tasted some level of acceptance (probably from his sister), which he longed for. Perhaps that constituted his hope. In his own words, Kip eloquently described the sequence of expectations leading to violations of expectations leading to violence, first against himself and then against others.

The ricocheting violations of expectations in Kip's family led to ever-increasing feelings of inadequacy, disappointment, and alienation on everyone's part. Kip moved toward increasingly perverse ways of asserting his presence in a world that was slipping from his grasp. By ages 13 and 14 he had become an expert bomb-maker, which brought him some attention from his classmates. By age 15 he had killed both of his parents and opened fire in his high school.

The day before Kip went on his killing spree he was caught in school in possession of a gun. He was taken to the police station and picked up by his father, who tried to enroll him in a boot camp for wayward boys. He was now faced with expulsion from school, having all his guns taken away, and being sent to a boot camp. Those were the proximal circumstances triggering his killing rampage. And even on that day, in his last diary entry before the final killing spree, he still seems to be concerned with what his parents might think of him and how he has shamed them and violated their expectations.

After shooting his parents, Kip wrote:

I have just killed my parents! I don't know what is happening. I love my mom and dad so much. I just got two felonies on my record. [This referred to the possession of a stolen gun on school property.] My parents can't take that! It would destroy them. The embarrassment would be too much for them. They couldn't live with themselves. I'm so sorry. I am a horrible son. I wish I had been aborted. I destroy everything I touch. I can't eat. I can't sleep. I didn't deserve them. They were wonderful people. It's not their fault or the fault of any person, organization, or television show. My head just doesn't work right. God damn these VOICES inside my head. I want to die. I want to be gone. But I have to kill people. I don't know why. I am so sorry! Why did God do this to me. I have never been happy. I wish I was happy. I wish I made my mother proud. I am nothing! I tried so hard to find happiness. But you know me. I hate everything. I have no other choice. What have I become? I am so sorry.

The story of Kip Kinkel is a tragic path from fussy baby to an eager-to-fit-in and be-accepted child, to a withdrawn, morose, isolated, young boy, to an increasingly depressed, increasingly isolated, angry, violent, suicidal, and homicidal adolescent. Clearly, his parents' sense of shame as well as his own played a role in the cycle of increasing despair, frustration, and violence. In retrospect, it is easy to see in how many instances a slight tilt toward recognizing Kip's longings for acceptance might have made a difference with respect to his expectations of himself and his life and how repetitive experiences of violation of expectations of affective responsivity led to his increasing violence.

From what we know of Kip Kinkel, there were no glaring problems until the age of 3. From that time onward, he plummeted on a downward spiral, propelled by his endowment (his learning difficulty), the social aspirations of his family (the year in Spain, their protected idyllic lifestyle), the homogeneity of the suburban community, and his relationship with his parents and their "demand" that he meet their expectations of "success." Gradually, Kip became an ever-increasing source of disappointment to his family, violating their hopes for and expectations of him. Kip Kinkel, just by "being," constantly evoked the disappointment and disapproval of his parents. His very being became a violation of their expectation. This cycle escalated in violence—from making bombs, to collecting guns, to throwing rocks off a highway overpass onto oncoming cars, to buying a stolen gun, to killing his parents and two high school classmates. Increasingly, the "violence" spread from his room into his home and, eventually, into his world.

Kip's violence was eruptive and expressive. It gained momentum as his expectations of acceptance in the family as well as in his school community were increasingly thwarted and violated. The only perceivable motivations in Kip's violence seem to be to redress long held feelings of shame, to avoid, once again, shaming his parents, and to revenge himself on all those who humiliated him. In his diary he explicitly aims to violate the expectations of his schoolmates. His eruption of violence makes it perverse by my definition. Furthermore, all of Kip's victims were "innocent," "unsuspecting," and "taken by surprise," which defined their role in the killer–victim interaction.

I have devoted this detailed discussion to violations of expectations in perversion to sharpen an understanding of the affective interaction that constitutes such violations. The study of these serial and mass killers illustrates the slow developmental trajectory of these extreme violations. Examining these lives closely raises the possibility that an intervention at any earlier time could have avoided a number of catastrophes. Typical of such missed opportunities is Kip Kinkel's teacher's comment "I'm concerned??" Similarly, in the life histories of serial killers one can find numerous early warning signs, and while we might find it difficult to view these as "cries for help" in adult killers, the killing sprees do not come early in the serial killer's career. Ted Bundy did not claim his first victim until he was in his 30s. Arthur Shawcross, another serial killer, escalated gradually out of a pattern of early school difficulties, including leaving signs such as collecting "road kills" as a young boy. His road kills were ignored as signals that something was wrong and his disintegration escalated.

The obliviousness, dissociation, and detachment, the "turning a deaf ear" of parents, school, and law enforcement authorities can all force a child with considerable self-regulatory difficulties, difficulties in affect and arousal, to deal with his or her disregulation on the child's own, without interactively provided resources. In reviewing the lives of serial killers, I believe they were abandoned specifically in the area of affect-regulating interactions. They were left on their own and ultimately created "inanimate" humans to regulate their states of distress. In addition they constituted for themselves a world of "still" but safe faces, people who would not betray, abandon, or shame them. At the same time they thereby succeed in turning themselves into violators of expectation, which is preferable to being the victim of that process. Experiences of actively violating expectations are sought by some who became creative artists, but their violation of expectations has a different basis. Rather than seeking to overcome feelings of being helpless and adrift, some creative artists violate expectations because they feel the world is their oyster.

8 Creative Artists as Violators of Expectations

In *Transforming Aggression* I discussed Henrick Ibsen's narcissistic injury when his play *Ghosts* was roundly criticized. With his expectation of critical and popular acclaim shattered, Ibsen responded by ridiculing his detractors and making them the thinly disguised characters of his next play, *An Enemy of the People*. In *Ghosts* Ibsen really violated his audience's expectations that a drama would uphold community standards of propriety and taste. *Ghosts* is not merely a tale of family secrets, it is a tale of family syphilis and thus inherited madness that in the end consumes the young hero and with him all possibility of familial redemption. In Ibsen's time it could not help but start a literary riot, even though quite quickly theater managers in other locals discovered that a bitter controversy sells more tickets. Even today, its shocking finale can stun an audience.

In this chapter I explore this theme of the artist's provocative relationship to his public, the artist as a violator of expectations. Audiences may respond antagonistically to having their dearly held standards and expectations violated or, on the contrary, respond with willingly suspended disbelief to enjoy the surprise of having their expectations safely violated. In this discussion I place the origins and development of some forms of creativity into a different context than the one proposed by

Kohut. In line with the general tenor of my reflections throughout this book, I am interested in the details of the process of transformation. That is, having placed affect at the heart of the process of transformation, I focused in the last two chapters on expectations and their affirmation and violation as the instigators of this process of affective engagement. In this chapter I connect expectations and their violation to creativity per se. Specifically, I propose that in some instances a profound experience of violating expectations can become an important wellspring for the creative endeavor. To illustrate this thesis, a series of anecdotal reports about a number of creative artists follows.

Some creative endeavors owe their appeal to the very fact that they shock and surprise: The artists who fashion these shocking works are violators, par excellence, of the expectations of their audience or onlookers. However, the dividing line between what is creative and what is perverse is at times quite permeable. What some consider "creative" may well be considered "perverted" by others. In fact, creative artists are frequently accused of perverting the very medium in which they create. Recall the reaction of the first-night audience at Stravinsky's *The Rite of Spring*. They were outraged at what Stravinsky had done to generally accepted conventions of music. Labeling that composition "perverse" was an expectable critical response given the cultural context, the prevailing customs, the zeitgeist. But over time customs change and yesterday's perversion may hardly raise an eyebrow today and become tomorrow's cliché.

For some artists the desire to cause a commotion through their work is quite conscious. For example, in his autobiography, Jean Cocteau explicitly announced what amounts to a program of shock: "When I write, I disturb. When I show a film, I disturb. When I exhibit my painting, I disturb, and I disturb if I don't. I have a knack for disturbing" (1991, p. 114). He speaks for many creative artists whose work disturbs and violates the expectations of audiences, listeners, and viewers.

The reports and anecdotes that follow were drawn from biographies and autobiographies of creative artists. The term "creative artist" is open to a variety of interpretations; to simplify matters for myself I have chosen a number of artists who achieved clear recognition and acclaim in their respective fields. Phenomena similar to the ones I describe may be found in patients who may be artists but also in others who express their creativity in a different way. Clearly, creativity can be seen in a variety of less public pursuits, including the one-on-one world of psycho-therapy. Furthermore, I am not proposing that violating expectations is a typical or universal motivation for all creative artists and their pro-ductions. Rather, I am proposing that to violate expectations is one powerful strand in the creative works of some talented people. Appreci-ating this connection can give us a glimmer of how creativity in general may be connected to the processes of self-transformation.

My sample of artists is more limited still as I consider violations of expectations from the point of view of the life of the artist within his family and their expectations. Specifically, I link certain creative artists' adult achievements to their having survived brushes with death in some form in their early childhood. My point is that as these near-death experiences became family lore, enduring myths sprang up that clung to the artist throughout his life. And conversely, these artists and their families evidently also clung to the myth. Later, these family myths emerged as nonconscious procedures for the artists in their relationship to the world and their art, as well as explicit themes in their works. They shadowed the artist's life, and they infiltrated his productions. As myths perpetuated within the family and later by the artist, they shape the self-experience of the artist in the form of an organizing theme: "I have come close to death and I survived! I am special! I expect the world, like my family, to celebrate my being alive."

I believe it is noteworthy that not just the artist felt he was excep-tional but so did his family. They too felt that something extraordinary had already happened to mark the artist-to-be as an individual beyond ordinary expectations. There was a family myth before there was a per-sonal one. A source of evidence that these events become family myths is that many occurred at or shortly after the birth of the artist. They could not have been "remembered" (except, perhaps, as bodily memories). I presume they were told within the family as the artist was growing up. Having been kept alive as family stories they emerge anew in the biog-raphies and autobiographies of the artists. I am not arguing for a causal connection between these early events and the artist's later creative works. Rather, I propose that these early events, model scenes of the infant and young child's triumph over a brush with death, have several effects. The child is celebrated as "special" in the eyes of the family and in his own eyes for having survived. Borrowing Tronick and Gianino's imagery (1986) again, by surviving the child succeeded in turning the "still faces" and "depressed faces" of his worried family, who feared the worst, into the animated and joyful faces that greeted the child's survival. The child's survival violated every family member's dreaded expectations. For some artists that role became a dominant expectation in their relationships. For those to be discussed, being violators of dreaded expectations also made its way in their art. In some form in their art, they try to recapture their success in turning "still faces" into the animated faces of a cheering audience.

Growing Up in the Shadow of Death

The myth of having cheated death can come about in a number of ways. Salvador Dali (1942) grew up and lived in the shadow of a dead brother. This brother died at the age of 7, 3 years before Salvador was born. The dead brother's name was Salvador and his parents gave his name to their new son, "a legacy that Salvador would have to live with for the rest of his life" (Brok, 2006, p. 7). Dali's parents dressed him in his dead brother's clothes, and gave him his dead brother's toys to play with. He "was a resurrected entity" (p. 8). Brok has suggested that Dali's "surrealistic paintings were an attempt to triumph over the uncanny quality of his identity" (p. 8). In the "unspeakable confessions" of his diary Dali wrote, "I lived through my death before living my life ... within my mother's womb. I could already feel the angst. My foetus swam in an infernal placenta. Their anxiety never left me" (Dali & Parinaud, 1976, p. 12).

Dali's identity was obviously encumbered with the presence of his brother from birth on, if not even prior to that moment in his parents' anticipation of his birth. But, there was also a profound difference between him and his brother, a reality that could not be obliterated. He lived; his brother did not. There was thus one quality to his identity that was indomitable: his aliveness. His parents' actions suggest that they pretended that their dead son's life was continuing through their newborn son. Looked at in today's light, their "pretense" constituted an extraordinary act of violence against Dali's identity and his sense of reality. Thus, just by being alive he violated parental expectations, defied their pretense, and asserted that he was real. Dali carried this self-assertion over to his surrealistic paintings, where he triumphed by taunting reality and by violating the artistic conventions of his audience. With photographic clarity he painted a desolate world of ants crawling over melting clocks. As art historian Sarane Alexandrian (1970) explained, "He tore off the mask which reason puts on reality, and behind it discovered a soft world which was subsiding or decomposing" (p. 103). It was not that painting had heretofore been without its surreal landscapes and its nightmare visions. Dali's work was unique in combining the clarity of his graphic style with bizarre images. From his special and unique place Dali could challenge reality, painting a bizarre, crystal-clear world shrouded in irony.

Igor Stravinsky, like Dali, violated the musical conventions of his audience and in his work. And like Dali, Stravinsky would appear to have derived his propensity for shocking the audience in part from the impact of a dying brother. For composing the ballet *Le Sacre de Printemps* (*The Rite of Spring*) Stravinsky was vilified for having destroyed Western music. Leonard Bernstein (1982) makes clear just how shocking this work was. It became "one of the most famous musical scandals of all time, a scandal which resulted in creating a public image of Stravinsky as a revolutionary, iconoclast, enfant terrible, and author of a work that would forever change music, and in the minds of some, possibly destroy it. And this fear existed even among certain serious musicians as well as the fashionable public at the Russian Ballet that memorable evening" (pp. 299–300). Stravinsky's music clearly shattered the expectations of those who attended the performance. But to Leonard Bernstein and later generations of music lovers, in his violation of expectations resides the kernel of Stravinsky's creative genius. The shock and outrage felt by the opening night audience became difficult for later audiences to recapture as the work entered the standard orchestral repertoire. And only a little more than 30 years after its premier, Walt Disney made the perverse *The Rite of Spring* part of pop culture by including it in *Fantasia*.

From what is known of Stravinsky's childhood years, according to his autobiography (Stravinsky, 1936) and his biographer (Walsch, 2002), his parents expected him to become a businessman and to study law. Although his father was a singer and young Igor heard a great deal of music in his home, there was clear family objection to Igor pursuing a career in music.

When Stravinsky was 15, however, his older brother died. The brother's health had been of great concern to the family for many years. After his death the family became overly concerned with, and placed enormous emphasis on, Igor's health. In fact, after his brother's death, whenever Igor traveled he was required by his family to send home detailed health bulletins. He thus finished out his adolescence as a "survivor," living in the shadow of his older brother's death. The intense focus on his health led to his lifelong obsession with illness.

During summer holidays in his later teen years, Stravinsky took piano lessons but kept this hidden in his letters to his parents. Given his family's very conventional aspirations for him, music continued to be a touchy subject and even at the age of 17 Igor constructed his letters home "specifically to gratify his parents' expectations" (Walsch, 2002, p. 2). That is, he omitted any reference in his letters home to the musical studies he had secretly undertaken. That he was earnest about his pursuit of music was in itself a defiance of their expectations.

Until his teen years Stravinsky only had a minor musical education; however, he did have the extraordinary good fortune later on in his teen years to be accepted as a student by the notable Russian musician Rimsky-Korsakoff. By that time he had made an agreement with his family. He would continue to study law, if he could also study music. When the family subsequently encountered some financial difficulties they were unable to continue to support Igor in his law studies. But the music continued.

Like many artists, Stravinsky embarked on a career in music against the expressed wishes of his family. *The Rite of Spring*, one of his earliest and certainly one of his most audacious and sound-barrier-breaking compositions, deals with the very topic of the anxious concern of his family: birth, death, sacrifice for the sake of renewal, and survival. The pagan, deliberately crude music of *The Rite of Spring* was thus a grand defiance, amplified fortissimo, of the restrictive, conservative expectations of his family and of his "extended family"—that is, his audience. Like his friend Picasso, who broke up traditional contours, perspectives, and concrete representations, Stravinsky continued to shatter traditional tonality and the long-standing musical convention of a key center for compositions.

The theme of having escaped death while his older brother succumbed and a conviction of being special, reinforced by his good luck at having Rimsky-Korsakoff as a tutor, merged in Stravinsky's consistently audacious compositions. His frequent and dramatic changes of style kept his audience off-guard. However, in his striving for artistic notoriety, he also shrewdly maintained a balance between adhering to musical traditions and violating them, and held on to his rapt audience while violating their expectations.

Portrait of the Artist as Stillborn

Norman Mailer (1996) opens his biography of Picasso with a flair characteristic of his writing and of Picasso's art as well. "Picasso, delivered at 11:15 PM in the city of Malaga, October 25, 1881, came out stillborn. He did not breathe: neither did he cry. The midwife gave up and turned her attention to the mother. If it had not been for the presence of his uncle, Dr. Salvador Ruiz, the infant might never have come to life. Don Salvador, however, leaned over the stillbirth and exhaled cigar smoke into its nostrils. Picasso stirred. Picasso screamed.... Such family accounts are open to exaggeration. Don Salvador may not actually have shocked the newborn into life. All the same, the story is agreeable" (p. 3).

Stillbirths were not uncommon in Picasso's day. Chagall, in fact, tells of a similar beginning of his life. However, the story of how Picasso survived, as Mailer suggests, is most likely an "agreeable" exaggeration by his family. As a family myth it may well have had the organizing power of a model scene in shaping Picasso's sense of himself. Like Stravinsky in music, Picasso changed his style many times in the course of his creative career. With considerable frequency he forced his audience not to expect the same-old, same-old from him, keeping them off-guard by constantly violating expectations of him that were based on his previous productions and on the prevailing trends of his day.

The myth of having violated the expectations of his family by surviving occurred for Marc Chagall as well. At the beginning of his autobiography Chagall states: "But, first of all, I was born dead. I did not want to live. Imagine a white bubble that does not want to live.... They pricked the bubble with needles, they plunged it into a pail of water. At last it emitted a feeble whimper. But the main thing was, I was born dead. I hope the psychologists have the grace not to draw improper conclusions from that!" (1994, p. 1).

What an amazing depiction by Chagall! It speaks of having learned through family lore that his survival after his stillbirth was utterly unexpected by his family. And what "improper" conclusions that psychologists might draw did Chagall have in mind? Perhaps Chagall would consider the model scene that I now draw from his account to be improper: "I came into the world and lived in spite of everyone's expectations. Defying the expectation that I would not survive is my triumph and is me. And so many sense modalities are stimulated: from immobile to mobile, from silent to whimpering, from lacking feeling to being pricked and plunged."

The model scene that I derive from Chagall's report depicts him as inert, immobile, and colorless; yet his very survival at birth defied those early impressions. In his art, Chagall repeats his unexpected survival, his early successful violation of expectations, through his depiction of defying gravity. In his paintings Chagall characteristically and blatantly violates the expectation that the force of gravity holds bodies to the ground and does not let them float through the air. Images depicting joy and love and remembering, images transcending and romanticizing his birthplace through floating figures, already appeared in Chagall's early works and remained his signature throughout his artistic career.

Even in paintings where he depicted the suffering of the Jews through references to pogroms and the Holocaust, the upward thrusting, floating, embracing, languishing figures of young Marc and his bride, Bella, dominate the landscape. In his paintings he takes the pain of the Jews and transcends suffering just as his whimper reversed his family's dread when he was brought to life.

A Really Dead Mother

Rene Magritte's paintings scream out: I want to violate what you expect to see. Meuris reports two events from Rene Magritte's early life that he considers to be "cautious explanations of Magritte's character and the foundation of the thinking that dominates his work" (2004, p. 12). Meuris stated that two close and long-standing friends confided these events to him; one event was well known, the other not. Both illuminate Magritte's creation of a paradoxical world and his artistic defiance of common sense. One event involved Magritte's first experience of what he later called the "sensation of mystery." Meuris reported, "A tethered balloon crashed on the shop where the family was living, it had to be got down from the roof, and this 'long soft thing' that stern-faced men in leather clothes and helmets with earflaps had to drag downstairs seemed very extraordinary to him" (p. 12).

The second event, well known to his friends but never discussed by Magritte, was his discovery of his mother's suicide when he was 14 years old. When his mother was 41 years old she drowned herself in the river Sambre near Chatelet where the Magrittes were living. "Magritte and his two brothers had gone to look for their mother and had found her body practically naked, but for a wet night-dress that had ridden up and was sticking to her skin" (p. 12). Meuris, who got this information from Louis Scutenaire, Magritte's biographer, speculates that this event was responsible for a further "sensation of mystery" experienced by Magritte, and at the same time—and for the first time—for giving him a sense of his own importance: He was, namely, "the son of a woman who drowned herself." Perhaps the experience also enhanced the malice that he apparently exhibited in his outbursts of "childish tyranny," as well as his "already strongly marked sense of the bizarre" (p. 13). In any case, a taste for the bizarre and the wish to defy expectations became central to his work. Bizarre juxtapositions, a woman's face with breasts instead of eyes and the pubic area in the place of the mouth (the painting *Nude*, 1919) or a man with a top hat in a room standing at a table with a large lion resting at his feet (the painting *Souvenir of a Journey III*, 1955) typify ways Magritte violated expectations and illustrated his sensation of mystery.

The evocation of mystery that infused Magritte's work seems to resemble an experience of dissociation and derealization. How the second event (finding his mother's dead body) was a traumatizing and character-shaping event is easy enough to imagine. But the balloon, with no additional clarifying information available, is mysterious in a different sense. What it meant to Magritte, and why it had such an impact on him, can only be conjectured. Perhaps, both events violated expectations—one of how adult men should behave, and the other of how mothers should behave: the grown men tugging at a caught balloon and the dead mother floating with her wet nightdress high up on her torso. They also contain an aspect of absurdity. Meuris linked the two events as marking Magritte as special. And, according to his biographer, as Magritte acquired an identity as the son of a woman who drowned herself, it was certainly a mysterious and special identity.

Was the mother's suicide the culmination of her depression? If so, Magritte, as the child of a depressed mother, may have been following the path of those children who try to animate their depressed mother. In a leading edge view of Magritte we can think of him as trying to "normalize" her depressed world as he did through the strange juxta-position of objects and people in his paintings. In discovering his mother's dead body, Magritte had his unique brush with death from which he too emerged with a sense of "specialness." Like Dali, Magritte placed himself into a special position as a commentator on reality and a violator of traditional views of the world. His art creates a world that defies common sense. It is a still world, disconcerting, that nevertheless contains an aura of menace.

A Mother "Almost" Wishing for Her Son's Death

In his autobiography, Richard Wagner describes an event that occurred shortly after his birth. He was found to suffer from an "ailment of infancy" that made him so sick that his mother, or so she later told him, almost wished him "dead owing to his seemingly hopeless condi-tion" (1983, p. 5). Wagner then adds, "I seemed to have surprised my parents by thriving" (p. 5). Like Chagall and Picasso, by the very act of living Wagner violated expectations by triumphing over his expected death. For him, too, defying expectations became a leitmotif, the leading theme of his artistic and personal life. Living when he had been expected to die was a personal triumph, causing his mother to rejoice. Wagner reported in his autobiography that his parents were astonished by his subsequent good health.

A second event described by Wagner may well have reinforced his sense of being the unique and extraordinary violator of expectations. Growing up, Richard had not been given music lessons, while his sisters had. His mother thought that young Richard lacked the apti-tude. When he was 9 years old Carl Maria von Weber, composer of the popular opera *Der Freischutz*, visited the family and asked Richard if he wanted to be a musician. His mother answered for him: Though young Richard was mad about *Der Freischutz*, she explained, she had noticed no musical talent and he was the only one of the children not given a musical education. However, on his own, young Richard figured out, perhaps even defiantly, how to finger the overture to *Der Freischutz* at the keyboard. Then, later that year as his father lay on his deathbed, Richard's mother distractedly asked the 9-year-old to play the piano for his father. He played two folk songs and an aria from *Der Freischutz*. Astonished, the dying man remarked, "Is it possible he has a musical talent?" (Wagner, p. 9).

The two myths–memories–fantasies, the one about his survival from near death and the other of his "surprising" musical talent, suggest a model scene for the young Richard Wagner: "I am destined to be special and a genius. The very fact that I am alive and that I have natural self-taught musical talent, is a miracle—I am the family's wunderkind." But, perhaps more accurately, as it turned out, he became a wunder-enfant terrible.

Wagner's enormous creativity stands in contrast to his abominable personal qualities. Commenting on Wagner's character, E. Newman wrote that "there was so much in Wagner that aroused ... dislike and distrust—his 'revolutionary' past, his vast ambitions, his ruthless driving power, his lack of conscience where money was concerned ... [he] was regarded by many people in that epoch and later as 'mad' with egoism, vanity, and lust for power" (1941, pp. 253–254). He seemed to have lived at the intersection of two roads: creativity and perversity.

Like Stravinsky, Chagall, Picasso, Magritte, and Cocteau, Wagner played with, teased, and violated the expectations of his audience. The libretti of many of his operas shock and mock conventionality. Their themes concern defying authority and common decency (as in the four operas of the *Ring of the Niebelungen*) as well as the betrayal of loyalty (as in *Lohengrin, Tristan und Isolde*). In his operas Wagner, as librettist, depicted violations of expectations in the form of betrayal of trust, conventions, and traditions; incest; infanticide; and all kinds of shocks and surprises. In his music he broke conventions but also taunted his listeners.

As the composer of what he termed "music dramas," Wagner violated the expectations of the characters in his plots, but he was even more gifted in his ability to violate the musical expectations of his listeners, as in the prelude to *Tristan und Isolde*. We are teased with a never-resolving chord progression at the beginning of the prelude and onward. It does not get its final resolution until the very end, in the love-death of Tristan and Isolde, the closing bars of the opera, 4 hours later. Furthermore, the libretto of *Tristan und Isolde* echoes a prominent theme in Wagner's life: violating expectations in the form of betrayal of a trust.

Examining all of Wagner's operas from the standpoint of violations of expectations and creativity would be profitable. However, I focus on a single one, *Die Meistersinger von Nuremburg* (*The Master Singers of Nuremburg*), his only "comic" opera. It specifically lends itself to this discussion because in the opera Wagner himself takes up my topic.

The theme of violating expectations and its relation to creativity opens, runs through, and closes *Die Meistersinger*. It is also considered to be Wagner's most autobiographical composition in which, on a grand scale, he avenged himself against the then-famous and powerful critic Eduard Hanslick.

Hanslick was a powerful and feared music critic in Vienna. Initially, he praised Wagner's earlier opera *Tannhäuser* and called him "the greatest living dramatic talent" (E. Newman, 1937, p. 30). Wagner thanked him in a long thoughtful letter and all was well until 1850 when Wagner published a virulent attack on the then-popular French composer Meyerbeer. The treatise was entitled *Jews in Music*. Offended and betrayed, Hanslick, a Jew, then turned against Wagner. We are now at the time when Wagner was writing *Die Meistersinger*.

Before falling out with Hanslick, Wagner had already conceived of one of the opera's central characters, Beckmesser, as a pedantic, unimaginative judge of the song contest held by the Meistersingers. Wagner now changed the name of that character to "Hanslich" and proceeded to read the libretto to a group that included Hanslick. Hanslick stormed out in a rage. Wagner later again renamed the odious character Beckmesser. Once Hanslick became his enemy, Wagner took great care to humiliate him in the opera. For example, Beckmesser was costumed as a Hassidic Jew, a custom that was altered only in relatively recent productions of the opera.

There are two heroes in *Die Meistersinger*, the young Walther von Stolzing, and the mature Hans Sachs. Walther is brash, impetuous, creative, and a bit undisciplined. He defies conventions. He has had some musical training, but considers himself to be a "natural" musician and is quite self-satisfied with his musical accomplishments. Hans Sachs, a cobbler and one of the Meistersingers, is wise, kind, and cautious, an ideal self-sacrificing mentor and "father figure." He is an upholder of conventions and traditions but also open minded. After hearing Walther sing, Sachs asks himself how Walther could have such extraordinary musicianship. He answers his own question: Like a bird's, the talent is natural. Both characters depict Wagner: Walther as he saw himself and Hans Sachs, as he wanted to be seen by others.

In these two personifications Wagner is also being both the father he wished he had had and the son who benefits from having had such a wise, guiding, protective, and encouraging father. There was an actual Hans Sachs, an author, cobbler, and Meistersinger who lived in Nuremberg from 1494 to 1576. So Wagner is also laying claim to a prestigious musical lineage for himself in the course of the libretto.

The very first scene of the opera sets the stage for violations of expectations. In church, Walther sees, flirts with, and falls in love with Eva, the daughter of a Meistersinger. Wagner inserts their sensual longings and furtive glances between the lines of the solemn hymn that the congregation sings with devotion. Between the lines of the chorale with organ accompaniment a solo violin and oboe accompany Walther and Eva flirting. Eventually, the flirty music, supported by Wagner's large orchestra, drowns out the end of the chorale. Tradition is challenged and trounced right from the start.

Walther learns that Eva's father will give her hand to the winner of a song contest that the Meistersingers will hold. Since only a Meistersinger may enter the contest, and since the only other applicant is the pedestrian Beckmesser, Walther decides to audition to become a Meistersinger. To do so, he must improvise a song according to strict rules of musical structure, rhyme, meter, and rhythm, in accordance with the Meistersinger tradition. He will be judged by Beckmesser as to his compliance with these rules.

Beckmesser applies the rules assiduously. Walther sings creatively but not according to the rules. As he sings, Beckmesser tabulates his "errors" by noisily running a piece of chalk across a blackboard. Lacking Walther's creativity, he can only try to destroy true artistic creativity. Walther accumulates more than the permissible number of errors and fails the audition.

Based on his training and arrogance (his name, "Walther von Stolzing," contains the word *stolz* which means "pride" in German), he had not expected to fail. Here is one violation of expectations that provides the motivation for much of the opera. It is inflicted by academic conventionality on the hero, whose musical talent is "natural." In addition, Walther's conviction that he is a creative and natural born artist is shattered. A narcissistic blow! There is an obvious parallel to the blow to Wagner's pride whenever his work was not received as enthusiastically as he felt he deserved.

Walther decides to defy the authority of the Meistersingers and to run off with Eva, but Hans Sachs wisely dissuades him. Later in the opera Walther has a dream about Eva. As he sings it, Hans Sachs writes it down. In this process a form of mentoring or supervision takes place. Sachs makes suggestions to Walther designed to make his work accept-able to the establishment. Beckmesser finds this paper and accuses Sachs of planning to enter the song contest himself. Sachs denies this and gives Beckmesser the paper with the words to Walther's song.

In the final act, at the song contest, Beckmesser, not having learned the song sufficiently, sings a ludicrous version of it and makes a fool out of himself. Sachs now leads Walther to the podium to sing his song. This time the Meistersingers and the people of Nuremberg are stunned. Having undergone a transformation in the course of the opera, Walther now, with Sachs's help, is able to shape his creativity in a more disciplined way.

Walther wins the contest and therefore the hand of Eva. The Meistersingers award him membership in their guild but, still offended by their initial rejection, he responds irreverently by telling them to "keep it." Herein is yet another violation of expectations: Walther does the unheard of: he rejects the Meistersingers. Hans Sachs again counsels him not to disparage the Meistersingers. Finally, Walther accepts membership in the guild and Eva's hand.

Wagner constructed the entire opera, *Die Meistersinger*, along the academically prescribed rules that had to be followed in composing a "master" song. These were the very rules that Walther had failed to follow when he auditioned for membership in the Meistersinger Guild. In composing an entire opera as though it was a master song Wagner responded to his critics with an "in-your-face" bravado, a tour de force in its own right. Specifically, however, in the depiction of Hanslick as Beckmesser, Wagner gave vent to both his outrage at his critics and detractors and his virulent anti-Semitism in one fell swoop.

Wagner's autobiography first appeared in 1911 and his biographers agree that portions are fiction. He rewrote his life in accordance with his belief in how the life of a genius should have unfolded. In fact, in the year that the autobiography first appeared, Irvine (1911) wrote a treatise on it entitled *Wagner's Bad Luck* in which he identified 800 errors in this autobiography. Thus, Wagner's autobiography is more revealing in its depiction of psychological truths and its rendition of the myths he perpetuated about himself than in its historical accuracy.

The actual events of Richard Wagner's earliest years must have been as confusing to him as they are to readers trying to follow them. The events of Wagner's birth (E. Newman, 1933) are shrouded in mystery. At the time of his birth his mother, Johanna, was married to Carl Friedrich Wagner. Geyer, an actor and friend of Carl Friedrich, frequently lived at the Wagner home and since Carl Friedrich often spent time in the arms of actresses who he felt gave life to his art, Johanna probably found solace in the arms of young Geyer. After Johanna recovered from her confinement, she left her husband and made a perilous journey of over 150 miles with six children and two babies, one being Richard, to see Geyer, who by then had left the household. Presumably, Carl Friedrich wanted nothing to do with young Richard. Evidently, Johanna and Carl Friedrich worked something out and Johanna and her family returned to Carl Friedrich, who then acknowledged Richard as his own. Three months later Carl Friedrich died of typhus. Nine months later Geyer married Johanna.

After Carl Friedrich's death, Geyer married Richard's mother and took care of her and her seven children. He became a devoted husband and father and was most caring of all the Wagner children. He died when Richard was 9 years old and it was at his deathbed that Richard performed at the piano. It was he who proclaimed that perhaps Richard did have some musical talent. Yet, years later, in his autobiography, Wagner altered and minimized the details of Geyer's role in his life. Wagner all along had apparently believed, accurately, that he was actually Geyer's son and confided this to Nietzsche. When Nietzsche read in the autobiography that Wagner now declared himself the biological son of Carl Friedrich Wagner, he called the autobiography "fable convenue, if not worse" (E. Newman, 1937, p. 616). "Fable convenue" can be translated as a "story made to fit" or better "a tall tale." Nietzsche knew that Wagner had always supposed that Geyer was his real father, and that Wagner was rewriting his own story.

After the death of Geyer when Richard was 9 and until he was 14, he had used the name Richard Geyer. After that he changed his name to

Wagner. Biographers as well as Nietzsche speculated that the reason for the shift was that Geyer might have had some Jewish ancestry. Probably for the same reason Wagner also changed the date of his baptism in the autobiography, pushing it up several months. In his autobiography Wagner wrote that he was christened 2 days after he was born—that is, while his biological father was still very much alive, thereby eliminating all connection to Geyer.

Richard's mother was 35 when he was born. In retrospect Wagner said of her, "I hardly ever remember being caressed by her, outpouring of affection did not occur in our family. [Rather] ... a certain impetuous, even loud and boisterous manner characterized our family" (Wagner, 1983, p. 11). Richard recalled being taken to bed one night by his mother and a visitor as she spoke with "strange zeal ... of the great and beautiful in art" (p. 11). But she did not include drama among these, only poetry, music, and painting. In fact "she came close to threatening me with her curse if ever I too were to think of going into the theater" (p. 12).

The threat of her curse seemed only to have made the theater more appealing. In an autobiographical essay quoted by E. Newman (1933), Wagner wrote, "What particularly attracted me to the theatre by which I mean also the stage itself, the rooms behind the scenes, and the dressing rooms—was not so much the desire for entertainment and distraction, as it is with the theatrical public of the present day, but the provocative delight of being in an element that opposed the impressions of everyday life, an absolutely different *world*, one that was purely fantastic, and with a touch of horror in its spell.... I felt that contact with [this world] must be a lever to lift me from the commonplace reality of the routine of daily life to that enchanting demon-world.... [I]t would make my heart beat wildly and fearfully" (pp. 39–40). In his provocative delight in participating in a different, fantastic world, opposing the impressions of everyday life, being lifted above the commonplace, Wagner acknowledged directly and consciously his delight in shattering everyday expectations.

Another incident, at age 10, further reveals aspects of him that were replicated over and over in the years to come: a pomposity that invited mockery and derision. Richard wanted to recreate Grillparzer's *Sappho* in a "spectacular performance" (Wagner, 1983, p. 12) in a puppet theater that his father had built. Richard's sisters discovered the manuscript of the play he had written and humiliated him for his pretensions and pomposity. His sisters would enrage him by tauntingly reciting his lines. These qualities—arrogance and pomposity—play a central role in the characters of Walther von Stolzing and Beckmesser. Walther's arrogance is rebuked but he is later totally vindicated. Beckmesser's arrogance and pomposity are resoundingly derided and he is publicly humiliated. It is as though Wagner is saying that Walther is essentially entitled to his arrogance due to his creativity, unlike Beckmesser, who lives off and undermines the creativity of others.

Wagner's fascination with the theater flourished during his early teen years. He wrote:

> The excitement of horror and fear of ghosts constituted a singular factor in the development of my emotional life ... I remember when I was alone in a room for any length of time and looked fixedly at such inanimate objects as pieces of furniture, suddenly bursting into loud shrieks, because they seemed to me to come alive. Until late in my boyhood no night passed without my awakening with a frightful scream from some dream about ghosts, which would end only when a human voice bade me be quiet. Severe scoldings or even corporeal punishment would then seem to me redeeming kindnesses. None of my brothers and sisters wanted to sleep near me; they tried to bed me down as far from the others as possible, not stopping to think that by so doing my nocturnal calls to be saved from ghosts would become even louder and more enduring, until they finally accustomed themselves to this nightly calamity. (p. 13)

From these early recollections emerged his fascination with the fantastic that fueled his libretti. In effect, he brilliantly transformed his night terrors into entertainment. From his autobiography and his biographers we get scant clues as to why Wagner should have suffered from such severe night terrors. Could they have been body memories rooted in his early near-death experience?

When he was 13 Richard and his family moved to Dresden where his older sister had obtained a singing engagement. Richard was sent to live in the home of school friends, where women including the sisters of his school friends who came to visit the family surrounded him. "I remember pretending to be in a state of stupefied sleepiness in order to induce girls to carry me to my bed, as I had noticed to my excited surprise that their attention in similar circumstances brought me into delightfully intimate contact with the female being" (Wagner, p. 16). The early rumblings of another theme that played a dominant role in his adult life emerge: deception, plotting, and subterfuge to win a woman that he wants. As an adult, he even went further in betraying his friends and cheating those who trusted him. In later years defiance and rebelliousness came to typify Wagner's relationships and life.

In Dresden, Richard was enrolled in a school and rebelled against the "arrogant pedantic system of instruction." Some time later, in Leipzig, he applied to the better of the two schools that were available to him, but the school authorities put him back half a year. He was outraged and felt deeply wounded. "I henceforth comported myself in such a manner as never to win the friendship of a teacher in this school. The hostile treatment I was accorded in return made me even more stubborn." As he grew he developed "an ever increasing love of rebellion for its own sake" (Wagner, p. 22).

Wagner's adolescence took on the quality of a grand defiance of academic expectations. He rebelled against schoolwork even when he realized that his neglect would lead to his expulsion from school. In secret he wrote a "masterpiece," encouraged by an uncle whom he idealized as a free spirit. They took long walks together and had deep conversations. He felt his uncle recognized his potential greatness and treated him as an equal. However, when he showed his "masterpiece" to the school authorities, he was roundly criticized for its over-the-top quality. The plot combined bloodshed and ghosts, yearnings for death and yearnings for love. In listening to his detractors, Wagner decided that his work could only be judged rightly if it were provided with music.

"From the age of 14 on, Wagner borrowed money as he needed it," from friends and acquaintances "on the ground that he thought himself, with some justice, entitled to financial support, private or public, in order that he might have the leisure and comfort necessary for him to produce masterpieces for the world" (E. Newman, 1933, pp. 48–49). Wagner notoriously betrayed the trust of these friends; after borrowing money he would "borrow" their wives. He returned neither.

Like Walther von Stolzing, Wagner was shocked and enraged when the musical world's response to his operas violated his expectations. He was similarly outraged when the response that he expected to his sense of entitlement from his friends and acquaintances was less than immediate compliance, obedience to his desires, or mirroring of his grandiosity. In these instances Wagner's expectations of living in a safe, predictable world were violated. But he defined his world as safe and affectively responsive according to his need to have his inflated sense of self, his unbridled sense of entitlement, and his grandiosity mirrored. He was enraged, uncomprehending, and bore lifelong grudges, as for example toward a colleague, a composer, who refused to forgo his own work when Wagner needed his company for several months in another city. Because he felt betrayed by his friend, Wagner felt justified in retaliating. Unlike in *Die Meistersingers,* where he turned his narcissistic injury into a creative triumph, in this instance Wagner turned his narcissistic injury into mean-spirited, vituperative, narcissistic rage.

To be the violator of expectations in life and in art virtually defined Wagner. His early near-death experience, when he shocked his mother through his survival, and the surprising emergence of his musical talent contributed to a conviction that he was "special" and to his expectation that he be treated as "special." He considered himself "entitled" to be given whatever (or whomever) he wanted and to be exempt from the rules of social behavior that others had to follow. Like his hero, Walther von Stolzing, Wagner considered that his talent was "natural" and that the conventions of society were as ludicrous as the rules established by the Meistersingers for their songs. Rules like that were made for pedants and plodders, not for truly creative geniuses. Yet, like Walther von Stolzing, he demonstrated that he knew those rules perfectly well, at least so far as music was concerned, but that his genius lay in knowing just how to break them. Walther von Stolzing, guided by Hans Sachs, followed the rules to win Eva. In Wagner's music, a Hans Sachs–like recognition of and respect for the value accorded to tradition was ever present. But, when it came to his personal life, Wagner had no Hans Sachs–like conscience. He ran off with and impregnated Cosima, the wife of his friend, Hans von Bülow. That was the perverse side of Richard Wagner. But in his composition, the dialectic between tradition and innovation vividly defined his creativity.

In some ways, Wagner's early life resembles Mayes and Cohen's (1996) description of the chaotic background of at-risk children. Recall his life-threatening illness shortly after his birth, the early loss of his two fathers, and his physically ill and affectionately undemonstrative mother. Given this background, his persistent night terrors into his puberty years are not all that surprising. In addition, he was unwilling or unable to adapt to the conventional expectations of those around him. However, unlike the children in the Mayes and Cohen study, with a combination of energy, talent, genius, and the backing of the family myths about his specialness, he could shape his world into one in which he became a celebrated violator of the expectations of others.

Wagner depicted himself as having been consistently at odds with his family's expectations. He was expected to possess no musical talent, but to everyone's surprise, at a young age he already showed unusual talent. Simultaneously, his survival and his extraordinary musical talent triumphantly violated the expectations of his family. Furthermore, although he had been told to stay away from drama, perhaps because his mother had bad experiences with her husband's dalliance with actresses, he elevated drama to music-drama in totally unique ways. His talents mingled with a sense of entitlement and this mixture of perversity and creativity remained intact for his life. For Wagner, the balance between having his expectations of living in an affectionately responsive, stable home violated and being the violator of the expectations of others clearly tilted in the latter direction. And his violations not only were surprising, but also were generally greeted with literal and figurative applause later in his adulthood, as he had evidently always expected they would be. His ambitions and ideals came to life in his music in an uncompromising way, but this same attribute made him a very difficult person to befriend. He seduced and befriended only eventually to abandon or betray those relationships.

I Disturb and I Refuse

I referred to Cocteau's repeated declaration "I disturb" at the beginning of this chapter. After coming across this quotation I was eager to find out whether he, too, had an early brush with death. In fact he did not. But in his autobiography he reports a very curious scene, a model scene, that was played out repeatedly and that in its own way was associated by him with a kind of "death."

Cocteau's autobiography was gathered together by Robert Phelps (1970) from autobiographical writings that span 74 years. In them

Cocteau described the recurrent scene that caught my eye and also a second event, both of which he named "the little death." Before proceeding further, that term, in its original French, *petit mort*, also refers to the orgasm. I will not discuss the numerous implications of the term except to say that Cocteau is clearly referring to an overwhelming excitement he associated with these events and that this excitement had its pleasurable, thrilling, and sexual dimensions.

In his autobiographical writings, he recalls, "Accursed were the occasions which, on Sunday, forced me out of my snug dreams ... Accursed except for two ... that provoked what we called 'the little death,' an exquisite and inextricable anxiety coveted, concealed, longed for, dreaded" (p. 18). This was the first: "clutching a smelly cup in my right hand, a mint drop in my left, I would refuse the Sunday-morning laxative. Coaxed, I would refuse. Threatened, I would refuse. Implored, I would refuse. No sooner had my mother's already terrible eyes sprung the trap of her still-charming voice, no sooner had the slap brushed my cheek, than *the little death* began" (p. 19). The similarities of the sentence structure and style of the "I disturb" quote and the "I would refuse" quote from the first *little death* are striking. I could not find that style in any of Cocteau's other writings.

Although he knew the scene well, Cocteau's account continues, *the little death* always took him by surprise. His grandfather's servant would thrust him into a sack that he then slung over his shoulder and he would run up and down the house until Cocteau was so dizzy that he no longer knew where he was. "I believed everything, savored my terror. My heart pounded, my tongue went dry, my ears buzzed, and I came out of the sack drunk on darkness and dreams, ready to refuse the laxative, having really crossed the river of the dead and squeezing in one hand, by way of a funerary obol, a half-melted mint drop" (Phelps, p. 19).

The second "little death" resulted from a reward: theatre tickets! "No sooner had I heard the great news [we were going to the theater] than the mechanism started up: a dim endless corridor, a corridor of the little death, opened in my fevered sleep, crossed Sunday morning and ended in broad daylight, opposite the tribunal of black-robed matinee ticket takers at the Chatelet" (Phelps, p. 19).

What are we to make of the juxtaposition of these two scenes? At the very least Cocteau linked his rousing ride in the sack and the heady excitement of being in the theatre as momentary overwhelming near-death experiences. They seemed to have evoked a sense of having triumphed by coming through the ordeal, the corridor of the little death. What does his linking this experience with his visits to the theatre tell us about his later career? Here's a theory. In his childhood his mother tried to force him to take the laxative, through this mock torture; in his artistic work he "forces" or "disturbs" his audience by figuratively putting them into a sack and disorienting them as he was disoriented. But, it was not a dangerous or really unpleasant ride for him in the sack, nor does he make it so for his audience. Recall Cocteau's film *Beauty and the Beast*. There is a shocking and unforgettable scene in which Beauty rushes along the dark corridor of Beast's castle. As she runs, candelabras held by human hands that stick out of the wall move to illuminate her way. Have we been transported into the dim endless corridor of the little death of Cocteau's childhood?

Although Cocteau knew the scene well, he reports that he was nevertheless surprised by being placed in the sack. That is quite a believable occurrence; it is similar to the "gotcha" game that evokes a surprise and laugh each time it is played. If anything, knowing the scene, expecting the "sack," probably makes for a degree of safety that reduces barriers and can make the experience all the more thrilling.

Unlike some of the other creative artists, Cocteau's "little death" story is not one of having survived a genuine life-threatening event. He has taken his obstinate refusal to be forced to take the laxative and the expected terror that would be instilled in him by the ride in the sack and converted them into a thrilling, perhaps even sexualized, adventure. He outwitted his adversaries by turning their threats into a "joy ride" akin to a roller coaster in an amusement park and yet he also maintained his adamant refusal to take the laxative. As with the other creative artists, Cocteau's little deaths reappeared in his creative endeavors.

Cocteau's story is clearly different from the other accounts of early brushes with death that I have discussed. In all the others I inferred a connection between the myths created by the artist's family around childhood near-death experience and aspects of the artist's later life and creative productions. In those artists I infer that the pattern of violating expectations was a nonconscious procedure that derived from the family myths. The way in which the pattern was inferred to have organized, implicitly, the relationships and products of these creative artists was different than it was for Cocteau. In his life and art he made it a deliberate strategy "to disturb." He was cognizant of what he was doing and took delight in it. Even Richard Wagner was not as direct and explicit as Cocteau in disturbing and violating expectations. So, in Cocteau we have an artist who consciously wants to violate expectations and, ironically, he makes up a "petit mort" out of a childhood experience.

Violations of Expectations in Perversion and Creativity

I have argued that violations of expectations play a role in many instances of both creativity and perversion but in quite different ways. In childhood, the creative person more likely becomes the beloved or at least astonishing violator of expectations of his family. In the illustrations presented, this violation began with the very act of surviving as in the cases of Chagall, Picasso, and Wagner. In other cases, this violation took a different form, living under the shadow of a dead brother and surviving as in the cases of Dali and Stravinsky, or the shock of discovering a mother's suicide, as in the case of Magritte, and considering oneself to be special on that account. It was not the event of survival that was crucial, but rather the myth that would inevitably be spun around the event.

The creative person can eventually own the specialness of being the violator of expectations. He will also have some awareness of the joy and thrilling surprise in having one's expectations violated. Both can infuse his creative output.

Creative persons, to use Tronick's paradigm of the "still face" mother metaphorically, have grown up in a world where they experienced the pleasure of turning still faces into joyful, surprised, animated faces. The perverted person by contrast grows up in a world populated by still faces, a world where mobile faces could be dangerous and angry. To remain within these metaphors, the creative person repeats his experience of turning potentially worried, sad faces into surprised, shocked, and thrilled faces; the perverted person alters his past experience by turning alive and potentially dangerous faces into dead and harmless faces. In fact, only under those circumstances can some serial killers find potency. In both of these instances we are considering the way in which violations of expectations transform affect, how they become part and parcel of the processes of regulation of affect and arousal.

The clinical material of previous chapters as well as the killers and creative artists depicted in this and the previous chapter can be placed along a metaphoric continuum. At one end are mobile, alive, responsive faces of families showing astonished, delighted, and surprised reaction to a child that had been feared to be too ill to survive, but who did. The child's resources and talents will be assimilated into this pattern. Here is a potential breeding ground for creativity and for a sense of self that soars but is also vulnerable and in need of large quantities of affirmation. Of course, not all children raised under these circumstances will become creative. In the next rung are those children who have experienced what Kohut called "the gleam in the mother's eye." This constitutes a positive reaction but is not connected with any extraordinary act of survival against all odds on the part of the child. It constitutes a joyful affirmation of the child and conveys a world that is welcoming.

Toward the other end of this continuum, but not quite at the end, are the still faces: the depressed, tense, and anxious faces of preoccupied and overwhelmed parents. These are the faces Carla and Nora encountered in their respective families. These faces may even be occasionally enlivened with gleams, but these gleams are not predictable and thus cannot be reliably anticipated. Still further down this continuum are the pervasively still faces. Although occasional mobility may appear in the face, the still face is considered safe. This was the face that Sally encountered in her mother. On the lowest rung are the animated faces that signal imminent danger, profound betrayals of trust and violence. At this end of the continuum we find the killers who turn animated, alive faces into still, dead faces. Here the sense of self plummets and requires concrete tributes to ensure some functionality.

The illustrations presented in the last two chapters account for two quite different routes to becoming the violator of expectations of others. In each instance, however, expectations on the part of both the child and parent are validated or violated. Once violations of expectations have become an implicit procedure in a person's repertoire of relationships, they become a magnet that attracts similar experiences that serve to reinforce and amplify this theme.

PART 3

Reflections

9 Disorders of Time

In this chapter on the acceptance of transience, and in the next chapter on wisdom, I consider qualities that are a consequence of maturation in the later years of life. They are not so much co-created in the therapist–patient dyad as they are achieved through engagement with the necessities, triumphs, adversities, losses, trauma, joys, and satisfactions of life. What we have acquired in our lifetime and bring to the experience of aging contributes to an acceptance of the transience of life and impacts our search for wisdom.

Acceptance of transience, like wisdom, comes from "having lived." But, although necessary, aging is not sufficient. And, at best, we navigate between accepting and rejecting transience. Kohut considered the acceptance of transience to constitute one of the transformations of archaic narcissism. Given a choice, I'd prefer any of the other transformations. But, that is exactly the point. There is no choice except to accept one's transience or to deny that life is transient and pretend that we are immortal.

One consequence of aging is the repeated experience of losing loved ones: parents, friends, a spouse, and sometimes even a child. After an initial period of shock, surprise, even outrage, we gradually move toward an acceptance of "I'll be neither the first nor the last to die." An acceptance of transience is also affected through separations from important people in our lives, not necessarily through death but through the vicissitudes of circumstances. Such experiences can also impart a sense of "nothing is forever." Recognizing the ticking away of time brings home the limits and impermanence of external attachments, though paradoxically this can increase the value we attach to them. In his essay, "On Transience," Freud (1916) even came to speak of "transience value," linking it to the extra value we place on things that are scarce": Transience value is scarcity value in time. Limitations in the possibility of an enjoyment raise the value of the enjoyment" (p. 305). Poets have known this only too well, linking thought of a loved one to thoughts of mortality and then back again to an even more intense cherishing of the loved one.

If, along with Erik Erikson (1959), we place acceptance of transience as a challenge for later adulthood, we also recognize that an acceptance of transience is unlikely to occur in the treatment of a young adult. But such recognition places us in a clearer position to address some problems presented by young adults that are troublesome for them in the present, but may also stand in the way of their accepting transience in later years. Early manifestations of a later difficulty in accepting one's transience appear as difficulties in attaining and maintaining a sense of self—specifically, maintaining temporal continuity. For example, the symptom of death anxiety would indicate having foreclosed the experience of time, of temporal continuity, which, in turn, will necessarily obstruct the acceptance of transience later in life.

Traditionally in psychoanalysis, death anxiety was understood as a telltale remnant of infantile aggressive wishes and was linked to narcissism. Analysts were directed to look for persisting death wishes with straightforward treatment implications: Unresolved infantile conflicts over aggression needed to be identified and confronted and the residuals of infantile omnipotence and grandiosity that had been retained by the person needed to be renounced. In 1980, when Bob Stolorow and I were young, in *Psychoanalysis of Developmental Arrest*s we offered a different perspective. We wrote about the emergence of death anxiety in the course of analysis as a developmental achievement. The idea was that not until you really had a sense of who you are could you feel anxious about extinction, nonbeing, or nonexistence. Death anxiety emerging in the course of an analysis, we argued, could indicate the successful resumption of a patient's developmental strivings. We proposed an alternative to the then-prevailing view that reduced adult anxieties to unresolved childhood conflicts. We argued that a patient's attempt to maintain or achieve a sense of self-integration could be reflected through the appearance of death anxiety.

Now, more than 25 years later, I think we were in the throes of youthful enthusiasm. Perhaps we were just a bit overoptimistic. Certainly, death anxiety can be a signal that one has reached a point in analysis where the fear of self-extinction indicates that a sense of self-cohesion, positive self-regard, and temporal continuity has developed. That is, having achieved a level of self-consolidation, the prospect of mortality can be newly dreaded. But this is only one among a number of explanations of this form of anxiety.

Kohut placed the acceptance of transience into the framework of developmental achievements through the transformation of archaic narcissism. In line with the arguments put forward in this book that transformations are primarily transformations of affect, the affect that is transformed in the acceptance of transience is "blissful comfort." That is the feeling often thought of as being shattered through trauma, whether "shock" or "strain" or a combination of the two (Lachmann, 2000; Sandler, 1967). Trauma is inevitable in the course of living a life and so our sense of "blissful comfort" is destined to undergo its unwanted transformations. Whether through the shock of a precipitous loss or through the strain of a process of slow aging, the fortress of one's feeling of safety and invulnerability is bound to be assaulted. At one extreme, trauma may crumble the conviction that we will live forever, as in death anxiety; at the other extreme we may increase defensively our fortifications of our omnipotence. One manifestation of this form of anxiety is that it interferes with one's ability to sustain a sense of self that is felt to be continuous over time. As Bob Stolorow, now also 25 years older, has put it: "The ecstatical unity of temporality—the sense of stretching along between past and future—is devastatingly disturbed by the experience of psychological trauma. Experiences of trauma become freeze-framed into an eternal present in which one remains forever trapped, or to which one is condemned to be perpetually returned through the Portkeyes supplied by life's slings and arrows" (2003, p. 160).

Maintaining a sense of self that is continuous in time is a necessary prerequisite for accepting transience but it is not sufficient. However, unlike the acceptance of transience, which requires a level of maturity, death anxiety and a loss of temporal continuity know no age limit. Thus, we can encounter problems in sustaining temporal continuity and manifestations of death anxiety, forerunners of an inability to "accept" transience, even in young adults.

Before elaborating these ideas clinically, I approach them from another side by making explicit a disclaimer. Three of the dimensions of the therapeutic relationship discussed so far—empathy, humor, and creativity, including metaphor, spontaneity, and play—are intrinsic aspects of the analytic dialogue. Therapist and patient incorporate these dimensions in their interaction and thereby expand the narrative envelope (Lichtenberg, Lachmann, & Fosshage, 1994). However, acceptance of transience and wisdom are conceptually of a different caliber. In one way or another, the vicissitudes of life and the acquisitions and the ravages of time contribute to shaping both. Thus, they cannot be placed on a par with empathy, humor, and creativity as intrinsic aspects of the therapeutic process. However, just as there are young adult patients who suffer from forms of death anxiety, there are aspects of treatment that involve the experience of temporality and thus pave the way for a more stable sense of self and the capacities that can eventually lead to acceptance of transience in later life.

A principal element on the road to accepting transience is the shared experience of the elapsing of time. In analysis this can be experienced over months and years, but it is also central to the immediate therapist–patient interaction within the hour. A shared experience of the moment and its rhythms over the short term are embedded in the co-creation of the analytic dialogue. A sense of time and memory, whether conscious or unconscious, procedural or bodily, contributes to empathic understanding and feeling empathized with. Both empathy and humor depend on timing. Being in synchrony or in syncopation with one's partner cements the connection. The "gotcha" game clearly illustrates the importance of timing. That is, any period of time other than a 3-second interval between the "I'm gonna getcha!" and the "gotcha," no matter whether it is a longer or shorter interval, can take the joy out of the experience. In studies of mother–infant self- and interactive regulations, the unit of time studied is also about 3 seconds. However, the unit of time implicated in the acceptance of transience is one's lifetime.

Whether over 3 seconds (as in the "gotcha" game) or over a lifetime (as in transience), both empathy and transience engage bodily rhythms that may be in tune, or at variance, with one's life and culture. Hence, when we look at the field beyond therapy in which transience and wisdom become players, we also encounter cultural and societal influences that may facilitate or obstruct the acceptance of transience and promote or devalue the search for wisdom. With respect to accepting transience, cultural and societal factors may enhance one's relationship to time, as, for example, in various rites of passage. However, they more often erect major obstacles.

Disorders of Temporality

Elissa Marder has approached the symptoms that arise through interferences with the sense of temporal continuity through an examination of the essays of Walter Benjamin. With Benjamin, she argues that an "overwhelming increase in external stimuli ... prevents the impact of particular experiences from becoming assimilated, processed, and remembered" (2001, p. 2). Benjamin referred to these experiences as "shock experiences" and attributed their detrimental effect to the enormous advances in technology, such as movies and photography and our modern modes of communication. These shocks overwhelm memory and have produced an "atrophy of experience." Older forms of communication, whereby information was narrated and communication of information took place in ways that respected our sense modalities, have been replaced by modern modes of communication. The older ones had a built-in respect for being patient and were conducted at a pace and intensity that facilitated their assimilation. Not so for the rapidity and high-intensity levels of current modes of communication. They are overwhelming in the speed at which they deliver information and the unrelenting pressure they exert to respond and react.

In the light of the place I have given to affect as the source of transformation, the work of Marder is particularly relevant. "Disorders of temporality," to use her term, ultimately manifest themselves in the denial of transience in later life and defensive filters that undercut one's relation to time at younger ages. To protect ourselves and ward off the pernicious effect of the shock experiences of everyday life, we interpose filters between our experience and our surround. But, the filters that we establish, such as dissociation and withdrawal, diminish affective experiences and expressive communication. These filters can lead to feelings of inauthenticity and unreality. Direct and intimate contact with the affective expression of another person can thereby be subdued. As a result of shock experiences that lead to the subsequent establishment of filters, our sense of others and of ourselves is dulled. Furthermore, the exposure to and the impact of a variety of shock experiences directly affect our memory of our life experiences. This process has been well documented in research that has linked the memory of an event to the affective context in which the event was experienced.

In a study by Singer and Fagan (1992), 2-month-old infants had a ribbon tied to one of their legs with the other end tied to a mobile. The infants learned that kicking their leg moved the mobile. In this phase of the study, infants were found to detect contingencies between what they did and what happened in the environment immediately following their actions. Detection of contingency facilitated the development of a sense of agency or effectance. This study provided the groundwork for further work that linked memory and affect. Using the same research setup, Singer and Fagan taught 2-month-old infants to kick in order to move a 10-item mobile. A two-item mobile was then substituted and half the babies cried. They were expecting a 10-item mobile. This two-item mobile was rigged also to move if the infants kicked, but the infants who cried didn't attempt to kick. Retested 1 week later with the original 10-item mobile, the infants who had cried did not remember the mobile well enough to kick it to get it to move. The infants who did not cry, however, remembered for up to 3 weeks that if they kicked, they moved the mobile. The researchers concluded that, for the infants who cried, the intense negative affect at the moment of learning seemed to have interfered with their memory.

The researchers then followed up their finding by giving the babies who cried a "reminder cue" by showing the infants the mobile and moving it. But they did not do so contingently. Nevertheless, given this cue, the babies who cried were then able to remember how to move the mobile with their kick 3 weeks after the first exposure. The researchers concluded that the problem for these babies was not the storage of memories but its retrieval. The heightened negative affect at the moment of learning interfered with their ability to access the memory: how to move the mobile by kicking it. Memories are viewed as permanent by these researchers. Instead of asking what is remembered, they are asking under what conditions retrieval is possible and what conditions interfere with the retrieval of memories.

The work of Singer and Fagan is relevant to the role of contingencies that are crucial in social interactions and in the organization of early representations (Beebe & Lachmann, 2002). The mode of communication is thus crucial in our ability to use—that is, to retrieve—information that we have already acquired. Communication is effective when it respects the individual's capacity to respond with a feeling of efficacy. Where it exceeds the receiver's ability to anticipate, absorb, master, and respond, it can evoke affect that disrupts the individual's ability to retrieve relevant and associated material. From infancy onward, reciprocal and modulated communication facilitates memory retrieval and thereby fosters a sense of one's continuity over time. But in our modern culture, reciprocal and modulated communication is everywhere replaced by experiences of "shocking" communication. Put differently, the life experiences or contexts that would make for acceptance of one's place in the flow of time and inhabiting one's life in the moment—necessary preconditions for sustaining a sense of temporal continuity—have been increasingly overwhelmed.

Among the "disorders of temporality," Marder identifies addictions and fetishism. But the patients described in this book who present aspects of self-pathology, particularly symptomotology that repeats the past and thereby "defies" the passage of time, also clearly suffer from disorders of temporality. They, too, exemplify the struggle to organize self-experience along a time dimension; they, too, struggle to attain a sense of temporal cohesion in the context of overwhelming unconscious pressures to the contrary. Such conflict weighs against accepting one's place in time, one's transience.

Given the increasing assault on one's sense of temporal continuity, it is noteworthy that the method of psychoanalysis can be thought of as implicitly addressing the very problems created by "shock experiences." Jean-Francois Lyotard (cited in Marder, 2001) notes that, by utilizing free association, psychoanalysis requires patience on the part of the patient, and thereby invites an essentially different relationship to time than that imposed by the shock experiences. In fact, Marder points out that the time-consuming process of psychoanalysis is itself a "possible method for resisting the prescriptions of ... temporal disorders" (p. 12). We are all aware that psychoanalytic treatment takes time and progress can be slow, but hopefully steady. In the context of temporality, perhaps there is an upside to this psychoanalytic limitation that may inadvertently pave the way for a gradual acceptance of transience.

Jason: A Disorder of Temporality

A somewhat cavalier attitude about time and transience might be anticipated from a 20-year-old, but not so with Jason (Lachmann, 1985). He began an 11-year analysis because of a constant dread of his own death. Although he was not cognizant of its connection to his death anxiety, another presenting symptom was his "impatience." He described flying into rages or becoming anxious and "spacey" at his work when he had to wait for phone calls or shipments of supplies he had ordered. However, the more pervasive manifestations of his disorder of temporality appeared in various aspects of his self-experience.

During the first weeks of his analysis Jason was most articulate about his constant feelings of alienation. "I feel like an outsider, damaged. I don't know how to experience reality. I am always pretending. A lot of the time I feel fear. I have no past to hold on to, to feel rooted in. Wherever I am—[with] friends, my girlfriend—I feel unprotected and alone."

Jason experienced time and his life as simultaneously standing still and rushing past him. Through dissociation, withdrawal, feelings of inauthenticity and unreality, he "filtered" his painful experience of being alive in a dead world so as to dull any impact on him. As it turned out, he failed to dull his pain and lost numerous opportunities for pleasure.

Jason's parents divorced when he was 7. For the first 6 months he lived with his mother, who had remarried, but then went to live with his father. Both parents died about 5 years prior to his coming for treatment. Subsequently, he became obsessed with the idea that he, too, would die "imminently," that his time was running out.

Jason was born into an unreal world, Hollywood. Both of his parents were in films, his mother on-screen, his father off-screen. Jason described life with his parents and their friends disparagingly. He had contempt for the frequent face-lifts by both men and women, and for the constant cross-generational pairings and shuffling of older men with much younger women and older women with much younger men. Both before and after his parents divorced his father "hung out with young chicks."

"Incredibly left out" is how Jason characterized life with his parents even prior to their divorce. In a dream at the beginning of treatment he depicted his "father and a woman running off together, like adolescents. I felt like an intruder. I had no effect." His father remarried four times until he died of a heart attack shortly after Jason's mother succumbed to cancer. She had remarried once. With all these adults Jason had conflicted relationships. He was not close to any of them, although for some years he did maintain "cordial" contacts with his mother and her husband. All in all, with both of his parents he felt like an intruder with no power to affect either one.

In Jason's world, holding on to one's youth or, conversely, denying the process of aging was paramount. Time was an enemy that could be vanquished surgically, chemically, or sexually. Withdrawing through disdain, fear, and envy began to shape Jason's experience even before his parents' separation and their later untimely deaths. The lifestyle of his family subjected Jason to continuous shock experiences, pummeling him from different sides. Increasingly, Jason lost access to his sense of continuity in time. Loewald (1980) proposed that the sense of self is organized along a time dimension; for Jason this was a scaffold with many missing rungs.

Jason's life after the divorce reinforced his sense of the transitory nature of relationships. In his experience significant relationships were continually aborted. The cast kept changing. It wasn't that his parents or their spouses abused him; rather, their indifference toward him and their apparent self-absorption kept him hungry for affective responsivity. It wasn't "still faces" or "depressed faces" that surrounded him; rather, it was the animated faces who were unresponsive to him that gradually and subtly undermined his self-cohesion.

Alienation from others, and alienation from himself in the form of standing at a distance both from "reality" and from inhabiting his life at the moment constituted the subjective, personal dimension of Jason's temporal disorder. In the context of his life, time was not permitted to pass; learning, practicing, and preparing were excruciating experiences for him. Although my impression was that he was quite bright, Jason had been a mediocre student. He did try his hand at painting but even that was pursued with little passion.

After the death of his parents, Jason inherited some money. He came to New York to study painting and met Leslie. She was a few years older, but she held a job with which she could support both Jason and herself. They began to live together and he enjoyed her maternal caring and support. She encouraged him to go into business in woodworking, cabinet making, and designing office space. She saw his talent in wood-working and hoped for the best. Jason worked as an employee for a contractor for a few years and then embarked on doing business on his own. What was remarkable about this period in his life was that while others could see his growing sense of competence and ability to function independently, he felt none of that.

Difficulties in tolerating the passage of time were evident in numerous aspects of Jason's life. However, they were nowhere more devastating than in his work as an independent contractor. Hired by architects and builders (some of whom were referred to him by Leslie), he had strained relationships with both the clients whom he served and the suppliers from whom he needed services and materials. In both directions, deliveries and services, communication had to be "instantaneous" to suit him. Jason's anxiety was expressed in a chronic sense of "impatience," and in petty rages. As we explored his anxiety, Jason realized he was afraid that he might not live long enough to complete a project if there was any delay. Realizing this, he struggled to keep his impatience in check but could do so only through another "grim belief." He countered his fear that he would die before the project's completion with an equally power-ful conviction that he was really still a "novice" in his profession with a lifetime of learning still ahead of him. Here was another assault on time. Time had stood still since the year his parents divorced. Furthermore, as a novice, he did not have the "right" or "status" to make demands on his suppliers or clients. In addition, though he could think of himself as a "novice," he could not think of himself as a "learner," or as ever being able to acquire competence and expertise through trial and error. All this would require a vastly different relationship to time since learning requires an acceptance of time; even learning through trial and error requires retaining a record of one's experience in memory. Only then can making the same error over and over again be avoided.

Each completed project thus fell into a "black hole" and disappeared from Jason's reservoir of memory and experience. Having an experience that was felt to be "now," "his," or one he "owned" vanished before it could be assimilated, processed, and remembered. He "learned" under a cloud of anxiety and duress and, subsequently, like the babies in the

Singer and Fagan study, he could not retrieve what he had learned. Each new project was a "start from scratch." Whatever knowledge he had acquired in one project, though used by him competently in the context of that project, was lost upon the completion of the project. In these circumstances past knowledge did not enrich his sense of self as a growing professional or move him beyond novice status in his own mind.

Jason continued to think of himself as a 7-year-old. The time just prior to his parent's separation was relatively better for him than the years that followed. Maintaining his self-image as a 7-year-old meant that he retained a view of himself as an easily intimidated, naive kid who needed to be cared for in a world of only intermittently caring adults.

More so in retrospect than at the time we were working together, I see how Jason's various difficulties all hinged on his "disorder of temporality." In retrospect, I see more clearly how his predivorce experiences of the parental fights and of the extent to which his family and immediate culture prized holding time still had set the stage for increasing feelings of "not belonging" and disorientation. Although at the time I did not see all the ramifications of his temporal disorder, we nevertheless did focus on the various ways in which his sense of continuity in time had been compromised and the ways in which his conviction that he would soon die appeared in his life.

As we explored the predivorce years, Jason also recalled more about his relationship with his parents from the time before their deaths. We saw the recovery of memories from this time as Jason beginning to fill in the blanks in his sense of temporal continuity. During this period of treatment Jason came to value his dawning ability to recall affective experiences of his childhood and early teens. This dawning ability to recall in turn increased his self-confidence. That is, he implicitly became aware of a developing sense of temporal sequences and of ordering his memories along this time continuum.

The memories were dispiriting. Jason's mother had been a moderately successful actress. She was perfectionistic and worked hard, but she did not enjoy her work. Her joylessness spilled over into her life and her relationship with Jason. By the time he was 7, she had already conveyed to him her "grave doubts that he would ever be able to survive financially in the world." Jason was shocked as he recalled her "doubts." He experienced them as a prognostication, as though there was no point in even trying to work. It was already too late; he was fated to fail.

Jason recalled his father as a financial "failure" and a "deeply humil-iated" person. His father complained endlessly about his unsuccessful forays into the film business, his otherwise unsuccessful law practice, and his four unsuccessful marriages.

The deaths of both parents reinforced Jason's sense of being frozen in time. This stance was even further reinforced in his desperate avoid-ance of the inevitable humiliations that throughout his developing years became associated with attaining adulthood. The terror of becoming an adult was contained in a dream image that reminded Jason of the conveyer belt scene from Charlie Chaplin's *Modern Times*. Becoming an adult meant stepping onto the conveyer belt of time, accepting the transience of life, the inevitable humiliations and failures of adulthood, and dieing in the midst of futile struggles for meager satisfactions. In his impatience, in clinging to his naïveté, in rejecting transience and temporal continuity, Jason stayed clear of his father's path of inevitable failure. He avoided his father's humiliations and his mother's prophesy with regard to what it takes and what he did not have to survive finan-cially in this world. In a memory recovered from about age 10 he said, "She wanted me to be somebody. She bought me all this mechanical stuff, templates, ovals, tape measures, architectural stuff. I didn't know what to do with it. Nobody helped me use it."

Most recollections of his life with his mother were painful: "She was always rehearsing. It made work look like an enemy. It intruded on me. Now when I see other people working and I get a glimpse of what life could be like, I get depressed and cut myself off."

Jason was aware that in our sessions I was working. This stirred up comparisons to himself as inadequate at work. After sessions he often felt depressed, humiliated, and overwhelmed. In fact, when we had a productive session—for example, when he recalled more affect-laden experiences from his life with his parents, in the sessions that followed he would often bring in dreams expressing anger toward me and feelings of inadequacy about himself. Over time, over a long time, however, he gradually began to feel more rooted and assertive.

When Jason was about 9 he left his mother's house and lived with his father. At that time his father was married to a woman with three children. Jason recalled that all the children slept in the same room and he slept in the same bed with his 12-year-old stepsister. He did not remember ever speaking to any of the others in the house and each night he cried himself to sleep. I said to him that I thought his sadness and his feelings of alienation were the only constants, the only stable memories he could carry with him in all the moves he made to all these places that felt so alien to him. I could understand he might be reluctant to leave these feelings behind.

About his father's marriage at that time, he told me, "That marriage lasted until I was about 13. But it was an awful time. I remember feeling trapped in that house and in those feelings. Always waiting, I never knew what I was waiting for. Initiating anything always felt 'as though.' Even now I get myself to do things rather than 'I do.'"

The treatment of Jason began in the 1970s when I had just become acquainted with Kohut's ideas and before the publication of Miller's description of Kohut's "leading edge" interpretations. But my recognition of Jason's painful affect states and their function in maintaining his self-continuity enabled him to begin to recognize their effect on his life. But, more important, his perspective on feeling so trapped by these feelings altered. We spoke of them as providing him with "company," with a feeling of "familiarity." Gradually in the sessions, his self-reflections were no longer tinged with excessive self-hatred but rather included his recognition that he paradoxically needed to rely on his alienation to provide himself with some stability. In a significant shift over the course of treatment, Jason reported a greater feeling of relief after sessions and a keener awareness of the extent of his "self-hatred." He said, "Sometimes I now look forward to coming to sessions. It takes me away from bad feelings. It's like my knowing it, and I will change."

We began to pursue the theme that his sadness and alienation was his connection to the time of his childhood and also contained his belief that he did not have to worry about the future because his parents would take care of him. He then labeled his feeling that he was unable to do anything as an "infection" that held him back from doing the work that it was time to do. Another series of dreams followed in which present-day friends, coworkers, and business contacts were in locales associated with his childhood. We understood these dreams as his forging connections between present and past as a way of not relying on his sadness and feelings of incompetence as the sole source of his connections. This series of dreams was capped by one in which he was in the driver's seat of a car. His girlfriend, Leslie, was in the back seat. Then he added, "No, my father was driving and then he was gone. The car began to waver; I reached out and helped to keep it straight. Father was not there and someone had to drive the car." A further series of dreams elaborated his acquisition of a greater sense of agency. For example, in a dream he is the narrator in a play, and he successfully narrates it—from memory. Then he dreamed he missed a session. "You were furious; I couldn't imagine how angry you would be. You said, 'If you ever do this again I'll never see you again.' I was shocked that you weren't warm and understanding." The salient issue in this dream, as we understood it, was that his presence or absence is important, recognized, and has an impact. He had begun to consider himself a presence in his life and my life, and in the life of others, here and now.

By the fifth year of his treatment, the connection between his impatience and his conviction that his death was imminent was in the forefront of the analysis. Jason became increasingly aware of the extent of his struggle against accepting transience and the consequence of this struggle in interfering with his sense of temporal continuity. The following year a pivotal development occurred, certainly unanticipated by me and surprising to Jason as well. Jason and Leslie bought a country house. Jason had saved enough money from his work so that they could contribute equally to the purchase. Jason developed a passion for gardening. He even planted perennials, reflecting a newly gained expectation that he might live long enough to reap the flowers in the seasons ahead. Even Jason had to admit that his interest expressed hope, an affirmation of his life, and represented an expansion of his sense of temporal continuity. The garden metaphorically extended into his past where he continued to recover emotionally rich memories and thereby finally harvested the fruits of his childhood labors.

As I was working with Jason I wondered how our exploration of his death anxiety, his impatience, and the many ways in which he maintained his temporal discontinuity would be translated into changes in his experience and life. I was concerned that the discussion of these issues in our sessions, while rich philosophically, might have been intellectualized and thus affectively distant. Certainly Jason was affectively engaged in the sessions, but I continued to wonder how his feelings would change. I never would have expected the emergence of a passion for gardening. One thing I was sure of. I would never have come up with that as a "suggestion." It was co-created only to the extent that I helped clear away the weeds and brush, thereby making the field receptive to new plants. Jason provided the seeds. This turned out to be true in more ways than one.

Leslie was a wonderful caretaker, friend, and work-coach. Most important, she had confidence in his ultimate ability to earn a living. Jason described her as "maternal." Even from the start of their relationship she had not been all that interested in sex, and by now she had lost all interest in it. Since she had taken such good care of him and was such a good friend, in the light of his conviction (and his mother's prophesy) that he would not be able to take care of himself financially, he thought about but rejected the idea of looking for someone else. Given her loyalty and her caretaking, he did not have the heart to leave her over this issue. But he did miss having sex.

After the joint purchase of the country house, Jason sometimes went to the house alone, during the week, to tend to his garden. On one of these train trips, he met Lizzy, a woman who was a few years older than him, very attractive, very rich, and very sexy. She owned a house in a neighboring community. With only some slight hesitation on his part, she succeeded in seducing him. His affair with her increased his passion for gardening. Tending his garden was more than an excuse to pursue the affair. The passion and earthiness of this woman, in contrast to the maternal but demur Leslie, seemed to increase his pleasures in the soil. Gardening became a link between temporal continuity and sexual passion. The affair dispelled some of the last vestiges of his naïveté and his feeling like an outsider. It also marked his emergence from the hiatus of age 7. The age difference between him and Lizzy, although slightly greater than between him and his Leslie, did not make her "maternal." What was crucial was that she was a woman, not a girl. She was mature, self-reliant, an executive in a business, and neither required nor offered caretaking. This was both the good news and the bad news.

Jason eventually, and guiltily, told Leslie about the affair. She told him that she would not continue to live with him while he was seeing another woman. Unsuccessfully, Jason tried to get her to agree to let him continue the affair. After all they did not have sex. But, she would not hear of it and so he ended the affair after several months. What also contributed to the end was that Jason felt that while the sex was great, he felt himself to be slipping into the role of a "sex toy"—not that there was anything wrong with that.

Subsequently, Jason and I continued to explore some remaining aspects of his impaired sense of temporal continuity, since his "death anxiety" had reemerged. It was now expressed as his worry that his perennials would not survive the winter. I said to him that indeed that might occur. I acknowledged that some perennials may not survive and that we were in the process of evaluating his relationship to such uncertainties. We had followed a route in the treatment from Jason's conviction of his imminent death and his impatience, to a recognition of his impaired sense of time, to an acceptance of the transience of his flowers and thus toward a widening of his temporal horizons. Then another tragedy occurred.

Jason had planted an enormous field of tulips. When they were just at the point where they were going to flower, he made a special trip to his house to see them in bloom. The night before someone had cut down and stolen all of his tulips. The sight of the field of tulip stems was shattering to him. He likened it to a heart attack or a cancer death. I could certainly commiserate with him about his shattered expectations and the massive violation of expectations that had again devastated his life. Just when he had begun to establish some perspective, just when he was starting to achieve a balance between hope and dread, an unexpected death struck again.

Once again we linked the death of his parents and his sense that his life was also over with the murder of his tulips. By this time the analytic work itself had become a reliable source for integrating past and present, and although he mourned the loss of his tulips he could begin to imagine a future for himself beyond his garden. A sense of himself with a temporal perspective had been acquired.

In Jason's treatment, death anxiety was understood as a way of freezing his attachment to his parents to a time just prior to his world falling apart when they were relatively more responsive and engaged with him than after their divorce. He acquired a beginning recognition of temporal continuity as his impatience, sadness, and anxiety were transformed through his surprise at my formulation of his sadness as his "company" in his lonely, alienated state. He furthered the transformative process unexpectedly and creatively on his own through his planting perennials. They signaled a future with hope.

I have said little about the vicissitudes of the transference in the course of this treatment. Jason had been referred to me through a friend of Leslie. The aura of potential nurturer, I believe, fell on my shoulders. In essence Jason "expected" very little from me, but feared that I would be critical and would, in some way, be ready to humiliate him by expecting little from him. In the early years of the analysis, simply describing these "expectations," derived from his relationships to both parents, sufficed to maintain the analytic work. Such dynamics as his parents' deaths evoking guilt over wishful fantasies of their demise that, in turn, had become the source of fear of his own imminent death were, so far as we could tell, not implicated in his sense of temporal discontinuity. When his disappointment and reactive anger toward his parents emerged he was quite comfortable in talking about it. It appeared to me that his attachment to them was in some ways shallow or, put differently, that he had detached himself gradually over the course of his childhood in response to their considerable self-preoccupation. Though recalling his mother's vote of "no confidence" in him evoked outrage, it led to our recognition of his gradually withdrawing and detaching himself from her long before this incident. The "cordial" relationship with his mother and her husband that he described at the start of treatment reflected the essence of his early relationship with both parents. He recalled their fights as centering on money (its absence) and his father's "affairs" (their presence). He kept out of their way, hiding in his room to avoid the shouting. He indicated that he might have tended to side with his mother, a factor that probably contributed to his decision to remain with Leslie.

During the period of the affair with Lizzy, we negotiated some sensitive transference issues. Jason expected me to be critical of the affair and judgmental of him for betraying Leslie. However, we also spoke about the affair being an affirmation of his growing up. It was an adolescent fantasy come true. Unlike the architectural supplies his mother gave him that nobody taught him to use, he was now discovering and retaining a new sexual sense of himself.

By the time we terminated the analysis, Jason had acquired a more stable and elaborated sense of himself that included learning and retention, self-assertion and self-reflection, and feeling present in the moment. All this pointed to his functional temporal continuity. How this will affect his acceptance of transience in his later years could not be seen when we terminated treatment when he was 31. His acceptance of time and his tolerance for its passage had increased. By the time he left, prompted by his affair and his newly acquired sexual skills, he and Leslie were having sex about once a month. Patience can pay off, a little.

10 In Search of Wisdom

For Kohut, wisdom was an achievement during the later phases of life. Wisdom entails accepting the limitations that aging imposes on one's physical, intellectual, and emotional powers in the context of stable attitudes and an overarching perspective toward life and the world. Kohut posited humor and acceptance of transience within a person's firmly held set of values and ideals as the major constituents of wisdom. By emphasizing an acceptance of transience and humor as well as ideals, Kohut differentiated someone who is wise from someone who is just smart.

I imagined that the topic of wisdom could be approached like creativity—not by finding a patient who developed wisdom in the course of treatment, but by finding a person whose life could be seen as the embodiment of wisdom. Inspired by Diogenes's search for an honest man and armed with Kohut's definition of wisdom, I began to search for a wise person, man or woman, who could fulfill the prerequisites for wisdom. To find such a person turned my task into a contest. As is customary in contests, relatives of those awarding the prizes or their associates and employees were not eligible to win. That criterion helped me to eliminate a large number of my relatives and colleagues without bruising too many psyches. In scanning the remaining list of friends and acquaintances, I recalled the father of a childhood friend who I thought qualified eminently as a candidate for wisdom. My friend and I have known each other since about age 9 and have maintained our friendship even though since beginning with college we have lived in different parts of the country. I had also maintained contact with his father, who died a few years ago at the age of 91.

My friend's father had become an internationally renowned celebrity in the music world, although at the time I first got to know him, at the age of 9, he had not quite yet achieved that status. My friend, his family, and I lived in the same building and later, when he moved, in the same neighborhood. We spent every day playing together outside and at each other's houses. One day as my friend tried to teach me to play some tunes on his piano his father chanced upon us. Very seriously, he gave me some pointers as I picked away with one or two fingers. He was already a bit of a music celebrity even then and I was astonished that he would take the time and show interest in my efforts at the piano. We would often talk but I can't recall what we talked about. I do recall feeling that he took me seriously and I felt like a grownup when we spoke. Later, during my teen years, I remember playing "what if" games with my friend and his father. "What if you were imprisoned unfairly, what would you do?" I remember this question because I was so surprised by my friend's father's response: "I would rattle the bars. I would scream and yell. I would not give up!" What struck me was that he was not thinking in ways to use his extraordinary intelligence to get out, but even so he was not going to go down without a fight. Apart from this one question, I don't recall what was said but I do recall that these "what ifs" led to very exciting discussions. All this occurred during the World War II era when the "what ifs" we came up with were not so far-fetched. My friend and his family, and my parents and I, had escaped from Europe just before we met in New York.

Over the years my friend and I maintained intermittent contact. We exchanged visits after we were separated by geography and I would attend concerts at which his father performed. In this way our friendship continued on an occasional basis as we both grew older. Meetings between my friend's father and me became more regular when chance brought us together during the 10 summers prior to his death.

In these later years our conversations were more on a par. My earlier and long-standing admiration of him was reinforced and I continued to be impressed by how his knowledge of history, philosophy, the arts, and human nature all came together in a charming cosmopolitan outlook toward life. In terms of the visions of reality I discussed earlier he combined ironic, comic, and romantic visions with a touch of the tragic. I think his perspective on life and the world was shaped by his flight from Europe before World War II; by his years of experience as a musician, mentor, administrator; and by a variety of forays into the public spotlight that required tact and sensitivity. He held humanistic values and ideals of honesty that were clearly consonant with Kohut's "firmly held ideals and values." I know that these values earned him enormous respect in his field, even as they may also have deprived him of some financial rewards that his positions might have otherwise earned for him. He held ideals above politics both on a national level and in his profession. Politically, he was fair and just, with a broad perspective that defied labels. He could be critical but without prejudice. His strong opinions were always expressed thoughtfully and in a kindly fashion. All this I gleaned over the years as we would talk occasionally, and it was brought home to me even more when we talked more consistently during his last 10 years.

An acclaimed musician, he retired from his post when he was in his late 70s because, he told me, he felt he no longer had the stamina to perform according to his professional standards. He was then invited to head the education department of a music festival for 1 year and became so beloved by the students that he was invited back each summer for the next 10 years. As the head of a music school he did the unprecedented. He attended classes with the students and lunched with them in the student cafeteria, where he shared with them his vast knowledge, expertise, and, most of all, his enthusiasm for music. His empathic understanding of the needs of the students was palpable. I could see the facial expressions of the students who spoke to him during concert intermission. They clearly felt that they were in the presence of someone special. He seemed able to balance the adoration and acclaim he received with a kind of reserve that somehow made it easy to speak or even argue with him.

My friend's mother had died just shortly after his father assumed the post as head of the music school. He was a vigorous 80 at the time and retained his optimism in terms of his expectations of life. Two years later he married an attractive woman in her late 40s. During his last year of life, at 90, his health began to fail and he was briefly hospitalized, several times, for a heart condition. During his last month, anticipating his death, he planned the music that was to be performed at his funeral. Was this an indication of his acceptance of transience? Or just a need to control the details of his funeral? Or perhaps a continuation of an enduring ability to make the most out of every moment of his life? Probably all of these.

His creativity was his strong suit and his contribution to the cultures of nations (although this was not exactly what Kohut had in mind with creativity) has survived and will no doubt continue to live. His sense of humor was implicit in his conversations and observations. All in all, he seemed to me to be a likely candidate for Kohut's definition of wisdom.

Having in mind that talking with my friend about his father would provide me with the details that I could only sketch broadly based on my feelings and impressions, I called him. I told him of my search for a person who would embody wisdom and I asked, in an open-ended way, whom he might consider to be a candidate for wisdom. He came up with a few names that we discarded. Either we did not really know enough about them or, as in the case of his suggestion of Primo Levy, we had some doubt about their acceptance of transience. Finally, I said to him, "What about your father?" And I told him what I had thought of. He said: "What? He did have all those qualities outside the house, but in his family he was impossible." "Well," I thought, "there goes empathy."

Empathy? Kohut didn't link wisdom and empathy. He just linked wisdom to humor and an acceptance of transience. But neither did he exclude it. In the discussion to follow I include empathy as relevant for wisdom. Recall that empathy, as I defined it, is co-created by one partner who conveys empathic understanding and another partner who presents a readiness to be empathically understood. Furthermore, both sides of an experience of empathy are known to both partners, although one side may be more dominant on occasion than the other.

In my survey asking various groups of friends, "Whom do you consider wise and why?" I discovered a notable absence of empathy in those deemed "wise." The results were invariably similar to my friend's report about his father. Wisdom and empathy are difficult to find in the same person. Biographies of Martin Luther King, Jr., Erik Erikson, Golda Meir, Simone Weil, and Gandhi, some of whose names were suggested, reveal their wisdom. But, with respect to their personal lives, it was either hard to tell, or their relationships with spouses and children seemed to resemble the story of my friend's father. Just as I had concluded in my discussion of Masud Khan that empathy and grandiose self-centeredness could live side by side, it now appeared that wisdom and grandiose self-centeredness could also live peacefully side by side. Yet, as certainly was the case for my friend's father, many of these nominees for wisdom were revered with affection and were empathically understood by those around them.

Through this book I have argued that three of the qualities that Kohut listed as transformations of archaic narcissism—empathy, humor, and creativity—are better placed into the ongoing therapist–patient dialogue. And even if an acceptance of transience can't comfortably be fitted into therapy, one's relationship to time can emerge in treatment in various ways. But wisdom? My anecdotal search led me to reaffirm my impression that Kohut's concept of wisdom must be on a different conceptual level than the other transformations he postulated. It also led me to question what the place of wisdom is in a therapeutic context. What can psychotherapy contribute to understanding or acquiring wisdom?

Defining "Wisdom"

Not satisfied by what I learned in my search for a wise man, I turned to the dictionary. The *Webster Dictionary* (1976) defines wisdom as "making the best use of knowledge, experience, understanding, good judgment, sagacity." Synonyms offered are "prudence, knowledge, sapience." I did not find this to be very helpful either, but on Google I came across an exhaustive review of the academic psychology literature on wisdom by Richard Trowbridge (2005). He surveyed and synopsized a wealth of studies on "wisdom" and how it might be defined. After surveying the literature and all the studies that tried to operationalize and define wisdom, Trowbridge concluded that in spite of the large number of empirical studies testing various definitions of wisdom, a comprehensive definition has yet to be formulated. He found some support for the idea that older people may excel in wisdom in contrast to earlier prevalent reports that aging resulted in general physical and mental decline. Other common assumptions about wisdom, such as equating wisdom with the way in which aging is approached, or with a way of approaching life challenges, or with how we conduct ourselves and see our life in the later years, were neither supported nor controverted.

Trowbridge cited a typical study (Jason et al., 2001) that found positive correlations between wisdom and life satisfaction and particular
personality traits such as openness, social intelligence, and moral
reasoning. Forty-three racially and religiously diverse adults (35 women)
with college or graduate degrees were asked to identify a person they
knew or knew of whom they considered wise, and to choose those
qualities from a scale that made that person wise. The qualities most
frequently mentioned were drive, tenacity, leadership, insight, and spiri-
tuality. In addition, qualities such as being smart, loving, reliable, and
practical were frequently listed. This study was typical of the level of
sophistication of wisdom research and Trowbridge was not particularly
impressed with it. Having independently conducted my own "wisest
person I know study" and seen the pitfalls in it, I was not particularly
impressed either. I also noticed that humor or an ironic view of life
and of human foibles was nonexistent in the responses of this group.
The young adults studied had seemingly not yet been touched by the
finiteness of human existence. If you want to know about wisdom, you
probably have to ask an older person, someone who had tasted life or
perhaps even been bitten by it.

The study of wisdom in relation to aging confronts us with a paradox,
one that Trowbridge noted in his survey of the literature: If wisdom is
one of the potential benefits of age, how can that be reconciled with the
deterioration, over time, of numerous brain functions, such as attention,
memory, mental flexibility, and speed of mental operations. In fact, as the
neurologist Elkhorn Goldberg (2005) has pointed out, the whole brain
shrinks as we age. Nevertheless, as we get older, Goldberg also argued,
we may gain wisdom, in the form of certain expertise and special competence, because simultaneously over time our skill in pattern recognition
increases. The cognitive capacities that diminish are compensated for,
in certain instances, by spreading an umbrella of preexisting templates
useful in problem solving that readily covers future cognitive challenges.
These templates enable us to engage in pattern recognition. Once established they require only slight modifications so that a broad range of
inputs will activate the relevant neural constellations.

Thus, Goldberg proposes that "those of us who have been able to form
a large number of such cognitive templates, each capturing the essence
of a large number of pertinent experiences, have acquired 'wisdom'
or at least a crucial ingredient thereof" (p. 106). Goldberg himself

acknowledged the "scandalous gross oversimplification [of his] admittedly narrow definition of wisdom" (p. 106). However, he does clarify that certain cognitive processes become increasingly adaptive in aging. Actually, these processes, involving the formation of large numbers of cognitive templates, are not confined to older people but have also been found when studying the brains of bilingual people, of professional musicians, and of London cab drivers. These three groups, Goldberg proposes, share certain neurological structures with older people indicating that these structures are probably necessary, but not sufficient to qualify for the dictionary definition of wisdom. Large numbers of cognitive templates and knowledge are good, and like wine, they get better as they age. But, there are no guarantees. In "senior moments," for example, we may be aware of the overall cognitive template ("I remember you are a relative of mine") but unable to recall the specific detail ("But I just can't remember your name").

So the question of what constitutes wisdom is left hanging. The dictionary, Trowbridge, and Goldberg point to wisdom as an attribute of a person—an attribute that requires certain necessary cognitive capabilities. But these capacities are not sufficient to account for wisdom. Perhaps the problem lies in trying to define wisdom as though it is a trait. Although Kohut thought of wisdom as a state of mind, in much of the preceding discussion wisdom is thought of as a trait or an attribute or even a capacity of a person. But based on my anecdotes and the survey and the empirical studies, I believe that understanding wisdom may require a different portal of entry.

How can we adapt the concept of wisdom to psychoanalytic treatment and consonant with the transformations of self-pathology? Wisdom as an attribute of a person clearly does not belong in the realm of psychoanalysis, but what about a person's relationship to wisdom? Can that find a place in psychoanalytic treatment? It might make more sense to consider how one goes about searching for and relating to wisdom, both as an ideal and as embodied in a person. Perhaps within self psychology we can find a place for the search for wisdom as an aspect of one's lifelong need for idealizing selfobjects.

My friend's father was clearly admired by the students at the music academy that he directed and by me. Was he idealized? Probably. In any case, feeling connected to a person like this who is seen as wise is a touching, enriching experience for both partners. I was surprised by my friend's description of his father's "other" side, although, knowing my friend, I have no reason to doubt it. Yet based on my experience of his father's respectful understanding of me, I made an empathic connection with him, and felt enriched by our contacts.

The capacity for empathy, although evidently not a requirement for wisdom, is crucial in the search for wisdom. Such a quest entails drawing the nectar of wisdom from its various sources. Odd as it may be, the search for wisdom requires empathy but wisdom per se seemingly does not.

From a different perspective, there may be a developmental basis for wisdom and empathy not residing comfortably together. Wisdom, it can be argued, is in part born of pain and suffering. In contrast empathy, as I discussed in earlier chapters, begins developmentally through the activation of hard-wired precursors as well as through learned procedures. This difference in their sources may put empathy and wisdom in a potentially conflicted relationship with each other. The precursors of empathy are numerous; for the development of empathy to be obstructed in a person's life, something must go wrong. But something going wrong is the very soil in which wisdom may grow. Thus, the very conditions that provide the soil for wisdom—pain and suffering—may well be the very ones that obstruct the development of empathy. In that case, psychotherapy may ameliorate the factors that interfere with experiencing and conveying empathy, but still the fate of wisdom may hang in the balance. Any number of treatments can document a burgeoning of the capacity for empathy, as in the treatment of Carla, who developed empathy not only for herself but also for her parents, or Nora, who developed empathy for her coworkers. This is not to say that either thereby became wise. In fact I am not aware of any clinical literature that documents the burgeoning of wisdom, however it is defined. Therapeutic work might more profitably set its sights on promoting curiosity as to where wisdom can be found. That curiosity is certainly co-created.

It is generally agreed that wisdom comes with age, if it comes at all. But what about Kohut's requirement that an acceptance of transience is a crucial aspect of wisdom? Furthermore, the acceptance of transience as bearable requires in turn a perspective on one's life laced with humor and irony. As I illustrated in the treatment of Jason, therapy can address a person's relationship to time and can thereby lay the groundwork for an acceptance of transience. In other instances we can make conditions ripe for a patient's sense of humor to blossom. But wisdom seems to require all of these and something more. And the "something more" may not be found in the therapeutic setting but rather emerge as a by-product of how psychotherapy reorganizes the intrapsychic landscape and prepares the person to engage with life experiences.

And another question: What about patients we treat who may not be old enough to be candidates for wisdom? Whereas the achievement of wisdom may lie in their future, their relationship to wisdom does not. When we move away from viewing wisdom as a "trait" and approach wisdom as a state of mind, as Kohut suggested, we can begin to see the preconditions for wisdom that actually constitute the beginning of wisdom: having a "decentered" view of life, and achieving a state of being in the world that involves self-understanding and self-acceptance. Self-acceptance includes accepting one's negative qualities; that is often euphemistically described as accepting one's humanness. Self-acceptance often emerges in life as humility without obsequiousness; it can be thought of as an empathy with oneself (J. Lichtenberg, personal communication, March 2006). Potentially, self-acceptance is achievable in the course of therapy. Whether it congeals as "wisdom" in a person is difficult to predict. Certainly self-acceptance was a quality that was prominent in my friend's father. His retiring from performing when he did plainly indicates a degree of self-empathy—he did not want to face the pain of performing at less than the level of professionalism he expected of himself.

Finding Solace

Many of the forgoing ideas came to me as I was reading Harold Bloom's (2004) book, *Where Shall Wisdom Be Found?* Bloom describes how a grave illness initiated a rereading of some of the great books of literature, books that he had previously taught over many years to his students. He portrays this private odyssey as his search for wisdom, a "quest for sagacity that might solace and clarify the traumas of aging, of recovery from grave illness, and of grief for the loss of beloved friends" (p. 1). Inadvertently, Bloom answered my question of how we might fit wisdom with the contributions of self psychology or, more specifically, with how therapy might transform self-pathology.

Bloom describes his depleted sense of self through illness, aging, and loss of his friends. He felt in need of solace to deal with these painful alterations of his affective state and he turned to the wisdom literature for self-restoration.

During his time of grave illness, Bloom's search took him to the "wisdom literature" as he defines it, to the works of Plato, Shakespeare, Cervantes, Goethe, Proust, and Freud, among others. As he plunged into this literature he embarked on a journey into wisdom and found solace and clarity in reading. He wrote, "The mind always returns to its needs for beauty, truth, and insight. Mortality hovers, and all of us learn the triumph of time" (p. 1). Holding on to "absolutes" evidently fulfilled a profound need as he reflected on his transience. He describes this quest for wisdom as coming from his "deepest motive for reading" (p. 101).

In his search Bloom reimmersed himself in literature that he had been teaching in university courses for decades. Although the context for this literature was the classes he had taught, he reread these works alone. Yet, at various points in his book, Bloom mentions his students, perhaps thereby dispelling his feelings of isolation, loss, and despair by surrounding himself with a familiar, affectively responsive human context. That context, his classes, and the imagined teacher–student dyad may well have provided an implicit but powerfully supportive background. Thus, the wisdom literature provided a double function. It served as a connection to a familiar, affectively enlivening past replete with wise "friends" as well as connecting him with a living present context in which he was the mentor to his students. Like Stravinsky, working alone on *The Rite of Spring* on the piano, reading the wisdom literature was a self-transforming process for Bloom. For him, the affective transformation went from despair to solace.

My friend's father and Bloom may have shared a similarity as well. Both sought and found a path toward strengthening their connection to a rich and valued past, one in literature and the other in music. Both served as teachers and mentors. There was a big difference, however; Bloom sought to find solace during his time of illness. I don't know about my friend's father, but it would be more consistent with what I knew about him to say that, rather than seeking solace, he tried to maintain his connection with his past strengths as best he could, and sought his rejuvenation through his continued actual connection with students. But, perhaps both were able to accept their transience, in one case the gradual physical decline of ageing, in the other a rapid decline through illness, by reexperiencing aspects of their life and intellectual history.

Following Bloom, I shifted from searching for a wise person or exploring how wisdom could be defined to the contemplating-enriching experience of *searching* for wisdom. Whether in literature, art, music, or nature, searching and finding, almost finding, and refinding are co-created even though to some to degree the successful end to a search necessarily is in the eye of the searcher.

Bloom's search for and discovery of wisdom in a diverse array of literature is instructive not merely to the extent that it provides a reading list for extricating oneself from the throes of that painful triad of aging, illness, and losses. Rather, Bloom presents a model for finding wisdom in a variety of places, including works of fiction even when the authors of these works may not have been personifications of wisdom themselves. Bloom distinguished, elaborated, and contrasted the wisdom found in poets, writers, the Bible, *Ecclesiastes, Hamlet, Don Quixote,* and many other sources. In this literature we are transported to a precious private place that is simultaneously a shared universal community where, as Schiller and Beethoven in the Ninth Symphony proposed, *"Alle Menschen werden Brüder"* (all mankind will be brothers).

An appreciation of and resonance with the search for wisdom in the world around us probably has long been implicitly included in psycho-therapeutic work, contributing to the transformative process. I do not mean that the analyst assigns the search for wisdom as a task for the analysand. Nor do I mean a kind of bibliotherapy, Rather, I think that a search for wisdom may be implicit as an attribute of the therapist's vision and may show itself, for example, as an attitude of skepticism about what is or what is to be, or curiosity about what could be and what has never been. Analytic staples like decentering, self-reflecting, and promoting self-acceptance, self-understanding, and self-empathy all can be thought of as fostering a search for wisdom, though they are usually implicitly included in the therapeutic process and don't neces-sarily become topics of explicit, verbal analytic discourse.

In this heyday of postmodern relativism, the wisdom literature seems to have become the last refuge of complex absolutes of truth, beauty, and insight into human nature. Whereas Bloom argued for the varied faces of wisdom as embodied in Plato, Homer, Yahweh, Shakespeare, Cervantes, Freud, or Proust, he also sided with relativism. After quoting William James to the effect that wisdom was learning what to overlook, Bloom concluded, "Truth, according to the poet William Butler Yeats, could not be known but could be embodied. Of wisdom, I personally would affirm the reverse: We cannot embody it, yet we can be taught how to know wisdom whether or not it can be identified with the Truth that might make us free" (p. 284). Thus, once we agree that wisdom is an elusive quality then the search for wisdom becomes an end in itself, whether or not wisdom is truth.

I doubt whether anyone embarks on psychoanalytic treatment to further his or her ability to search for wisdom. But, as a resource, the search as well as the literature is a powerful transformer of painful affects. Bloom found the solace with which to face illness and loss of friends that comes with the territory of aging. But, that cannot be the only benefit from searching for wisdom. There are other benefits to this search as well, as I discuss next.

In searching through the wisdom literature, Bloom contrasts Falstaff and Sancho Panza to illustrate vastly different contexts of wisdom. Both of these men were delighted in being just themselves and prized their own version of knowledge. Rather wistfully, Bloom commented, "I would rather be Falstaff or Sancho Panza than a version of Hamlet or Don Quixote because growing old and ill teaches me that being matters more than knowing" (pp. 97–98). Kohut makes precisely the same point—that is, knowledge is acquired in youth but wisdom comes through the seasoning of time. For both Bloom and Kohut the role of aging and dealing with the experience of transience is an integral part of acquiring wisdom.

There are numerous similarities between Bloom's and Kohut's approaches to wisdom. For Kohut wisdom is acquired through development and maturation. Certainly Kohut would not rule out the contribution that reading makes to one's wisdom. Kohut posited living a life that includes a personally evolved "wisdom" derived through transforming "archaic narcissism." Whereas Bloom does not discuss archaic narcissism, per se, he implies residues of it in his depleted state. He looked at the process of searching among varieties of wisdoms as an enriching, stimulating, calming, eye-opening, and morally instructive and constructive endeavor. For Bloom the search itself was transformative. He presented us with a rainbow of wisdoms as embodied in authors and literary characters. From each we can derive something that is not available from the others. And the variety of wisdoms can speak to us at different times in our lives and in different voices.

Teaching the wisdom literature was Bloom's occupation. Important in his thesis for the current discussion is not whom or what he nominated as works of wisdom. Rather, it is his personal, affectively intense relationship to these authors and their works. He has co-created a personal bond that was not the property of the works, or their authors, or Bloom himself, but rather emerged from his entering into their worlds. Similarly, through aging, illness, and loss of friends, we may feel a need for finding solace in literature, music, art, or nature. All of these can offer solace and rejuvenation, but also an opportunity to transcend our limitations and losses. Simultaneously, we can reconnect with others in whom we can find aspects of our own aspirations and a grander vision of life and the world, as well as reconnect with, and affirm, our ideals.

Searching for "Transcendence"

When we read *Don Quixote* or attend a performance of *Hamlet* or *Die Meistersinger,* we also long for and search for transcendent experiences. Any one of these works can be enjoyed on many levels but their ability to touch so many people over many centuries speaks to their universal quality. They stretch human knowledge by expanding our experience of being human. Their wisdom resides not in what their authors say directly but in the fictional characters that they have contrived, characters that embody human nature, sometimes even in exaggerated form. Hamlet, Falstaff, Don Quixote, and Sancho Panza speak a "truth" that we recognize, that we resonate with, and that we can share with them and others.

Ask an opera enthusiast which characters in an opera should be nominated as embodying wisdom and the chances are that it would be Hans Sachs in *Die Meistersinger* (see chapter 8) and the Marschallin in Richard Strauss's opera, *Der Rosenkavalier.* I don't know what criterion of "wisdom" opera lovers use, but the outstanding quality of the Marschallin in *Rosenkavalier,* an "older woman," is her extraordinary empathy with both the young lover who leaves her as well as the younger woman for whom he leaves her. She is painfully attuned to the passage of time, her transience, and the folly of trying to hold on to one's youth. She understands the relationships between men and women, and having been forced into a loveless marriage at a young age, she does not want to have the same fate befall even her rival. She embodies an ideal combination of empathy, an acceptance of transience, and a sense of bemused, ironic humor, a combination that qualifies for wisdom. In the opening scene of the opera, after she and her young lover have spent a passionate night together, her lover proclaims that nobody knows how wonderful she is. She responds, "Would you want everyone to know?"

The nuanced depiction of this character underscores the distinction between the literary characters that move and inspire us to feel we are in the presence of wisdom, and the authors of this literature. Richard Strauss, the composer, and Hugo von Hofmannsthal, who wrote the libretto of *Der Rosenkavalier,* were not especially noted for their wisdom. Similarly, relatively little is known about the character of Shakespeare, but the play *Hamlet* has proven to be a transcendent experience, including all the different ways in which this role has been interpreted, over the last 500 years. And wisdom did not seem to be the strong suit of Richard Wagner (see chapter 8), yet he created the wise character Hans Sachs in *Die Meistersinger.*

Some of the writers of wisdom literature were as flawed as the wise people I eliminated as illustrative of wisdom earlier in this chapter. So we are clearly addressing their creative products as the sources of our admiration. And in the search for wisdom, to engage with these creative products in literature, art, or music does require our capacity for empathy, as Robert McKee proposed, our capacity to experience a character as "like me." Recall McKee's discussion of empathy and that it is through empathy we connect with a character in a drama. By making this human connection we derive an emotional catharsis through the drama. But with the wisdom literature—for example, with the characters of Hamlet and Don Quixote—emotional catharsis is not the only goal. There is something more, and that is transcendence. These characters, as well as some poems, Biblical passages, paintings, or music, evoke feelings akin to admiration and awe for their embodiment of some ideal transcendence of the human condition.

Ordinarily, when we think of "transcendence" we think in spiritual or philosophical terms. I am using it to connote a sublime, almost uncanny experience tinged with awe as illustrated in an essay by Leonard

Bernstein (1982). He described an uncanny transcendent experience as he browsed through the Kaballah:

> I was suddenly aware of a strange, hidden memory that this was in some way a forbidden book, and I went on reading it; and I came across something that added a new dimension to me.... In the revelation of Rabbi Shimeon it is pointed out that the total manifestations of God are to be understood as Wisdom, or *Chachmah*, but that this cannot exist except in the dual form of male and female; and so *Chachmah* is the father, and Binah, or Understanding, is the Mother.... The two are not separate—but that this is the mystical necessity; they are indivisible.... What a marvelous paradox ... the mother is, after all, a Son of God, just as the Father is: therefore they are one. (pp. 174–175)

Bernstein alludes to a reverence for wisdom, a reverence that is accorded to it in the Kaballah by placing it in the deity, a reverence that Bernstein feels anew as he encounters this passage. Judaism, however, is not the only religion to revere wisdom. Ecclesiastes, part of the Old Testament wisdom literature that Bloom also places in his wisdom literature, reflects Greek influences in its origins and its greatest literary impact has come from the translation to be found in the King James Bible.

Bernstein found himself in particular relationship to wisdom: a position of awe and wonder at ideas that are so simple and yet so profound that they gave him "a new dimension." He gives wisdom a spiritual slant. When Bloom wrote of the wisdom literature, he gave wisdom a secular slant. Yet no less than Bernstein he marveled at the insights about life and the human condition that he encountered. The distinction between spiritual and secular views of transcendence is really only superficial. In both cases being in the presence of transcendence is uplifting. In this search for wisdom and transcendence, empathy is engaged. Both require openness to being so moved; the relationship to the text clearly demands active engagement. Without the wisdom seeker's active participation, exposure to the wisdom literature, art, or music would fall on closed minds.

My point is that the wisdom cannot be passively acquired; rather, the search for wisdom is an active pursuit requiring the inclusion of empathy for its co-creation. And just as the wisdom literature incorporates ideals that are picked up by the empathy of the reader, empathic understanding in treatment potentially opens the doors to inspiration and solace, as well as pointing to a change in perspective: from self-centeredness and despair to inclusiveness and self-acceptance. So, we really cannot engender wisdom in our patients, but we may be able through the co-created treatment process to include glimmers that can potentially inspire and equip a patient to search for wisdom. One more question: Do patients (or analysts, for that matter) really search for wisdom in treatment? I think the answer to that question may depend on which vision of reality is dominant in the responder. Undoubtedly the answer would also rest on cultural and family background and friendships. My friend's father had an impact on me that I have not until now put into words. I believe once we have sensed this elusive quality, wisdom, in another person, book, or work of art, we are prompted to search for more of it.

The wisdom literature includes some incredible humor and we marvel at how wisdom is delivered in these writings. *Don Quixote* would probably be on most lists of the top 10 works of wisdom, if not number 1. This work is hilarious and has brought untold joy to its readers. Although written almost 500 years ago, its humor is timeless because it depicts human nature in ways that have not changed. The qualities Cervantes depicts in Don Quixote, Sancho Panza, and the people they encounter on their quest are still prevalent: greed, pride, self-delusion, and a thirst for revenge. The brilliance of Cervantes lies in his ability to depict these qualities in ways that make them instantly recognizable, anywhere, anytime, in ways that make them "like me."

Cervantes injects an ironic twist into many of Don Quixote and Sancho Panza's adventures. He skewers all shades of the political spectrum. For example, Don Quixote sees a group of men held captive. However, freeing these captives is made absurd when these captives, who appeared to be honorable soldiers and travelers, turn out to be criminals. Once Don Quixote frees them they rob him and Sancho Panza.

Freud (1905b) noted that Don Quixote himself possessed no sense of humor but took himself with utter seriousness. But, if Don Quixote did not depict and take to an absurd extreme truths about human nature, we would not laugh at him and simultaneously at ourselves. He would not be the personification of wisdom as seen through the lens of irony. And, ironically, in our own search for wisdom we can wander alongside Don Quixote who, himself, was the quintessential searcher. Don Quixote never found his Dulcinea, but what a search that was!

11 What Happens to Theory?

In these chapters I have explicitly delineated a theory of treatment focused primarily on the co-creation of nonverbal, implicit, and procedural communications between infants and caretakers, patients and therapists. My emphasis on these dimensions of organization is not intended to downgrade the explicit, verbal, symbolic, and dynamic contents of psychoanalysis, but rather to draw attention to an equally powerful but subtle and often neglected dimension of the treatment relationship.

The implicit, procedural dimension of the therapeutic encounter is contained within an evolving "implicit relational knowing" and a "dyadic expansion of consciousness" that accompany therapist and patient throughout the treatment process, inform each about himself or herself and the other, and further the treatment process implicitly and nonconsciously. To highlight their seminal contribution to therapeutic action, I have placed these dimensions of analyst–patient communication into the foreground and the better known, more traditional psychoanalytic interventions and interpretations into the background.

I am not advocating that explicit, verbal, dynamic interventions be eliminated or ignored. On the contrary, there are numerous instances in the preceding clinical discussions that include dynamics, content-sensitive conflicts, as well as the importance of cognition. However, my emphasis does differ from traditional psychoanalytic perspectives that focus on conflict, defense and compromise, transference and counter-transference, the co-construction of meanings, and selfobject ties.

My overarching conceptual framework used Kohut's work, in particular, "Forms and Transformations of Narcissism," as a springboard. I reframed Kohut's propositions with respect to transformation of the pathologies of the self to emphasize the co-creation and circularity of this process and suggested conceptualizations that would further and clarify "therapeutic action."

Transforming narcissism is a process of transforming affect through empathy, humor, creativity, and expectations met, affirmed, or violated. I am not simply prescribing empathy or humor or creativity as therapeutic tools. Rather, I propose recognition and respect for the unique, individualistic styles of patients and therapists in negotiating their implicit relational knowing. Styles of relating, like visions of reality, do not constitute pathology, but they are indivisible from one's sense of self. Yet they can also obstruct a dyadic expansion of consciousness, and cement a narrow view of oneself and one's relationship to the world.

When Kohut proposed that archaic narcissism is transformed, he was still hovering on a border between conceptualizing transforming structures through analysis, and analysis as a transformative process per se. A transformative process means that two partners are emotionally engaged, and whatever emerges in their interactions is co-created—the property of neither one partner nor the other. As a consequence of their interaction, the two partners are affected by each other and by their own behavior.

A refresher of self- and interactive regulation may be useful here. Self-regulation refers to the individual's continuing regulation of his or her state, affect, and arousal via implicit procedures such as heightening attention or diminishing vigilance. Interactive regulation refers to the impact that therapist and patient have on each other—for example, by leaning toward or away from the partner to regulate degrees of emotional closeness and distance. Both forms of regulation are continually present throughout treatment, whether they are thought about or not—and for better or worse. By attending to this process we are in a better position to understand how the dyad is continually evolving and transforming itself. The same is true of the other two principles—disruption and repair and heightened affective moments, which are also derived from empirical infant studies. These processes that form the bedrock of therapy are seen as a process that works by transforming affect in both partners.

Structures and Process

When Freud (1937) asked whether or not analysis was terminable, and when Kohut (1984) asked how analysis cures, thinking in terms of psychological structures prevailed for both. Even though Rapaport's (1960) definition of structure as process with a slow rate of change predated Kohut's theorizing, it took a number of years until psychoanalysts shifted significantly from static structural formulations toward recognizing processes and systems theories (Lachmann, 1994, 1998).

In these chapters dyadic systems theory (Beebe & Lachmann, 2002; Lachmann, 2000; Thelan & Smith, 1994) has provided the silent and also not so silent scaffold for the examination of the process of treatment. Conceptualizations derived from the empirical infant literature have been extrapolated to apply to the therapist–patient interaction. Prime examples include not only the aforementioned three principles of the organization of experience, but also the establishment of expectations of affective responsivity, the consequences of violating expectations, and the ongoing accompaniment of implicit relational knowing and the dyadic expansion of consciousness that inform the experience of both therapist and patient. However, since these concepts were derived from infant research, they are rooted in nonverbal implicit and explicit dimensions of communication.

Enactments as Communications

In the treatments described in this book, several of the nonconscious procedures engaged in by therapist and patient were discernable through enactments. Usually in discussion of enactments one can discern a patina of criticism attached to the use of this concept. There is a sense that an enactment should not have occurred but that, once it has, perhaps we can learn something about the patient (and ourselves), so maybe it was useful after all. In addition, too often "enactment" is how one therapist describes the work of another therapist to explain why that therapist's patient got worse or got "spuriously" better. Enactments are often used to describe some "unanalytic" behavior by therapist and patient that reeks of transference–countertransference. In usual discourse, enactments are constituted by verbal, symbolic elements, representative of a dynamic unconscious, and as requiring verbal exploration and interpretation and negotiation for their resolution.

However, Karlen Lyons-Ruth's proposition that certain kinds of procedural knowledge can only be expressed through their being enacted leads to a broader view of enactments in the clinical setting. In this view the potential for enactments is ever present. Enactments may constitute communications on a procedural nonverbal level and serve as a legitimate (perhaps the only) way in which the patient can reveal nonconscious, implicit relational themes. As these implicit relational themes become enacted the potential arises for a heightened affective moment. In this book I have described a number of affectively salient moments that determined the subsequent direction of several treatments. Seen from this perspective, whether these nonconscious procedures benefit from, or are made redundant by, translation into words cannot be determined a priori. Neither the "Duck Lake" intervention with Nora nor the "assuming I have grown up" intervention with Sally was subsequently discussed. Both interventions, I believe, did their work and further probing about how each patient felt about my having made these interventions could have poured cold water on their positive affective impact.

My "I don't do windows" comment, however, did require considerable subsequent discussion. Similarly, both Carla's "head banging" and Sally's gift of "the birthday chocolates" were further investigated. The context in which Sally brought the chocolates led me to see the gift in a positive light, yet its meaning was not clear. It had not been self-evident to either of us that she now wanted to share a positive experience with me, even though it entailed seizing sweet chocolates from the jaws of bitter transience. The lead-ups to both Sally's and Carla's enactments were co-created, yet their meaning within the therapeutic process was ambiguous, and hence in need of clarification.

I am making a strong case for the legitimization of enactments as a valuable entry into the subjective life of the patient. But, not all that is "enacted" between analyst and patient is worthy of such respect. Whether a particular enactment qualifies as the best or only way a particular nonconscious, implicit procedure or communication could be brought onto the analytic dialogue is a matter of clinical judgment. My point is that whether a patient–therapist interaction constitutes a communication of hitherto implicit nonconscious procedures or an analytic faux pas needs an on-the-spot assessment. The delicate status of enactments requires distinguishing whether a nonconscious, implicit theme has appeared in the treatment or whether analyst and patient have acted in ways that communicate unconscious motives—for example, of a denigrating or seductive nature.

Nothing in analysis gets a free pass that can be cashed in anywhere, anytime. Placing emphasis on implicit process alters the shape of explicit interventions and interpretations and thus affects therapeutic action. The kind of insight-delivering interpretations that once characterized psychoanalysis is no longer so evident in the cases described. This is not to say that in the treatments illustrated there were any contentless interventions, but rather that the nature of the content as well as the delivery of the interventions has changed. Recall the treatment of Nora and her grandiose "swan" self or Jason and his withdrawal, alienation, and dissociation. For Nora, my description of a Mother's-Day-card model scene was inadvertently sufficient to further an ongoing, self-motivated process that enabled her to address the relevant childhood memories and their current consequences. Interpretations or confrontations of her "grandiosity" or "covert hostility" were unnecessary. For Jason, recognizing a function of his sadness and self-hatred enabled him to become more self-reflective, thereby gradually disentangling himself from the web of childhood experiences that immobilized him.

Experience Near and Experience Distant

And another question: When psychoanalytic treatment is considered in the terms that I have been proposing—principles of salience in the organization of experience, implicit relational knowing, or enactments as communication—how do we relate these conceptualizations to previously established notions of what constitutes psychoanalytic knowledge? That is, what happens to theory? To address this question I think it is helpful to turn to Robert Waelder's (1962; see also Bergmann & Hartman, 1976) schematization of psychoanalytic constructs. A contemporary of Kohut, Waelder placed Freudian psychoanalytic constructs into a hierarchy of increasing abstraction and distance from clinical material. That is, he categorized psychoanalytic formulations from experience near to experience distant. Waelder's hierarchy extends along six levels, observations being the most experience near and the analyst's philosophy of treatment being the most experience distant.

An implication of Waelder's hierarchy is that psychoanalytic theory should be built from the bottom up with the experience nearer levels providing the base upon which the higher levels rest. Metapsychology and philosophy should rest on an empirical and clinically observable base. Of course, that never happens. Philosophy, including the analyst's private implicit philosophy, the analyst's *Weltanschauung,* as well as the analyst's adherence to a particular theoretical framework, invariably trickles down to color clinical observations. Then these theory-saturated observations lead to interpretations that, in turn, ultimately reinforce the analyst's philosophy. Nevertheless, Waelder's levels provide a useful framework for thinking about clinical data and interpretive formulations. I have adapted this hierarchy to provide an organization for the constructs used in the treatments I presented.

Waelder's Level 1, the level of observation, comprises both what the patient reports, including biographical information, and what the analyst can observe directly, such as vocal inflection, facial displays, and body language. For example, Sally's report of her mother's violence, her father's exciting appearances and disappearances, and her abandonment by her husband, as well as her gloomy, detached stance in relation to me, all constitute clinical observations. My dawning awareness of an increasingly less distant relationship that finally emerged in our "intimate" session also qualifies as an implicit observation that was crucial in guiding the treatment. When it surfaced, we co-created an enactment. Following Lyons-Ruth, our evolving implicit relational knowing could only be enacted; Sally had no language to convey it. Sally's hitherto detached stance had gradually morphed into a greater capacity for intimacy with me as she moved on from the beginning phases of her treatment. Initially and for a considerable time into the treatment she protected herself from repeating her traumatization at the hands of her mother and her father, the latter having let her down through his unexpected appearances and disappearances. Gradually, she reconnected with procedures of relating to others that stemmed from her earlier life with both parents and from the positive experiences with her father.

For Sally, more intimate ways of relating had previously been revived in her relationship with her ex-husband. When he abandoned her, that style of relating was again suppressed. The capacity for play and intimacy slowly resurfaced as Sally and I gradually worked our way through the overriding traumatic relationship to her mother and suppressed disappointment in her now-here, now-gone father. Level 1 thus includes not only the observable information from the patient but also the implicit nonverbal relational patterns that emerge and then become apparent through enactment.

On Level 2, observations are organized into clinical interpretations. For example, verbally and explicitly I connected two sources of Sally's fear. She was afraid to alienate her father if she were to express her disappointment at his unexpected arrivals and too quick departures, and she was afraid to alienate her ex-husband were she to complain about his alcoholism. In my interpretations I connected two "reports" by Sally to identify a long-standing organizing theme in her life: accommodating to others lest she be abandoned altogether. Further interpretations addressed her dread that her father would abandon her to the dangerous and unpredictable world of her mother. Consequently, when she failed to prevent her husband from leaving her, this dread was reawakened and confirmed. She failed to hold him and he abandoned her to New York, which turned into the present-day personification of her psychotic mother. These formulations and interventions addressed dynamic connections and conflicts. Simultaneously, through this explicit interpretive process, our implicit connection grew. She could notice me as differentiated from her potentially psychotic mother against whom she had to protect herself by being ever vigilant. She no longer needed to stay prepared to run from me as she once kept herself ready to run for her life should her mother burst into her room at night. These automatic self-protective relational procedures had previously accompanied and constrained our verbal discourse.

Clinical interpretations on this level also can take the form of enactments when these are accommodated within the dyad. The accommodation need not be verbalized. When Sally asked me the question: "Did you grow up in New York?" she implicitly and nonconsciously signaled a decisive shift toward expectations of positive affective responsivity. Therefore, she risked being retraumatized either by encountering her psychotic mother or her abandoning father. The implicit relational patterns described in Level 1 had gradually been transformed though our self- and interactive regulations, repair of disruptions, and heightened affective moments. In my humorous response I implicitly interpreted her fear of retraumatization by conveying that I welcomed her attempt to risk a more intimate contact with me. My surprising and humorous response thus was my "interpretation," and the only interpretation I offered on this occasion.

Level 3 is the level of clinical generalizations. In classical Freudian theory the Oedipus complex would occupy this level. However, here affective and procedural memories come into play more directly. For Sally, her fear and hatred of her mother and her idealization of her father could indeed qualify as an Oedipal struggle. But, in working with Sally I was focused on understanding how her distance from me derived from a vast self-protective effort. She had to survive on her own and avoid retraumatization at all cost. Her mother dramatically shattered her expectations of living in a safe, affectively responsive world—expectations that had apparently been met during the first 6 years of her life.

Thus, my clinical generalizations in this case were focused on the resulting self-pathology. Sally's self-pathology was characterized by persistent depressive affect and anxiety, by self-doubts and self-depreciation, and by a dread of abandonment. Her relational procedures worked against her having experiences that would disconfirm expectations of being endangered and abandoned. Such expectations had been engaged implicitly in the treatment process. Gradually, these expectations and her anxious, depressive affect had been transformed through my empathic understanding, humor, play, and spontaneity, as well as through meeting expectations of affective responsivity and enactments.

In moving from Level 1 to Level 3 I am taking advantage of hindsight to no small degree. Yet, even during the treatment, I did try to remain anchored in the realm of clinical process as best I could. I sensed when she was ready to move beyond the point where the world was divided between the dangers associated with her mother and the safety and adoration associated with her father. In retrospect, it is clear to me now how implicit relational knowing had made its way into our dialogue. She had assumed that she needed to keep the same self-protective distance from me in the sessions that she had developed over the years and that had lately become massively reinforced by the shock of her husband's departure.

Level 4, clinical theory, contains the constructs that provide the scaffold for thinking further about the aforementioned processes as they appear in the treatment. In Waelder's schematization of classical Freudian theory, the transference neurosis, seen as a product of the patient's infantile neurosis transferred to the analyst, was placed on this level. Rather than thinking of the transference as solely a displacement or projection on the part of the patient, the assumptions that governed these cases were that the therapeutic dialogue, transference, and model scenes are all co-created. Recall that co-created does not mean that analyst and patient contribute similarly, equally, or symmetrically to the emergent dialogue.

What I have proposed about other aspects of the patient–therapist dialogue can be thought of as at the level of clinical theory as well. For example, differentiating between leading and trailing edge formulations in this dialogue is part of clinical theory. The same can be said for the concept of expectancies and their relation to expectations. Recall that infants develop expectancies based on experiences as to how a particular interaction will go and what they can anticipate. Expectancies are early, presymbolic interaction "structures" but, truth be told, whereas they do have a certain stability, they really fulfill Rapaport's definition of undergoing a slow rate of change. How these expectancies congeal in any given moment into expectations and how these expectations are affirmed, surpassed, or violated, with whatever consequences, take us into the realm of clinical theory.

Perhaps some readers will find evidence of Level 5, metapsychology, in these chapters but I did my best to stay clear of that level of abstraction. I think that psychoanalysis can get along very well without metapsychology clogging up its theory. Level 6 consists of the personally held philosophy or vision of the world, reality, and human nature of the analyst. As I indicated earlier in this book, I have tried to include and balance all four visions.

We can't really get the analyst's vision or visions of life out of treatment or even out of theory. The best we can do is to be brutally precise in how our assessment of our vision impacts our behavior and our theory. Now, as I look back on these pages, I find somewhat to my surprise that my interest in the four visions that Schafer delineated has surfaced in the emphasis I placed, respectively, on the possibility of transforming narcissism (comic), the role of empathy forging a bond (romantic), the necessity for humor (ironic), and the importance of recognition of transience (tragic).

The Centrality of Affect

In my emphasis on affect in this book I join the vast literature that holds that affect is the crucial point of contact for change to occur in psychoanalytic treatment. Affect can be transformed directly, without verbally transmitted meanings, as in music, and it can also be transformed in the music of the analytic dialogue, whether through tone and inflections or through the myriad of nonverbal, procedural, implicit communications. Affect is also stirred up through the symbols and meanings of verbal discourse. However, unless that discourse with its interventions and interpretations evokes an affective resonance, nothing can get transformed. I am stating here what has been well known in psychoanalysis and discussed as far back as Fenichel's (1941) dictum that for an interpretation to be effective it must come at an affectively urgent moment. What I have added is an emphasis on pathways to that affective change that have not been so well accepted or recognized. The implicit dimension of the evolving therapist–patient interaction, which is neither an aspect of the transference–countertransference dimension of the therapeutic relationship nor a "real" relationship (Greenson, 1967), provides a powerful, constant, nonconscious and nonverbal connection that develops subtly as the treatment progresses. If it grows, it does so with the speed of a blade of grass and yet it crucially provides gradual implicit input into the experience of both therapist and patient, to themselves and about each other.

The notion that changes in affect are the means whereby transformation occurs is also implicated in the use of humor, play, and metaphor in treatment. Indeed, in a theory that emphasizes implicit verbal and nonverbal communication in the transformative process, there is also room for humor, play, spontaneity, and the use of metaphors. These are not "parameters" that can be introduced on the condition that they can be "eliminated" through analytic work. Rather, they are a genuine part of the therapeutic dialogue no matter whether they emerge overtly, as with Eric and his written spoof on his therapy, or whether they come in the form of enactments, the culminating manifestations of procedural enactive representations that have been interactively organized by therapist and patient.

In fact, as I now reflect on these issues, it seems to me that the engagement of enactive representations lies close to the very heart of play, humor, and the therapeutic use of metaphor. These enactive interactions carry the treatment forward by providing an avenue of communication through jointly organized procedures. They open a level of communication that would not have been possible through narrative alone. They are clearly affectively engaging and can serve as powerful implicit or indirect confrontations and interpretations.

If the analyst's use of humor once got a bad rap in psychoanalysis, the analyst's use of imagination got an even worse one. Imagination tended to be relegated to "fantasy" or "phantasy," both of which were seen as overflowing with id derivatives and thus deserving of serious analytic attention. Patients might be encouraged to fantasize, but in general analysts only offered fantasies about what they imagined their patients might be fantasizing. The analyst's imagination was placed in a straightjacket, although analysts were allowed to make analogies. Recall that in my consultation with Judy she reported that her analyst had asked her if she had been on her high school debating team. Had a patient asked this of her analyst, it would have been (and rightly so) open to analytic inquiry.

In my treatments, I use my imagination and play with metaphors. I am in agreement with Spezzano, who comments, "Imagination is the name we give to the human capacity to generate metaphor and metaphor is the primary link between affect and word" (1995, p. 31). And that's the point: The analyst's use of metaphor and of his or her imagination is best used in the service of promoting a process that facilitates affective change. It is in this sense that I used metaphors in my treatment with Nora.

The context for my "Duck Lake" comment was co-created at and for the moment. Her use of the swan–duck metaphor had opened the door, but I then entered and joined her "fun." In my follow-up comment to her about a prospective date with a "dangerous" man that it would be like the swan inviting a vulture for dinner, I rushed past a more detailed discussion of the shift to a humorous interaction while imaginatively reaching for an even broader, more playful context. In this instance, although the context was one of playfulness and we were both giving our imaginations free reign, the topic we addressed was serious: Nora's aversion to boredom and the lengths to which she had gone to avoid boredom and maintain excitement in her life. The consequences of these endeavors were highly problematic and self-defeating in her life. But, our dialogue was now being carried on simultaneously on two levels: playful and serious. This enabled us to address, head on, issues that were shame ridden and that Nora had avoided in her prior treatment. We were engaged through humor and play; that, in turn, allowed for something like the aesthetic distancing that occurs in the theater in the form of a "suspension of disbelief." For the moment we agreed to play while also engaged in serious work. Our "agreement" was implicit and signaled by Nora's enjoyment as our dialogue continued. Our humor had shifted into creative and imaginative play. The emerging imagery took off from her serious comments and concerns and then served as a source of pleasure while promoting further affectively laden explorations of her aversion to "boredom."

Play in psychoanalytic treatment has similar functions to children's play. It provides a rehearsal or practice space for engaging in life conflicts, and allows for competition and cooperation in highly regulated, controlled, and therefore safe conditions. Play allows for a range of affective experience at a modulated level; in play, expressions of affect can thus be freer and more varied. Playful interactions in treatment follow the same rules implicitly. The implicit acceptance of a situation as playful makes possible the suspension of disbelief and reinforces the patient's trust; it also conveys the therapist's trust that the playfulness will be experienced by the patient in the spirit in which it is offered. Playing thus not only can be an intimate experience for therapist and patient but also can convey the therapist's respect for the patient as a trustworthy player. Knowing how to play and when to play occurs at the level of implicit relational knowing. Contrary to some analysts' expectations that humor and play can conceal negative feelings of patient and analyst, my point is that humor, play, and metaphor can also expand the narrative envelope (Lichtenberg, Lachmann, & Fosshage, 1992).

An emphasis on the implicit relational aspects of process is, however, crucial to understanding therapeutic action. Attending to process at this level changes what is said; the kinds of insight-delivering interpretations that characterized classical psychoanalysis are no longer so evident. Not that the content they contained is absent or ruled out, but the delivery has changed. Recall the treatment of Nora and her "grandiose self" or Jason and his withdrawal, alienation, and dissociation. For Nora, my description of the Mother's Day–card model scene was sufficient to further a process that enabled her to address the relevant childhood memories and their current consequences. For Jason, my recognizing a function of his sadness and self-hatred enabled him to become more self-reflective and thereby gradually to disentangle himself from the web of childhood experiences that immobilized him.

Expectations and Violations of Expectations

I have given expectations and violations of expectations a key role in both the development of pathology and of creativity and in promoting affective transformation in the course of treatment. Nora grew up with two contradictory sets of expectations. As the brightest, highest functioning, and most ambitious member in her family, she developed an expectation of having her "specialness" recognized. This expectation led to lifelong interpersonal difficulties that brought her into treatment. Simultaneously, as depicted in the Mother's Day–card model scene, she was subject to painful disappointments not only in her expectation of being seen as "special" but also as a hopeful recipient of ordinary affective responsivity. As is always the case, Nora became familiar with both roles in the world of violated expectations. Her difficulties with her coworkers centered on the extent to which she violated *their* expectations of affective responsivity.

Sally's expectations, evolving in her first 8 years, were of living in a physically safe, nurturing environment. Her mother's apparently rapidly developing psychosis then shattered that sense of safety and security. Thereafter, she was not even physically safe in her home. She turned to and clung to her father. In consequence, she felt devastated, abandoned, and in literal danger when he left—a repeated violation of her hopes. In her marriage, a sense of safety derived from her earlier years was revived, and she also experienced the thrill and security of refinding her father when in the arms of her husband. Sally shielded herself from the shakiness of her security by closing her eyes to aspects of her father's emotional and financial unreliability. Later she did the same with her husband's alcoholism. She sought to insulate her sense of safety and security from being violated by shock trauma at the expense of continuing strain trauma (J. Sandler, 1967).

Viewing these treatments with respect to the place that violations of expectations occupied in the formation of a person's *Weltanschauung*, character style, and self-defeating patterns offers several therapeutic benefits. First, it provides an empathic entrée into painful, disappointing, and yet crucially formative aspects of the person's life. Second, it can contribute to the co-creation of model scenes that can integrate meanings derived from affect-laden images and visceral bodily experiences. Third, it can open a window for the therapist's sensing opportunities to include joyful, humorous surprises, co-creating new contexts. These therapeutic violations of expectations can enhance and further transform an intimate affective responsivity between therapist and patient. The violation becomes a heightened affective moment in the best sense. Fourth, expectations and violations of expectations are basic to establishing a sense of presence in the world, of inhabiting a world that to the child permits an expansion of a sense of agency and autonomy as well as increasing comfort and familiarity with the world one inhabits. The familiarity is derived from repeated and generalized early and lifelong experiences of affective responsivity. Organized from infancy onward, these experiences provide a template for interactions between self and others. In that context, experiencing violations of expectations by others establishes new expectations that violations can be dealt with and are not necessarily emotionally fatal, but occupy a range that can be discriminated. Similar benefits accrue from certain violations of expectations and disruptions in the therapeutic process. Chief among them is the developing of expectations that surprises can be pleasant and that even untoward violations will eventuate in efforts at repair and, ultimately, in therapist and patient coming closer together rather than the patient's expectations of abandonment by the therapist.

Balancing expectations of affective responsivity and violations of expectations is basic to establishing a sense of one's presence in the world. To the adult it entails the ability to suspend disbelief and enjoy surprises and some thrills. Expectations and violations of expectations are central organizing principles that touch a variety of character traits. Organized from infancy onward, they provide a template for interactions between self and others. Such "others" may range from significant family members or their representatives, groups of people, audiences, and strangers. Under adverse developmental conditions, classes of people (young children, classmates, music critics) may become targets for either triumphing through violating their expectations or for inflicting the humiliation and pain of having one's expectations violated.

Self-Transformation

At times, throughout this book I have considered the possibilities of self-transformation, a process in which a person derives feedback from his or her own activity, and that this, in turn, causes the person to shift in ways that are new. The shift eventuates in a new creation or a new idea that subtly or even dramatically continues to shift or "transform" the person. The now transformed person then continues along a new path. This can be as simple as hitting a handball against a wall and becoming more and more excited about one's adeptness, the changes of angles, and the increasing skill in keeping the ball in play. However, my favorite example, and the one I keep coming back to, is of Stravinsky composing *The Rite of Spring* at the piano. In composing this piece, playing it, hearing himself play it, and reacting to the wondrous sounds he was hearing transformed the composer/pianist. As in Sameroff and Chandler's transformational model, from one moment to the next neither Stravinsky nor the music he was composing remained the same. They were both transformed. The expressions Stravinsky's friend observed on Stravinsky's face leave no doubt that this was an affective transformation.

Self-transformations of this kind are frequently reported as part of the process of artistic creation. Obviously, it is rare for another person to be present and to be in a position to report such an event. However, recall the film *Pollack* about the life of Jackson Pollack. It contains a vivid scene of the painter becoming more involved and excited, agitated and enthralled, as he experiments with ever more daring, yes, and artistically defiant ways of applying paint to the canvas. That's another example of a self-transformation. Of course this scene was a co-creation of an author, director, and actor, but, I believe, based on reports that this scene corresponded to an experience in Pollack's life.

When I began writing about transformation as a co-created process I had in mind "two people." Along the way I began to see that self-transformation needs to be given its just due because it can and does happen, not only in the arts but also in psychoanalytic treatment and in the process of writing. When working alone, one's partner in the co-creative process is the material that provides the feedback: the music produced by the piano, the paint on the canvas, the words one hears oneself say to the patient or that one has placed on the paper. Once the first new sound is made, the first new splatter of paint has been dripped on a canvas, the first new newly formed connection has been uttered to a patient or recorded on paper, the transformative process has been set in motion.

Much of the time we, artists and analysts, work in a methodical if not plodding way. That's not self-transformation. But sometimes we become engaged in our own experience in a new way that makes the feedback from what we have been doing a surprise, a "violation of our own expectation." And we are momentarily thrilled. We embark on an affectively moving process of self-transformation.

In writing this last chapter and reviewing the earlier chapters for a final time, I began to look back in a different way at the cases I reported. Some of the discussions in this chapter went far beyond what I understood about the treatments at the time. As these new views on old material popped into my mind, I felt exhilaration but also regret. The regret was that I had not had this particular understanding earlier, in the course of those treatments. The exhilaration was that I had discovered something new, now. The changes in my view of some of these cases were affectively moving to me. So, transformation remains a co-created process but the partner in that process can even be oneself—oneself with a piano, with an easel, or with a word processor.

Termination

Does the centrality of process impact on the question of the terminability of analysis? Does attention to process dull the analyst–patient relationship by making it less "authority" dominated? Or, does it heighten the relationship because it is more egalitarian? Does a focus on process increasingly enmesh analyst and patient, prompting both to feel more connected to each other and more "moved" by the ongoing treatment, hence making termination more painful? Or, does it take the wind out of the analytic sails and make termination a nonevent?

There are no general answers to these questions, only a case-by-case assessment. In the treatments I described, some terminations were "forced" because patient and family left New York; others were expected, as when Eric married and became a father. I met Jason several years after we terminated and he was visibly less anxious and quite satisfied with his life. The termination had been comparatively uneventful and when we met, by chance in the street, he did not speak of missing me. Another patient, however, said to me in his last session, paraphrasing Humphrey Bogart in *Casablanca*, "I'll always have Frank." In some cases therapy was resumed some years after terminations, as when Nora returned after she was diagnosed with multiple sclerosis. She responded to this news with remarkable resilience.

Leo Tolstoy begins *Anna Karenina* by announcing: "All happy families are alike; each unhappy family is unhappy in its own way." Our patients, often the children of unhappy families, undergo a treatment process that is geared to recognizing each patient's "own way." The termination of these treatments follows along the same line. They are all unique and proceed in their own way.

Coda

It's been more than 50 years since the Bellevue seminar and psychoanalysis has undergone some major transformations. I use the term *transformations* as I have throughout this book. The changes in psychoanalysis have come from several directions. The one, of numerous changes, that I credit here is in the psychoanalytic consumers. It's not that the patients who seek treatment have changed so remarkably. In fact I made this point in the preface. It's their expectations that have changed and they demand a more affectively engaged analyst. And they are right to do so. If affect is the quality that can be transformed, then a treatment approach whereby the analyst conceals his or her affectivity, even if for consistent theoretical purposes, misses the boat.

As an experiment, I told one of my study groups the same story that the analyst at Bellevue told the seminar. I told them that I had dinner with a group of colleagues at a restaurant, saw and greeted a patient of mine, who then proceeded to pay for everyone's dinner. I asked the group what they thought of this. They immediately asked me about the patient, what was my relationship with him, the transference, what had been happening in the treatment. They thought there was no way of understanding this event without that context. I was delighted by their responses. I was as proud of the members of my study group as the analyst at Bellevue appeared to have been of his seminar participants. We have certainly changed as analysts. Like analysts a half century ago, we no doubt continue to miss the boat or make analytic faux pas. But I think we are more likely to see these as co-created and search to see how, where, and why we participated as we did.

References

Alexandrian, S. (1970). *Surrealist art*. London: Thames & Hudson.

Allen, W. (2006). *Scoop*. Focus Features (Film).

Arlow, J. (1969). Unconscious fantasy and disturbances of conscious experience. *Psychoanalytic Quarterly, 38*, 1–27.

Aron, L. (1996). *A meeting of minds*. Hillsdale, NJ: The Analytic Press.

Aron, L. (2006). Analytic impass and the third. *International Journal of Psycho-Analysis, 87*, 349–368.

Balint, M. (1969). Trauma and object relations. *International Journal of Psycho-Analysis, 50*, 429–435.

Bargh, J. A., Chen, M., & Burrows, L. (1996). The automaticity of social behavior: Direct effects of trait concept and stereotype activation in action. *Journal of Personality and Social Psychology, 71*, 230–244.

Basch, M. (1983). Empathic understanding: A review of the concept and some theoretical considerations. *Journal of the American Psychoanalytic Association, 31*, 101–126.

Beebe, B., & Lachmann, F. M. (2002). *Infant research and adult treatment: Co-constructing interactions*. Hillsdale, NJ: The Analytic Press.

Beebe, B., Lachmann, F. M., & Jaffe, J. (1997). Mother–infant interaction structures and presymbolic self- and object representations. *Psychoanalytic Dialogues, 7*, 133–182.

Bergmann, M., & Hartman, F. (1976). *The evolution of psychoanalytic thought*. New York: Basic Books.

Bernstein, L. (1976). *The unanswered question*. Cambridge, MA: Harvard University Press.

Bernstein, L. (1982). *Findings*. Simon and Schuster: New York.

Bloom, H. (2004). *Where shall wisdom be found?* New York: Riverhead Books.

Bodansky, R. (2004). *The benefits of humor in psychoanalysis*. Paper presented at European Federation for Self Psychology, Oslo, Sweden, May 21.

Boston Change Process Study Group, Stern, D., Sander, L., Nahum, J., Harrison, A., Lyons-Ruth, K., Morgan, A., et al. (1998). Noninterpretive mechanisms in psychoanalytic therapy: The "something more" than interpretation. *International Journal of Psycho-Analysis, 79*, 903–921.

Boston Change Process Study Group, Bruschweiler-Stern, N., Harrison, A., Lyons-Ruth, K., Morgan, A., Nahum, J., Sander, L., et al. (2002). Explicating the implicit: The local level and the microprocess of change in the analytic situation. *International Journal of Psycho-Analysis, 83*, 1051–1061.

Brok, A. (2006). A brief Dali-ance: The mystery of the Freud portrait. *Round Robin Newsletter, 21*, 7–8, 20–24.

Bucci, W. (1985). Dual coding: A cognitive model for psychoanalytic research. *Journal of the American Psychoanalytic Association, 33*, 571–608.

Bucci, W. (1997). *Psychoanalysis and cognitive science*. New York: Guilford Press.

Buchsbaum, H., & Emde, R. (1990) Play narratives in 36-month-old children—Early moral development and family relationships. *Psychoanalytic Study of the Child, 45*, 129–155.

Chagall, M. (1994). *My life*. New York: Da Capo Press.

Chasseguet-Smirgel, J. (1984). *Creativity and perversion*. London: Free Association Books.

Cocteau, J. (1991). *Diary of an unknown*. New York: Paragon House.

Cohen, J., & Tronick, E. (1983). Three-month-old infant's reaction to simulated maternal depression. *Child Development, 54*, 185–193.

Cormier, S. (1981). A match–mismatch theory of limbic system function. *Physiological Psychology, 19*, 727–730.

Dali, S. (1942). *The secret life of Salvador Dali*. New York: Dial Press.

Dali, S., & Parinaud, A. (1976). *The unspeakable confessions of Salvador Dali*. New York: W. H. Allen.

Darwin, C. (1871). *The expression of emotion in man and animal*. London: Murray.

Davidson, R., & Fox, N. (1982). Asymmetrical brain activity discriminates between positive and negative affective stimuli in human infants. *Science, 218,* 1235–1237.

Dawson, G. (1992). Infants and mothers with depressive symptoms: Neurophysiological and behavioral findings related to attachment status. *Infant Behavior and Development,* Abstract Issue, *15,* 117.

Demos, V. (1984). Empathy and affect. Reflections on infant experience. In J. Lichtenberg, M. Bornstein, & D. Silver (Eds.), *Empathy 2* (pp. 9–34). Hillsdale, NJ: The Analytic Press.

Demos, V., & Kaplan, S. (1986). Motivation and affect reconsidered: Affect biographies of two infants. *Psychoanalytic Contemporary Thought, 10,* 147–221.

Dimberg, U., Thunberg, M., & Elmehed, K. (2000). Unconscious facial reactions to emotional facial expressions. *Psychological Science, 11,* 86–89.

Dimen, M. (2001). Perversion is us? Eight notes. *Psychoanalytic Dialogues, 11,* 825–860.

Ekman, P., Friesen, W., & Ancoli, S. (1980). Facial signs of emotional experience. *Journal of Personality and Social Psychology, 39,* 1125–1134.

Ekman, P., Levenson, R., & Frieson, W. (1983). Autonomic nervous system activity distinguishes among emotions. *Science, 221,* 1208–1210.

Eliot, S. (2003). A clinical example of perversions and the regulation of self. *Psychoanalytic Dialogues, 13,* 313–326.

Emde, R. (1990). Mobilizing fundamental modes of development: Empathic availability and therapeutic action. *Journal of the American Psychoanalytic Association, 38,* 881–913.

Erikson, E. (1959). The problem of ego identity. *Psychological Issues, 1,* 101–164.

Feldstein, S., & Welkowitz, J. (1978). A chronography of conversation. In defense of an objective approach. In W. Siegman & S. Feldstein (Eds.), *Nonverbal behavior in communication* (pp. 329–377). Hillsdale, NJ: Lawrence Erlbaum Associates.

Fenichel, O. (1941). Problems of psychoanalytic technique. New York: Psychoanalytic Quarterly Press.

Fenichel, O. (1955). *The psychoanalytic theory of neurosis.* London: Routledge & Kegan Paul Ltd.

Ferenczi, S. (1933). Confusion of tongues between adults and the child. In E. Jones (Ed.), *Final contributions to the problems and methods of psychoanalysis* (pp. 156–167). London: The Hogarth Press [1955].

Field, T., Healy, B., Goldstein, S., Perry, D., Bendell, D., Schanberg, S., et al. (1988). Infants of depressed mothers show "depressed" behavior even with nondepressed adults. *Child Development, 59,* 1569–1579.

Fonagy, P., & Target, M. (1998). Mentalization and the changing aims of child psychoanalysis. *Psychoanalytic Dialogues, 8,* 87–114.

Fonagy, P., Gergely, G., Jurist, E., & Target, M. (2002). *Affect regulation, mentalization, and the development of the self.* New York: Other Press.

Fosha, D. (2000). *The transforming power of affect.* New York: Basic Books.

Fosshage, J. (2003). Contextualizing self psychology and relational psychoanalysis. Bidirectional influences and proposed synthesis. *Contemporary Psychoanalysis, 39,* 411–448.

Fosshage, J. (2005). The explicit and implicit domains in psychoanalytic change. *Psychoanalytic Inquiry, 25,* 516–539.

Freud, A. (1972). Comments on aggression. *International Journal of Psycho-Analysis, 53,* 163–171.

Freud, S. (1905a). Three essays on the theory of sexuality. *Standard Edition* (7, pp. 125–243). London: Hogarth Press [1953].

Freud, S. (1905b). Jokes and their relation to the unconscious. *Standard Edition* (8, pp. 3–249). London: Hogarth Press [1960.]

Freud, S. (1913). The claims of psychoanalysis on the interest of the non-psychological sciences. *Standard Edition* (13, pp. 176–190). London: Hogarth Press [1953].

Freud, S. (1916). On transience. *Standard Edition* (14, pp. 302–307). London: Hogarth Press [1957].

Freud, S. (1927a). Fetishism. *Standard Edition* (21, pp. 147–157). London: Hogarth Press [1961].

Freud, S. (1927b). Dostoevsky and parracide. *Standard Edition* (21, pp. 177–196). London: Hogarth Press [1961].

Freud, S. (1937). Analysis terminable and interminable. *Standard Edition* (23, pp. 221–253). London: Hogarth Press [1964].

Gazzaniga M., & LeDoux, J (1978). *The integrated mind.* New York: Plenum.

Gladwell, M. (2005). *Blink.* New York: Little, Brown and Company.

Glover, E. (1959). *The technique of psycho-analysis.* London: Balliere, Tidall & Cox.

Godley, W. (2001). Saving Masud Khan. *London Review of Books, 23,* 22 February, 3–7.

Godley, W. (2004). Commentary. *International Journal of Psycho-Analysis*, *85*, 42–43.

Goldberg, A. (1995). *The problem of perversion: The view from self psychology*. New Haven, CT: Yale University Press.

Goldberg, E. (2005). The wisdom paradox: How your mind can grow stronger as your brain grows older. *Cerebrum*, *7*, 103–121.

Green, A. (1983). The dead mother. In *On private madness*. Madison, CT: International Universities Press.

Greenson, R. R. (1967). *The technique and practice of psychoanalysis*. Madison, CT: International Universities Press.

Grey, A. (1992). On being a male analyst: The reluctant discovery of a troublesome goldmine. *International Forum of Psychoanalysis*, *1*, 20–29.

Grotjahn, M. (1957). *Beyond laughter*. New York: McGraw–Hill.

Hadley, J. (1983). The representational system. A bridging concept for psychoanalysis and neurophysiology. *International Review of Psychoanalysis*, *10*, 13–30.

Hadley, J. (1989). The neurobiology of motivational systems. In J. Lichtenberg, *Psychoanalysis and motivation* (pp. 227–372), Hillsdale, NJ: The Analytic Press.

Hanley, M. A. F. (Ed.). (1995). Papers on masochism. New York: New York University Press.

Irvine, D. (1911). *Wagner's bad luck*. London: Watts & Co.

Jacobs, T. (2001). On misreading and misleading patients: Some reflections on communications, miscommunications, and countertransference enactments. *International Journal of Psycho-Analysis*, *82*, 653–669.

James, W. (1890). *Principles of psychology*. New York: Holt.

Jason, L. A., Reichler, A., King, C., Madsen, D., Camacho, J., & Marchese, W. (2001). The measurement of wisdom: A preliminary effort. *Journal of Community Psychology*, *29*, 585–598.

Khan, M. R. (1960). Regression and integration in the analytic setting: A clinical essay on the transference and counter-transference aspects of these phenomena. *International Journal of Psycho-Analysis*, *41*, 130–146.

Kohut, H. (1957). *Death in Venice* by Thomas Mann: A story about the disintegration of artistic sublimation. In P. Ornstein (Ed.), *The search for the self* (Vol. 1, pp. 107–130). Madison, CT: International Universities Press, 1978.

Kohut, H. (1959). Introspection, empathy and psychoanalysis: An examination of the relationship between mode of observation and theory. In P. Ornstein (Ed.), *The search for the self* (Vol. 1, pp. 205–232). Madison, CT: International Universities Press, 1978.

Kohut, H. (1966). Forms and transformations of narcissism. In P. Ornstein (Ed.), *The search for the self* (Vol. 1, pp. 427–460). Madison, CT: International Universities Press, 1978.

Kohut, H. (1968). The psychoanalytic treatment of narcissistic personality disorders—Outline of a systematic approach. In P. Ornstein (Ed.), *The search for the self* (Vol. 1, pp. 477–510). Madison, CT: International Universities Press, 1978.

Kohut, H. (1971). *The analysis of the self.* Madison, CT: International Universities Press.

Kohut, H. (1972). Thoughts on narcissism and narcissistic rage. In P. Ornstein (Ed.), *The search for the self* (Vol. 2. pp. 615–659). Madison, CT: International Universities Press (1978).

Kohut, H. (1977). *The restoration of the self.* Madison, CT: International Universities Press.

Kohut, H. (1982). Introspection, empathy, and the semicircle of mental health. In P. Ornstein (Ed.), *The search for the self* (Vol. 4). Madison, CT: International Universities Press, 1991.

Kohut, H. (1984). *How does analysis cure?* Chicago: University of Chicago Press.

Lachmann, A. (2001). The theme of cuckoldry in *Othello*. In A. Goldberg (Ed.), *The narcissistic patient revisited: Progress in self psychology* (Vol. 17). Hillsdale, NJ: The Analytic Press.

Lachmann, F. M. (1985). On transience and the sense of temporal continuity. *Contemporary Psychoanalysis, 21,* 193–200.

Lachmann, F. M. (1990). On some challenges to clinical theory in the treatment of character pathology. In A. Goldberg (Ed.), *Progress in self psychology* (Vol. 4, pp. 59–67). New York: Guilford.

Lachmann, F. M. (1994). From narcissism to self pathology: New pathology or new perspective on pathology. *International Forum of Psychoanalysis, 3,* 157–163.

Lachmann, F. M. (1998). From narcissism to self pathology to ...? *Psychoanalysis and Psychotherapy, 15,* 5–26.

Lachmann, F. M. (2000). *Transforming aggression: Psychotherapy with the difficult-to-treat patient.* Northvale, NJ: Jason Aronson.

Lachmann, F. M. (2001). Dialectics forever: Reply to commentaries. *Psychoanalytic Dialogues, 11*, 213–219.

Lachmann, F. M. (2003). The devil is in the details. *Psychoanalytic Dialogues, 13*, 326–341.

Lachmann, F.M. (2004). Beyond the mainstreams. *Psychoanalytic Inquiry, 24*, 576–592.

Lachmann, F., & Lachmann, A. (1992). Mary Tyrone's long day's journey. *The Annals of Psychoanalysis, 20*, 235–244.

Lachmann, F. M., & Lichtenberg, D. (1992). Model scenes: Implications for psychoanalytic treatment. *Journal of the American Psychoanalytic Association, 40*, 117–137.

Lashley, K. S. (1951). The problem of serial order in behavior. In L. A. Jefress (Ed.), *Cerebral mechanisms in behavior: The Hixon symposium* (pp. 112–136). New York: Wiley.

Lemma, A. (2005). The many faces of lying. *International Journal of Psycho-Analysis, 86*, 737–753.

Levitin, D. J. (2006). *This is your brain*. New York: Dutton.

Lichtenberg, J. D. (1984). The empathic mode of perception and alternative vantage points for psychoanalytic work. In J. Lichtenberg, M. Bornstein, & D. Silver (Eds.), *Empathy II* (pp. 113–136). Hillsdale, NJ: The Analytic Press.

Lichtenberg, J. D. (in press). The clinical power of metaphoric experience. *Psychoanalytic Inquiry*.

Lichtenberg, J. D., Lachmann, F. M., & Fosshage, J. (1992). *Self and motivational systems*. Hillsdale, NJ: The Analytic Press.

Lichtenberg, J. D., Lachmann, F. M., & Fosshage, J. (1994). *The clinical exchange*. Hillsdale, NJ: The Analytic Press.

Lichtenberg, J. D., Lachmann, F. M., & Fosshage, J. (2002). *A spirit of inquiry*. Hillsdale, NJ: The Analytic Press.

Loewald, H. (1980). *Papers on psychoanalysis*. New Haven, CT: Yale University Press.

Lyons-Ruth, K. (1999). The two-person unconscious: Intersubjective dialogue, enactive representation, and the emergence of new forms of relational organization. *Psychoanalytic Dialogues, 19*, 576–617.

Lyons-Ruth, K. (2003). Dissociation and the parent–infant dialogue: A longitudinal perspective from attachment research. *Journal of the American Psychoanalytic Association, 51*, 883–911.

Lyons-Ruth, K., Bruschweiler-Stern, N., Harrison, A., Morgan, A., Journal, N., Sander, L., et al. (1998). Implicit relational knowing: Its role in development and psychoanalytic treatment. *Infant Mental Health Journal, 19*, 282–291.

Mailer, N. (1996). *Portrait of Picasso as a young man.* New York: Warner Books.

Marder, E. (2001). *Dead time.* Stanford, CA: Stanford University Press.

Mayes, L. C., & Cohen, D. J. (1996). Children's developing theory of mind. *Journal of the American Psychoanalytic Association, 44,* 117–142.

McKee, R. (1997). *Story.* New York: Harper Collins.

Meltzoff, A. (1985). The roots of cognitive and social development: Models of man's original nature. In T. Fields & N. Fox (Eds.), *Social perception in infants* (pp. 1–30). Norwood, NJ: Ablex.

Meltzoff, A. (1990). Foundations for developing a concept of self: The role of imitation in relating self to other and the value of social mirroring, and self practice in infancy. In D. Cicchetti & M. Beeghly (Eds.), *The self in transition: Infancy to childhood* (pp. 139–164). Chicago: University of Chicago Press.

Meltzoff, A., & Borton, R. (1979). Intermodal matching by human neonates. *Nature, 282,* 403–404.

Meuris, J. (2004). *Rene Magritte.* Cologne: Taschen.

Miller, J. (1985). How Kohut actually worked. In A. Goldberg (Ed.), *Progress in self psychology* (Vol. 1, pp. 13–32). New York: Guilford Press.

Mitchell, S. (1993). *Hope and dread in psychoanalysis.* New York: Basic Books.

Mithen, S. (2006). *The singing Neanderthals.* Cambridge, MA: Harvard University Press.

Murray, L. (1991). Intersubjectivity, object relations theory, and empirical evidence from mother–infant interactions. *Infant Mental Health Journal, 12,* 219–232.

Murray, L., & Trevarthen, C. (1985). Emotion regulation of interactions between 2-month-old infants and their mothers. In T. Field & N. Fox (Eds.), *Social perception in infants* (pp. 137–154). Norwood, NJ: Ablex.

Nabokov, V. (1989). *Speak, memory.* New York: Vintage Books.

Newman, E. (1933). *The life of Richard Wagner* (Vol. 1). Knopf: New York.

Newman, E. (1937). *The life of Richard Wagner* (Vol. 2). Knopf: New York.

Newman, E. (1941). *The life of Richard Wagner* (Vol. 3). Knopf: New York.

Newman, K. (2004). *Rampage: The social roots of school shootings*. New York: Basic Books.

Newton, M. (1992). *Hunting humans: The encyclopedia of serial killers* (Vol. 1). New York: Avon.

Norris, J. (1988). *Serial killers*. New York: Dolphin.

Olson, J. (1993). *Misbegotten son*. New York: Dell.

Ornstein, A. (1995). The fate of the curative fantasy in the psychoanalytic treatment process. *Contemporary Psychoanalysis, 31,* 113–123.

Ornstein P., & Ornstein, A. (1985). Clinical understanding and explaining: The empathic vantage point. In A. Goldberg (Ed.), *Progress in self psychology* (Vol. 1, pp. 43–61). Hillsdale, NJ: The Analytic Press.

Patel, A. (2003). Language, music, syntax and the brain. *Nature Neuroscience, 6,* 674–681.

Phelps, R. (1970). *Professional secretes: An autobiography of Jean Cocteau*. New York: Farrar, Straus & Giroux.

Pizer, S. (1998). *Building bridges: The negotiation of paradox in psychoanalysis*. Hillsdale, NJ: The Analytic Press.

Poland, W. (1990). The gift of laughter: On the development of a sense of humor in clinical analysis. *Psychoanalytic Quarterly, 59,* 197–225.

Purcell, S. (2006). The analyst's excitement in the analysis of perversion. *International Journal of Psycho-Analysis, 87,* 105–124.

Rapaport, D. (1960). *The structure of psychoanalytic theory: A systematizing attempt*. Madison, CT: International Universities Press.

Reik, T. (1962). *Jewish wit*. New York: Gamut Press.

Renik, O. (1993). Analytic interaction: Conceptualizing technique in the light of the analyst's irreducible subjectivity. *Psychoanalytic Quarterly, 46,* 466–495.

Rotenberg, C. (1992). Optimal operative perversity: A contribution to the theory of creativity. In A. Goldberg (Ed.), *New therapeutic vision: Progress in self psychology* (Vol. 8, pp. 167–187). Hillsdale, NJ: The Analytic Press.

Rule, A. (1989). *The stranger beside me*. New York: Signet.

Sadie, S., & Tyrell, J. (Eds.). (2001). *The new Grove dictionary of music and musicians* (Vol. 24). Oxford: Oxford University Press.

Sameroff, A. (1983). Developmental systems: Contexts and evolution. In W. Kessen (Ed.), *Mussen's handbook of child psychology* (Vol. 1, pp. 133–156). New York: Wiley.

Sameroff, A., & Chandler, M. (1976). Reproductive risk and the continuum of caretaking casualty. In F. D. Horowitz (Ed.), *Review of child development research* (Vol. 4, pp. 187–244). Chicago: University of Chicago Press.

Sandler, A.-M. (2004). Institutional responses to boundary violation: The case of Masud Khan. *International Journal of Psycho-Analysis, 85,* 27–41.

Sandler, J. (1967). Trauma, strain, and development. In S. Furst (Ed.), *Trauma* (pp. 154–176). New York: Basic Books.

Sato, W., & Yoshikawa, S. (2005). Spontaneous facial mimicry in response to dynamic facial expressions. *Proceedings of 2005 4th IEEE International Conference on Development and Learning.*

Schafer, R. (1976). *A new language for psychoanalysis.* New Haven: Yale University Press.

Schlesinger, K. (1979). Jewish humor as Jewish identity. *International Revue of Psychoanalysis, 6,* 317–330.

Schwaber, E. (1984). Empathy: A mode of analytic listening. In J. Lichtenberg, M. Bornstein, & D. Silver (Eds.), *Empathy II* (pp. 143–172). Hillsdale, NJ: The Analytic Press.

Sears D. (1991). *To kill again.* Wilmington, DE: Scholarly Resources Books.

Seitz, E. (2005). Igor Stravinsky, *The Rite of Spring,* notes for the Boston Symphony Concert July 29.

Silverman, L., Lachmann, F. M., & Milich, R. (1982). *The search for oneness.* New York: International Universities Press.

Singer, J., & Fagan, J. (1992). Negative affect, emotional expression, and forgetting in young infants. *Developmental Psychology, 28,* 48–57.

Spezzano, C. (1995). "Classical" versus "contemporary" theory: The difference that matters. *Contemporary Psychoanalysis, 31,* 20–46.

Stein, R. (2005). Why perversion? "False love" and the perverse pact. *International Journal of Psycho-Analysis, 86,* 775–799.

Stern, D. (1983). The early development of schemas of self, of other, and of "self with other." In J. Lichtenberg & S. Kaplan (Eds.), *Reflections on self psychology* (pp. 49–84). Hillsdale, NJ: The Analytic Press.

Stern, D. (1985). *The interpersonal world of the infant.* New York: Basic Books.

Stern, D. (1994). One way to build a clinically relevant baby. *Infant Mental Health Journal, 15,* 9–25.

Stern, D. (2002). *The first relationship.* Cambridge, MA: Harvard University Press.

Stern, D. (2004). The present moment in psychotherapy and everyday life. New York: W. W. Norton.

Stern, D. (2005). Keynote presentation at 28th Annual International Conference on the Psychology of the Self, Baltimore, MD, October 20.

Stern, D., Sander, L., Nahum, J., et al. (1998). Noninterpretive mechanisms in psychoanalytic therapy: The "something more" than interpretation. *International Journal of Psycho-Analysis, 79,* 903–922.

Stern, I. (1979). *From Mao to Mozart.* Independent Film.

Stolorow, R. D. (2003). Trauma and temporality. *Psychoanalytic Psychology, 30,* 156–161.

Stolorow, R. D., & Lachmann, F. M. (1980). *Psychoanalysis of developmental arrests.* Madison, CT: International Universities Press.

Stolorow, R. D., Brandchaft, B., & Atwood, G. (1987). *Psychoanalytic treatment: An intersubjective approach.* Hillsdale, NJ: The Analytic Press.

Stravinsky, I. (1936). *An autobiography.* New York: W. W. Norton.

Taerk, G. (2002). Moments of spontaneity and surprise: The nonlinear road to something more. *Psychoanalytic Inquiry, 22,* 728–739.

Teicholz, J. (1999). *Kohut, Loewald, and the postmoderns.* Hillsdale, NJ: The Analytic Press.

Teicholz, J. (2006). Qualities of engagement and the analyst's theory. *International Journal of Psychoanalytic Self Psychology, 1,* 47–77.

Thelan, E., & Smith, L. (1994). *A dynamic system approach to the development of cognition and action.* Cambridge, MA: MIT Press.

Tomkins, S. S. (1962). *Affect, imagery and consciousness: The positive affects.* New York: Springer–Verlag.

Tronick, E. (2003). "Of course all relationships are unique": How co-created processes generate unique mother–infant and patient–therapist relationships and change other relationships. *Psychoanalytic Inquiry, 23,* 473–491.

Tronick, E., & Gianino, A. (1986). Interactive mismatch and repair: Challenges to the coping infant. Zero to three. *Bulletin of the National Center Clinical Infant Programs, 5,* 1–6.

Tronick, E., Als, H., Adamson, L., Wise, S., & Brazelton, T. (1978). The infant's response to entrapment between contradictory messages in face-to-face interaction. *Journal of the Academy of Child and Adolescent Psychiatry, 17,* 1–13.

Tronick, E., Bruschweiler-Stern, N., Harrison, A., Lyons-Ruth, K., Morgan, A., Nahum, J., et al. (1998). Dyadically expanded states of consciousness and the process of therapeutic change. *Infant Mental Health Journal, 19,* 290–299.

Trowbridge, R. H. (2005). *The scientific approach to wisdom.* Unpublished doctoral dissertation. Union Institute & University, Cincinnati, OH.

Waelder, R. (1962). Psychoanalysis, scientific method, and philosophy. *Journal of the American Psychoanalytic Association, 10,* 617–637.

Wagner, R. (1983). *My life* (Grey, A., Trans.). Cambridge, UK: Cambridge University Press. (Originally published in German as *Mein Leben,* 1963, Munich: Paul List Verlag.)

Walsch, S. (2002). *Stravinsky.* New York: Macmillan.

Webster unabridged international dictionary. (1976). New York: The Publisher's Guild Inc.

Weiss, J., & Sampson, H. (1986). *The psychoanalytic process.* New York: Guilford.

Winnicott, D. W. (1960). Ego distortions in terms of true and false self. In M. Kahn (Ed.), *The maturational processes and the facilitating environment* (pp. 140–152). Madison, CT: International Universities Press [1965].

Woodruff, J. (Interviewer) (May 1998). The killer at Thursden High. Frontline [television broadcast]. New York and Washington, DC: Public Broadcasting Service.

Index

Communication
    humor in, 89–90
    and music, 17–18
Compassion vs. empathy, 74
Contingencies in social interactions, 189
'Creative artist' term, 158–159
Creativity
    defined, 9
    and perversion, 133–136, 158
    role in transforming narcissism, 9
Cross-modal transfer
    in infants, 58–59
    language and music, 59–60
    in musicianship, 65–67
    and priming, 24–25

D

Dali, Salvador, 159–160
Death anxiety, 184–185
Declarative knowledge, 54–55
Depressed mothers, 115–121
Despair expressed as aggression, 5
Disruption and repair
    defined, 15
    as principle of organization, 14
    'still face' study, 15–16
Don Quixote, 216
'Duck Lake' intervention, 14–15, 113,
        220, 227–228
Dyadic systems theory, 219

E

Einfuhlung, 48, 84
Empathic hero, 73
Empathic listening perspective, 56
Empathic understanding, 50–51, 69ff,
        80–86
Empathy
    abuse of, 74–76
    by analyst, 49–50
    background vs. foreground, 69–72
    as bidirectional, 48

bidirectional, 56–57
vs. compassion, 74
defined, 9, 48
development of, 47ff
lapses in, 15
'like me', 73
precursors to, 47ff, 80–86
role in transforming narcissism, 9
as skill, 52–53
transmission of feeling state, 61–62
uses of, 49
and vision types, 51–52
and vocal rhythm, 62–63
and wisdom, 208
Enactive procedures, 35
Enactments, 219–221
Eruptive aggression, see Aggression
Expectancies, defined, 14
Expectations, 113ff
    defying by survival, 159ff
    in infants, 114–120, 121–122
    violations in therapy interactions, 114
    violations leading to violent
        behavior, 144ff
    violations of, 229–231

F

Facial expression, 60–62
'False self' organizations, 120
Fantasy, 227
Freudian theory and vision types, 34
'Friends of empathy', 48

G

Gaze and head aversion, 117–118

H

Heightened affective moments
    effects of, 16
    as principle of organization, 14

Humor, 87ff
    boundaries, 91–94
    and communication, 89–90
    development of, 87–88
    gone awry, 106–106
    as inappropriate in therapy, 91
    Jewish, 90
    therapist defensiveness, 91–92
Humor lens, 97

I

Imagination, 227
Implicit communication, 26–27, 94–95
    and therapy, 23
Implicit relational knowing, 34–36
Infant research, 10, 11, 60–61
    on expectations, 114–120, 121–122,
        188–189
    'still face' study, 15
Inner organization, 14
Interactive regulation, 14–15, 218–219
Interpretation and transformation, 18
Ironic vision, 34

K

Kinkel, Kip, 147–155
Kleinian theory and vision types, 34
Kohut, Heinz
    as basis for this work, ix
    early influence by, 4

L

Lacanian theory and vision types, 34
Language and music, 59–60
'Leading edge' interpretations of
        aggression, 5–6
'Little death', 177–179
Lucas, Henry Lee, 144–146
Lying, 125–127, 129, 131, 132

M

Magritte, Rene, 164–166
Maturity, as transformation of archaic
        narcissism, 10
Metapsychology, 225
'Mirroring validation', 17
Model scenes, 83, 85
Mothers, see Infant research
    depressed, 115–121
Mother's Day-card model, 103, 106,
        114, 229
Music
    illustrative of transformative process,
        18
    language and, 59–60
    training and cross-modal transfer,
        65–67
    transformation of affect by, 17–18

N

Narcissism
    and aggression, 5
    archaic, defined, 8–9
    terminology history, 7
    transformation process, 218
    transformations of, 8
Narcissistic vulnerability
    and aggressive reaction, 5
    as metapsychological construct, 7

O

Object love, 7, 8
Object relations, 7, 8
Oedipal struggle, 224
Ongoing regulations, 218–219
    defined, 14
    as principle of organization, 14
Organizations, 'false self', 120